THE MAKING OF
THE ANGLO-IRISH AGREEMENT
OF 1985

Sir David Goodall GCMG

The Making of
THE ANGLO-IRISH AGREEMENT of 1985

A Memoir by

DAVID GOODALL

With Contributions by

MORWENNA GOODALL,

MICHAEL LILLIS, ROBIN RENWICK,

CHARLES POWELL, STEPHEN COLLINS

AND MAURICE MANNING

* * *

Edited by Frank Sheridan

NATIONAL UNIVERSITY OF IRELAND
2021

First published 2021
by the National University of Ireland
Ollscoil na hÉireann
49 Merrion Square, Dublin 2, Ireland

www.nui.ie

ISBN 978-0-901510-86-0 HB
ISBN 978-0-901510-87-7 PB

Cover design, text design and
typesetting by Lyn Davies *www.lyndaviesdesign.com*
Text in Garamond Oldstyle FS 11½/14 pt
Titles set in *Monotype Garamond italic* 18 & 28 pt
Printed in Ireland
by CRM Print + Design

Contents

Foreword

The National University of Ireland has not been in the habit of conferring honorary doctorates on retired British civil servants. Yet on 2 December 2015 in the Royal College of Surgeons in Ireland, I was privileged, as Chancellor of the University, to confer an honorary Doctor of Laws degree on Sir David Goodall.

The main reason why the University Senate agreed to confer this honour and the reason why NUI is very pleased to publish Sir David's memoir *The Making of the Anglo-Irish Agreement* is our recognition and appreciation of the very significant, part-unsung and largely unrecognised, role he played in making a reality of one of the most important and history changing agreements in Anglo-Irish history – one that transformed the relationship between our two countries at a dangerous and difficult time.

The distinguished historian and member of the NUI Senate, the late Professor Ronan Fanning, in his elegant citation that day captures the centrality and essence of Goodall's role:

> The basic equation underpinning the Agreement has been best described in the Goodall memoir: 'according the Irish some form of political involvement in Northern Ireland in return for a formal Irish recognition of the Union'. It marked the moment when, again in David's words, 'an inter-governmental relationship that had been adversarial became co-operative'.
>
> The other essential element of the Agreement was its immunisation against the fate of the Sunningdale Agreement of 1973: that what the two governments had agreed could never be overturned by the opposition of Northern Ireland's unionist majority. Unionists were consequently persuaded that sharing power with the nationalist minority was their only escape route from the Irish government's continuing involvement in the governance of Northern Ireland. And unionists know to this day that the Hillsborough Agreement remains the default position of both governments if the power-sharing executive under the terms of the Good Friday Agreement of 1998 were to collapse.

Sir David's memoir is supplemented in this publication by a number of other contributions from both the British and the Irish point of view. Inevitably there is a degree of repetition in these contributions which however serve the purpose of enriching the central narrative and providing some other perspectives on the Agreement and those centrally involved in its negotiation.

NUI has another motive in publishing this memoir and that is to acknowledge the central role of our fourth Chancellor, my predecessor, the late Dr Garret FitzGerald. The Anglo-Irish Agreement was the high point of his political career, the greatest of his many achievements and something which we in NUI are proud to honour through this publication. His autobiography *All in a Life*, referenced frequently by David Goodall, provides the most comprehensive account, apart from this memoir, of the background to the Agreement.

Frank Sheridan has done an excellent job in preparing this exceptional memoir for publication. Dr Emer Purcell has expertly completed the process of bringing the publication into print.

MAURICE MANNING
Chancellor,
National University of Ireland

Abbreviations

AIGC	Anglo-Irish Governmental Council
AIIC	Anglo-Irish Intergovernmental Council (later became the Anglo-Irish Intergovernmental Conference).
BIA	British-Irish Association
CDS	Chief of the Defence Staff
GCMG	Grand Cross (Knight or Dame) of the Order of St Michael and St George
EC	European Council
ECST	European Convention on the Suppression of Terrorism
FCO	Foreign and Commonwealth Office
GOC	General Officer Commanding
IRA	Irish Republican Army
KOYLI	King's Own Yorkshire Light Infantry
MBFR	The Mutual and Balanced Force Reductions talks (a series of negotiations between NATO and Warsaw Pact countries, Vienna, 1973–75)
NIA	Northern Ireland Assembly
NIO	Northern Ireland Office
PIRA	Provisional IRA
PUS	Parliamentary Under Secretary
RUC	Royal Ulster Constabulary
SDLP	Social Democratic and Labour Party
UDR	Ulster Defence Regiment

Acknowledgements

Credit for the publication of Sir David Goodall's memoir must be given to a small number of determined people.

The first is Morwenna, Lady Goodall, widow of Sir David, who holds the copyright on the memoir. Following the death of her husband, she accepted the view put forward by his friend and lead British negotiator, Robert Armstrong, Lord Armstrong of Ilminster, that the memoir, which holds up a mirror to the legacy of Sir David and others in addressing a deep division mired in history, should be made available to the public and published.

The second is Robert Armstrong himself, the former British Cabinet Secretary, who sadly passed away in April 2020. A third is Michael Lillis, one of the Irish negotiators of the 1985 Agreement and the Irish opposite number of Sir David during the negotiations.

Before Sir David died, Michael Lillis and the surviving Irish negotiators, Noel Dorr and Seán Donlon, who had the privilege of reviewing the document on a confidential basis when first written, were convinced that it provided exceptional insights into the dynamics of the challenging process leading to the Agreement and should be published.

In early 2019 Michael Lillis called on Robert Armstrong in London to ask him to raise the issue of the document's release with Lady Goodall. This he did and she was immediately supportive – as she was throughout the whole process of securing the release of the document and preparing it for publication. And the introduction, which she wrote, sets a solid base for the fascinating story which follows. Lord Armstrong also contacted a successor in the Cabinet Office, Sir Mark Sedwill, who confirmed that there was no objection to the release of the memoir.

And that allowed for an approach by Lady Goodall to Churchill College, Cambridge, where Sir David had deposited the document for safekeeping. The Chief Archivist at Churchill College, Andrew Riley, not only quickly released the memoir to her and ultimately to me, as editor, but also most helpfully assisted me, during a lockdown and while working from home, in converting what was essentially a photographed version of the memoir into a formattable text.

A conversation about Sir David and the memoir between the late Professor of Modern History, Ronan Fanning, and Maurice Manning, Chancellor of the National University of Ireland (NUI) (following the granting of an honorary degree by the university to Sir David in 2015), led to an offer by Maurice to have the memoir published by NUI, an offer accepted by Lady Goodall.

On contributions, I am most grateful to Lord Renwick of Clifton, who readily agreed to allow the inclusion of his chapter on Northern Ireland from his book *A Journey with Margaret Thatcher: Foreign Policy under the Iron Lady*. Thanks are due also to Lord Powell of Bayswater, who was Margaret Thatcher's Private Secretary during the negotiations and who responded positively to a request from Michael Lillis for a contribution. Stephen Collins too agreed to the request from Maurice Manning for an essay, which sets an informative Irish backdrop to the memoir.

In terms of assistance and guidance with the editing process, of which I had no prior experience, I am indebted to Michael Lillis for his constant engagement which kept the process on the rails. And I am grateful too to Michael Kennedy of the Royal Irish Academy, who, in response to my query as to whether my approach was appropriate for a publication of such substance, promptly responded and gave me fullest assistance.

The main sources for the biographical notes in the book are 1. the Oxford University Press *Who's Who* and *Who Was Who*; 2. *The Dictionary of Irish Biography*; 3. the online directory of British diplomats by Colin Mackie (2013); and 4. the Internet generally. Any errors are unintentional and regretted.

FRANK SHERIDAN
21 January 2021

Introduction

The Anglo-Irish Agreement, signed at Hillsborough Castle on 15 November 1985, is now generally perceived as a turning point in the current peace process in Northern Ireland. This account of it is written from the perspective of a British official. It explains how the Anglo-Irish Agreement actually came about; the figures involved in driving forward the negotiations, the spirit in which they engaged with one another; the manner in which political demands intersected with their work and the practicalities involved in getting the Agreement over the line amidst controversy and contention.

In 1982 my husband, David Goodall, was appointed to the Cabinet Office and in this position, under – and together with – the Cabinet Secretary, Sir Robert Armstrong, was involved in the whole process. He thought it would be valuable, therefore, to have an account of this important negotiation from his own perspective. The text published here is the result. It was drafted between 1992 and 1998, following his retirement and about a decade after the events which it describes. It sits between an attempt at objective history and a personal perspective on events. It is for this reason that he has subtitled it 'A personal account'. He would have emphasised that such an approach was particularly apposite in the context of Anglo-Irish relations, where so much ultimately comes down to individual viewpoints. Significantly, he makes no attempt to assess the impact of the Agreement, which he felt was a matter for posterity to judge.

When this account was finished, he was keen for the family to read the text, which they all did. This was not to garner criticisms or corrections, but to make us all aware of what the Anglo-Irish Agreement had meant to him and entailed. That aside, he was very circumspect about making it available and determined that it should not be publicly read while many of those described in it were alive. With this in mind, and in reflection of his understanding of it as an official record, he deposited the manuscript in Churchill College, Cambridge, under the thirty-year rule. This delay intentionally echoed that of the release of official government papers.

The thirty years since 1985 have now long expired and current political events make the negotiation of the Anglo-Irish Agreement topical once more. It is for this reason that I have agreed to publish the manuscript. Before doing so, in 2018, I cleared this decision both with Lord Armstrong, who led the British negotiating team, and also, through him, with the then Cabinet Secretary. Slightly to my surprise Sir Robert had never seen my husband's account. Having read the text, he wrote me a long letter dated November 8, 2018. One section of it is worth quoting at length:

> The account of the negotiations reminded me of much that I remembered, and of much that I had otherwise forgotten, about that experience. It brought back that extraordinary feeling that we were conducting not one negotiation but two, simultaneously: one with our Irish counterparts and another with the Prime Minister. David was obviously wondering, just as I was, whether she really wanted an agreement, and whether she would see it through. I think she did want it. She thought that something needed to be done about Northern Ireland, and that she needed to be seen to be doing it, in view of the loss of lives and the injuries resulting from PIRA terrorism and in view of the economic and financial cost of the troubles. Jim Prior's 'rolling devolution' policy was not getting anywhere. Though her instincts were unionist, she had become disenchanted with the Northern Irish politicians. She thought an agreement would please Reagan and the Americans. And she basically liked, and almost trusted, Garret FitzGerald. Once she had started the process, she did not want it to end in failure. But it had to be on her terms. In particular, there had to be no dilution of sovereignty.
>
> The other thing that the account brings back to my mind is the pleasure of working with David on the negotiations, and the strength of the friendship which our work together created. We shared a belief in what we were trying to achieve, and we were able to work together harmoniously. Even when it was arduous and seemed to be at risk of collapse, it was fun (in the sense that Edward Bridges used to use that word) to be doing it together. And we were helped by our cross-border friendships: David with Michael Lillis and mine with Dermot Nally. I think both of us thought that this was the best thing we had done or were likely to do in our careers.

In this last regard my husband would unquestionably have agreed. Throughout his life David was deeply interested in Ireland. As part of that interest, he researched his family connections there and published several articles on episodes of Irish history. In retirement he also became chairman of the British Irish Association and President of the Irish Genealogical Research Society. The Anglo-Irish Agreement was, therefore, an undertaking very close to his heart. He also regarded it as an enormous privilege to negotiate, largely because of what it achieved, but also because of the people he met and the opportunity it afforded – rare in civil-service life – to see through to the finish a major project with tangible positive effects. This account, and the care he took over its compilation, make his commitment to it clear.

MORWENNA GOODALL
November 2020

David Goodall

A BIOGRAPHICAL NOTE

Sir Arthur David Saunders Goodall, GCMG (9 October 1931 - 22 July 2016) was a British diplomat, the only child of Arthur William and Maisie Josephine Goodall (née Byers). He was born in Blackpool, Lancashire. Both of his grandfathers were born in Ireland – he did extensive research on his Irish roots, publishing articles in the journals of the Irish Genealogical Research Society (he was its President from 1992 to 2012) and of the Wexford Historical Society.

Goodall, a Roman Catholic, was educated at Ampleforth College, a prominent Roman Catholic boarding school in north Yorkshire and later at Trinity College, Oxford where he studied Classics and obtained a first-class degree in 1954. For his military service, he served as a 2nd Lieutenant in the King's Own Yorkshire Light Infantry from 1954 to 1956, serving in Kenya and Cyprus.

In 1956 he entered the diplomatic service in the Foreign Office (renamed the Foreign and Commonwealth Office, or FCO, in 1968). He married Morwenna Peecock in 1962, and they had a daughter, Elisabeth, and two sons, Dominic and John.

In his career in the foreign service, David Goodall served in Nicosia in 1956; was assigned to the Foreign Office (FO) in 1957; the Embassy in Djakarta from 1958 to 1960; the Embassy in Bonn 1961–63; the FO again 1963–68; the High Commission in Nairobi 1968–70; the FCO 1970–73; he was a member of the UK Delegation to The Mutual and Balanced Force Reductions (MBFR) talks (a series of negotiations between NATO and Warsaw Pact countries) Vienna, 1973–75. He served as Head of the Western European Department at the FCO from 1975 to 1979; Minister Plenipotentiary (Deputy Head of Mission) at the UK Embassy in Bonn 1979–82. From 1982 to 1984 he was seconded (loaned) to the Cabinet Office with the title of Deputy Secretary from 1982 to 1984 and was promoted Deputy Under-Secretary at the FCO from 1984 to 1987. His last assignment in the diplomatic service was as British High Commissioner (this title is given to the ambassador of one Commonwealth country accredited to another) in New Delhi from 1984 to 1987.

It was while at the Cabinet Office that Goodall became involved in the secret negotiations which led to the Anglo-Irish Agreement of 1985. His report on proposals put to him by the Irish diplomat, Michael Lillis, with the approval of Taoiseach, Garret FitzGerald in September 1983, that the political, security and judicial resources of the Irish State be involved in the government of Northern Ireland in order to mitigate the widespread alienation of the nationalist community there, led to the Prime Minister, Margaret Thatcher, authorising the negotiations led by the Cabinet Secretaries in London and Dublin that culminated in November 1985 in the signing of the Anglo-Irish Agreement. Even when assigned back to the FCO in 1984 with a heavy workload, Goodall continued to be involved at the heart of the negotiations.

Goodall explains in his memoir that he 'had felt for a long time that relations between our two islands were a historic mess' that he had no 'sympathy with the idea that the unionists of the North could or should be pushed into a united Ireland against their will' but that 'there had to be some compromise whereby continuance of the Union could be assured while at the same time the character of the Northern State was reformed so as to legitimise nationalist aspirations and give them a link of some kind with the Republic'. His views were broadly shared by his superior at the Cabinet Office, Sir Robert Armstrong, and together they drove an agenda for change in Northern Ireland, working with a Prime Minister who was by conviction a British nationalist and a unionist. Mrs Thatcher's frequently dogged reluctance and obduracy throughout the negotiations made the conclusion of a Treaty agreement between London and Dublin all the more remarkable.

Goodall and Armstrong were in the tradition of senior, gifted British civil servants, seeking to offer to their political masters creative solutions to historically intractable problems. Their knowledge of the deep historical roots of the crisis in Northern Ireland and its continuing legacy of conflict did not deter them from trying to find ways forward and transforming the situation there from being, in Goodall's words to his Prime Minister in 1983, 'the only place in the world where British soldiers' lives were being lost in anger'.

Both Armstrong and Goodall regarded the 1985 Agreement as the highlight of both their careers. Goodall, as he outlines in his memoir, saw it as neither promoting nor preventing Irish unity, but rather taking account of the uniquely complex relationships between the two parts of Ireland and between the two countries. Speaking at an event in Trinity College Dublin in 2015, to mark the 30th anniversary of the signing of the Agreement, Goodall said that it had 'fundamentally changed the chemistry of the relationship between our two governments'.

Goodall was described by one obituarist as 'clever, cultured, witty and successful', by another as 'dapper and intelligent' and by another as a George Smiley type – ironically Goodall served in the British Embassy in Bonn with John le Carré (David Cornwell) and they remained friends thereafter. Goodall was, like Smiley, short of stature, bespectacled and slightly owlish in appearance, recalling for yet another obituarist 'the penetrating innocence of Father Brown'. It was probably this slightly 'monkish' appearance and personality which earned him Mrs Thatcher's teasing sobriquet 'my favourite clergyman'.

It was during his schooldays at Ampleforth that Goodall first discovered the talent that would make him a celebrated watercolorist in later life. His works were repeatedly exhibited and collected internationally; they were published as two books *Remembering India* (1997) and *Ryedale Pilgrimage* (2000).

THE NEGOTIATORS

Chevening (Country residence of the British Foreign Secretary) April 1985.

FRONT ROW *(left to right)*

Sir Alan Goodison, UK Ambassador to Ireland; Dermot Nally, Secretary to Irish Government; Sir Robert Armstrong, UK Cabinet Secretary; Noel Dorr, Irish Ambassador to UK.

SECOND ROW

Sir David Goodall, Deputy Permanent Secretary at Foreign and Commonwealth Office (FCO); Tony Brennan, Deputy Permanent Secretary, Northern Ireland Office (NIO); Seán Donlon, Secretary General, Irish Department of Foreign Affairs; Andrew Ward, Secretary General, Irish Department of Justice; Michael Lillis, Assistant Secretary General, Irish Dept. of Foreign Affairs; Tony Stevens, Deputy Permanent Secretary, NIO; Declan Quigley, Secretary General, Irish Attorney General's Office; Sir Christopher Mallaby, Deputy Secretary to UK Cabinet.

BACK ROW

Henry Darwin, Legal Adviser at the FCO. (Absent: Sir Robert Andrew, Permanent Under Secretary NIO)

The Making of

THE ANGLO-IRISH AGREEMENT OF 1985

(The Hillsborough Agreement)

A Personal Account

by David Goodall

*

I

THERE ARE MANY different perspectives on the negotiation which led up to the signing of the Anglo-Irish Agreement at Hillsborough Castle on 15 November 1985. The two protagonists have published their own accounts: Margaret Thatcher a grudging and somewhat waspish one in *The Downing Street Years*, and Garret FitzGerald a long, uniquely detailed and authoritative one in *All in a Life*. Geoffrey Howe, another key participant, has devoted a chapter to the negotiations in *Conflict of Loyalty*. These are accounts 'from the top', so to speak, which describe what happened from a political perspective. But although the decisive bargains were struck, and the outcome shaped by the political leaders on both sides, the detailed negotiations were carried on by a very small group of British and Irish civil servants, meeting frequently and intensively over a period of more than two years.

What follows gives the story from the standpoint of one of the British members of that group, who was, by virtue of his position, preoccupied with the cut and thrust of the negotiations but in ignorance of much that was happening on the political level to affect them. So, the pressures on Mrs Thatcher from her private contacts with unionist sympathisers, including Ian Gow and Enoch Powell, figure only peripherally in this account, as does the influence exercised by President Reagan and senior members of the US Administration.[1]

For my impressions and anecdotes, I have drawn on memory, supplemented by entries in the short daily diary which I kept throughout the period. But classified information was not confided to the diary; so in tracing the detailed course of the negotiations, especially in their later stages, I have relied heavily on the factual record compiled in 1986 by Ted

1. Although the need to ward off American pressure over Northern Ireland was always an important consideration in Mrs Thatcher's approach to the negotiations, I do not think it was the decisive factor which led her to conclude the Agreement. But when I asked privately in July 1992 if she was still happy with the Agreement, she thought for a moment and then said dismissively that it had 'helped a lot with Reagan'.

Hallett of the Research Department of the FCO, who was given access to all the papers relating to the negotiations then held in either the FCO or the Cabinet Office (including those on my own private files) and quotes from them verbatim. It hardly needs saying that a history of the negotiations based on Northern Ireland Office files would no doubt have a rather different flavour.

To the extent that my account does less than justice to the contributions of my colleagues – and in particular to the skill, tact and ingenuity at every stage of Robert Armstrong – that is simply because (as Virginia Woolf observed) 'in reporting conversations one's own sayings stand out like lighthouses'.

In December 1982, six months after being seconded to the Cabinet Office from the Foreign Office, I attended a small dinner party at No 10 Downing Street given by Mrs Thatcher for Lord Shackleton, who had been engaged in making recommendations about the future economic development of the Falkland Islands. After the other guests had gone, Mrs Thatcher invited me to join her and her Private Secretary (John Coles) for a drink by the fire in the White Drawing Room. She equipped herself with a large whisky and soda, which she sipped at intervals during the conversation until, like an hourglass, it signalled by its emptiness the time to go to bed.

From the Falklands the conversation turned to Ireland, and what seemed to me the often overlooked and scandalous fact that the only place in the world where British soldiers' lives were being lost in anger was in the United Kingdom itself. Earlier in the year, I had been struck by Mrs Thatcher's outspoken distaste for Jim Prior's 'rolling devolution' proposals and her unconcealed reluctance to endorse them. This time, although there was no mistaking her lack of sympathy for, or understanding of, Irish nationalism, what impressed me was the seriousness of her interest in the problem of Northern Ireland and the extent of her background reading on the subject, including several books on the Treaty and Dervla Murphy's *A Place Apart* (1979), which she said she had found 'fascinating'.

I suggested that relations between England and Ireland were complicated by the interpenetration of our two populations: so many people in England being of Irish or partly Irish descent and vice versa in Ireland. Her eyes flashed: 'I am completely English', she said. I said that both my grandfathers had been born in Ireland, and there were thousands of English people who could say the same. Her face was shadowed by a momentary doubt: 'Well, I suppose I am one sixteenth Irish: my great grandmother was a Sullivan'.

She spoke of her debt to Airey Neave and the discussions she had had with him about devolved government for Northern Ireland; and she wrestled repeatedly and frankly with the thought that there could perhaps be no final settlement in Northern Ireland until the British withdrew and left the two communities there to come to terms with one another. The conversation ended with her saying reflectively 'If we get back next time' (looking ahead to the forthcoming General Election in 1983) 'I think I would like to do something about Ireland'.

In the event, the initiative came from the Irish side. Margaret Thatcher's temperamental dislike of things Irish, fuelled by the whole IRA terrorist campaign, by Airey Neave's assassination, and by the mutually embittering tensions of the Hunger Strikes, had been sharpened into a sense of personal affront by the anti-British stance adopted by the Haughey government in the Falklands War; and relations between London and Dublin had been in deep freeze ever since. But in early 1983 Mr Haughey fell from power and was replaced as Taoiseach by Dr Garret FitzGerald. Then in June 1983 Mrs Thatcher won her comfortable election victory. Despite the ungenerous tone which she adopts towards Dr FitzGerald in *The Downing Street Years*, she had at the time a high regard for his integrity and indeed a degree of affection for him personally: he was one of those who she could 'do business with'.

Garret FitzGerald had entered politics fired with a determination to bring about a reconciliation between the two parts of Ireland: and with governments in place in London and Dublin looking likely to be secure in office for the next three or four years, he saw an opportunity for achieving his ambition. By good fortune this chimed in with Mrs Thatcher's quite differently motivated feeling that it was time to 'do something about Ireland', if only to stop the drain on British lives and treasure.

As soon as the British election was over, the Secretary to the Irish government, Dermot Nally, was despatched to London to propose to his British opposite number, Sir Robert Armstrong, the activation of the Anglo-Irish Intergovernmental Council – a grandiose name for regular meetings between the two heads of government, to be serviced by a joint 'Steering Committee' of officials. The entity had been agreed upon between Mrs Thatcher and Mr Haughey in 1981 during their brief political honeymoon, but aborted by the subsequent differences over the Falklands.

As we sat around the table with Nally and his colleagues in the Cabinet Secretary's large and elegant office, the sound of martial music and military commands was wafted into to the room from the Horse Guards Parade, where soldiers in scarlet could be seen rehearsing for a Beating of Retreat – 'England's cruel red' making an ironical background to this first overture to a new attempt at Anglo-Irish reconciliation.

It was agreed that the Steering Committee should be mandated simply to identify practical areas for closer Anglo-Irish cooperation and report to a Summit Meeting of the two heads of government the following autumn. Although it was to meet occasionally at the Armstrong-Nally level, the detailed work was to be done by a 'coordinating committee' of officials from the interested departments within both governments. The Irish team was to be headed by the Assistant Secretary for Anglo-Irish Affairs at the Department of Foreign Affairs, Michael Lillis. I was deputed to lead the British team, as a function of the Cabinet Office's coordinating role within Whitehall, given that the NIO and the FCO had an equal interest in the outcome and neither would have been happy to let the other take the lead. It was in this way that the controlling role in what proved to be the negotiations leading to the conclusion of the Anglo-Irish Agreement was assumed by the Cabinet Office, although we had at that stage no knowledge that the Irish were contemplating any major new initiative beyond an intensification of high level political and official contacts.

So, it was a considerable surprise when, at the first meeting of our coordinating committee in Dublin at the beginning of September 1983, Michael Lillis invited me to take a quiet walk with him along the Grand Canal and proceeded to sketch out the possibility of radically new arrangements for Northern Ireland. In essence, he envisaged unequivocal Irish acceptance of the Union and of a revived Stormont Parliament, in return for the participation of Irish security forces in operations in the North and of Irish judges in terrorist trials there.

Michael explained that these ideas were not those of the Irish government; but they were being canvassed within the SDLP and had the backing of the Taoiseach. He said they stemmed from the recognition that unification by consent was not a realistic goal for the foreseeable future; and a fear that unless the Catholic minority in Northern Ireland could be brought to identify themselves with the institutions of law and order there (from which they were profoundly alienated), Sinn Féin would replace the SDLP as the legitimate representative of nationalist opinion in the North, with disastrous consequences for the stability of the island of Ireland as a whole. With this anxiety paramount, the Taoiseach believed that outright acceptance of the Union would be a price worth paying for measures which, by addressing the concerns of Northern nationalists in regard to policing, the administration of justice and the need for a visible Irish Dimension on the ground, would end their alienation from the institutions of the state in the North.

I had no previous dealings with Michael Lillis; and being a complete newcomer to the Anglo-Irish political scene, I was uncertain what to make of these (to me) astonishingly far reaching ideas or whether they were to be taken seriously; and I had some difficulty in believing that I was the channel chosen for conveying to London a major new initiative by the Taoiseach. I asked Michael if he wished me to report what he said, and he confirmed that he did. I had little doubt that any suggestion of Irish troops or police operating in the North would be a non-starter in London. At the same time, it seemed to me that unequivocal acceptance of the Union by the Republic would be a step of sufficient political and symbolic importance to justify the introduction of a significant 'Irish Dimension' into the Northern Ireland administration (something Mrs Thatcher had refused to contemplate in any form in the context of Jim Prior's 'rolling devolution' proposals).

Meanwhile I remained sceptical about the extent to which Michael's exposition really reflected the considered thinking of the Taoiseach himself. Although Michael had the reputation of being a confidant of Dr FitzGerald, I knew that he was regarded in Belfast and London with considerable suspicion, and I began to wonder how my report of our conversation would be read in Whitehall. In talking to me he went out of his way to make it clear that he was, by background and conviction, a strong Irish nationalist with his fair share of historic resentments of the British role in Ireland; but he impressed me as being an essentially honest man, as well as an extremely intelligent and persuasive one with a capacity for being both imaginative and objective. In the course of the intensive contacts between us over the next two years, I never had cause to revise that opinion; and I like to think that the mutual confidence which grew up between us (and which never precluded vigorous disagreement) was a factor in the eventual success of the negotiations.

Michael and I met again a few days later at the annual conference of the British-Irish Association at Balliol College, Oxford, which gave me my first experience of Irish political and academic opinion en masse. In one of the working groups into which the conference divided itself there was a discussion of neutrality. The atmosphere was informal and the discussions were taking place 'under Chatham House Rules', which means that views expressed are personal and unattributable. I rather frivolously suggested that Irish neutrality, ostentatiously pursued from a position safely within the NATO area but without the obligations of NATO membership, was a way of getting the Republic's national security on the cheap. What I had intended as a tease was related by some of the unionists present to Enoch Powell, who later attacked me by name in a public speech to illustrate his thesis that there was a longstanding conspiracy between the Foreign Office and the US State Department to push Northern Ireland into a united Irish Republic in exchange for the Republic joining NATO. At the time I was innocent enough to be unaware that there was such a thesis; and I have never before or since come across the slightest shred of evidence to support it.

Another unionist encounter at Balliol was with Edgar Graham, a young law lecturer at Queen's University, Belfast, who was pointed out to me as being a graduate of my own college and as representing the 'new generation' of unionist politicians, from whom some degree of flexibility might be expected. Over breakfast on the first morning, he assured me with apparent seriousness that, as a Trinity man, nothing would induce him to spend a night under Balliol's roof, so he was staying next door. His contribution to the general debate then took the form of an impassioned statement that he would never sit down at the negotiating table with people who were in public life to destroy all he believed in (i.e., the Union). It was borne in upon me that in a Northern Ireland context, flexibility did not connote any readiness to compromise.

As well as affording insights into unionist attitudes, the BIA Conference introduced me to the perils of Irish hospitality in the shape of an after-dinner free bar provided (I think) by the Irish government. After high words with the redoubtable John A. Murphy about Britain's role in Ireland and some rousing singing (by him) of Irish ballads, matched by an antiphonal rendering of 'Ilkley Moor', I tried to keep a clear enough head to probe Michael further about the Taoiseach's thinking on Northern Ireland in the course of a stroll through Oxford in the small hours. In this I thought I was just about successful; so, I was not sure whether to be gratified or dismayed when Ruth Dudley Edwards remarked to me some days afterwards 'You certainly did a lot for the reputation of the Brits by staying up and getting drunk with the boys at Balliol'.

The reports of my conversations with Michael were received in the FCO with scepticism and in the Northern Ireland Office with incredulity. I was told that Michael Lillis was devious, anti-British and unreliable; that there was no evidence that he was a trustworthy guide to the Taoiseach's thinking; and that it was implausible to suppose that Dr FitzGerald or the SDLP could be harbouring such farfetched ideas, which it would in any case be politically impossible for them to deliver. Jim Prior minuted that nothing of the kind had been floated with him by John Hume. This scepticism was echoed to some degree by the Prime Minister herself, who nevertheless wanted to know more about the terms in which the Irish might be willing to recognise Northern Ireland's status as part of the United Kingdom.

A further talk with Michael Lillis in Dublin, as we strolled in autumn sunshine round St Stephen's Green, left me in no doubt that he was speaking with Garret FitzGerald's authority and that the Taoiseach was prepared, if the package was right, to carry recognition of the Union to the point of a referendum to amend Articles 2 and 3 of the Irish Constitution.[2] On the basis of this further conversation, as reported to her by Robert Armstrong, the Prime Minister asked for a detailed study by officials of

2. These Articles read: '2. The national territory consists of the whole island of Ireland, its islands and territorial seas. 3. Pending the re-integration of the national territory, and without prejudice to the right of the Parliament and Government established by this constitution to exercise jurisdiction over the whole of that territory, the laws enacted by that Parliament shall have the like area and extent of application as the laws of Saorstát Eireann and the like extraterritorial effect.'

the implications of the Irish proposals, while recording her fear that they looked more likely to lead to an increase in violence than to its reduction. The first definitive signal that the Prime Minister's interest had been engaged and that a serious negotiation might lie ahead had thus been given.

Anyone who knew Whitehall under Mrs Thatcher will realise that things would never have progressed so far if my judgement of the genuineness of Lillis's proposals had not been endorsed by the Cabinet Secretary and presented by him to the Prime Minister as meriting serious (if sceptical) consideration: similar reports presented to her with mandarin-like detachment – or reaching her (for example) through the Foreign Office – would probably have got short shrift. But by good luck (though critics of the Anglo-Irish Agreement might see it differently) Robert and I shared an interest in Ireland and a conviction that it was time to move the Irish Problem back to the top of the British political agenda. We enjoyed (I speak for myself) one another's company and Robert, I believe, had confidence in my professional competence and reliability.

Robert always had his own clear view of how to proceed, although his mind was never easy to read. But in the next two years of intensive negotiating activity, he backed my judgements, shared ideas and accepted my help with a consistency and a generosity which resulted in real and lasting friendship. On my side I greatly admired the combination of integrity and presentational skill with which he kept Mrs Thatcher focussed on the feasibility and desirability of an eventual agreement. The combination of openness and tactical address which won him the confidence of the Irish negotiators, and the fertility of mind with which he circumnavigated so many reefs in the drafting of the Agreement itself, were equally impressive. Clearly, the Anglo-Irish Agreement owes its existence in the first place to Garret FitzGerald and Margaret Thatcher herself; but there can be no doubt that the single other person on the British side without whom it would never have been concluded was Robert Armstrong.

The interdepartmental study of the Irish ideas by officials, which I chaired, was heavy going. The reluctance of the Northern Ireland Office to take the ideas seriously was reinforced by a feeling that their responsibility for a very difficult and potentially explosive situation in the Province was being jeopardised by ill-judged interference from Cabinet Office officials (and me in particular) who had no first-hand experience of the problems or feel for what was happening on the ground, and who would not have to carry the can if their bright ideas ended up (as they infallibly would) by making things worse. This attitude of mind was entirely understandable. On the other hand, one did not have to be a Northern Ireland expert to be aware that the NIO appeared temporarily at least to have run out of fresh ideas or to sense that Garret FitzGerald's overtures, however unacceptable they might be in detail, marked a sea change in the attitude of successive Irish governments to the Northern Ireland problem and that simply to turn them down as unacceptable could be to miss an unrepeatable opportunity.

Some may argue that neither Robert nor I, as officials, were entitled to push our own view of the need for some fresh initiative in Northern Ireland in this way. But we were, of course, acting in the knowledge that the Prime Minister herself thought that the time had come 'to do something about Northern Ireland' and recognised, albeit with reluctance, that the days of simple majority rule in Northern Ireland were over. As for the preconceptions with which we approached the negotiations, Robert Armstrong is on record (Martin O'Brien's unpublished MA thesis, 'Margaret Thatcher and Northern Ireland', [QUB, 1993], p. 31) as saying that he was motivated by a desire to make amends for Britain's ill-treatment of Ireland down the centuries; and I certainly shared the same desire.

I had felt for a long time that relations between our two islands were a historic mess; and that for this mess the British carried the main (though by no means the sole) responsibility. My interest in Irish history had originally been kindled by reading the horrendous accounts of the Famine in Cecil WoodhamSmith's *The Reason Why* and *The Great Hunger*; and I shared her view that '... the English, normally kind, behaved in Ireland as they behaved nowhere else' (*The Reason Why*, p. 110). By doing so, we had created a legacy of hatred, alienation and mistrust in a country whose natural relationship to us in terms of culture and propinquity was of belonging to the same family of nations as the rest of the United Kingdom.

My own descent – from the Catholic branch of an originally English Protestant family in Co Wexford – and my researches into family history had given me a feeling both for what it was like to be an Anglo-Irish Protestant and for what it was like to be a Catholic nationalist. I never had any sympathy with the idea that the unionists of the North could or should be pushed into a united Ireland against their will: rather it seemed to me that the long-term aim should be to bring the whole island of Ireland freely back into some closer relationship with England, Scotland and Wales. The nature of that relationship could not be defined in advance. It would have to evolve over time, probably over generations. Meanwhile I thought that the circumstances of Northern Ireland were such as to make it impossible for it to function contentedly either as an integral part of the United Kingdom tout court, or as part of a united Ireland, or on the basis of simple majority rule. There had to be some compromise whereby continuance of the Union could be assured while at the same time the character of the Northern State was reformed so as to legitimise nationalist aspirations and give them a link of some kind with the Republic.

In September 1983 I doubt if I could have formulated my views as clearly as this: I simply thought that a start had to be made in this general direction, and that the shape of what was feasible would emerge in the course of negotiation – provided that the negotiation could be kept going long enough.

Given the differences of view and interest between the departments involved, the detailed study of the Irish proposals commissioned by the Prime Minister was able to reach only tentative conclusions, most of them negative, about the feasibility or attractiveness of the Irish ideas. Joint judicial arrangements were thought to be fraught with constitutional difficulties and the objections to joint policing only marginally less insuperable (though neither was unequivocally ruled out). Formal acceptance by the Republic of the Union would be welcome, but was thought to be beyond the Taoiseach's power to deliver except in return for concessions on our part going beyond anything we could consider. There was, however, unanimous and unqualified agreement that anything which smacked of 'joint sovereignty' must be excluded. For the rest, the most important recommendation was that at the forthcoming Anglo-Irish Summit it would be tactically advantageous not to reject Dr FitzGerald's ideas out of hand.

My assistants in the Cabinet Office thought this a depressing outcome; but I was content with the tactical recommendation, since I was pretty sure that, once serious talking started between the Prime Minister and the Taoiseach, the process would take on a life of its own and things presently unthinkable would become starting points for compromise. This turned out to be correct.

II

When robert and I visited Dublin together immediately before the impending Anglo-Irish Summit, Dr FitzGerald saw Robert alone and explained his ideas along the lines already outlined by Michael Lillis, thus putting to rest any suggestion that Michael had not been a reliable interpreter of his views. Robert intimated that the Prime Minister was primarily concerned to reduce the level of violence and would not be willing to consider anything affecting Northern Ireland's status as part of the United Kingdom or involving 'joint sovereignty'.

The Summit took place at Chequers on 7 November. At our briefing meeting with her beforehand, the Prime Minister was tired, on edge and dismissive. She was convinced that the Republic was half-hearted in its opposition to the IRA and the security battle against it. Her overriding interest was to improve crossborder security cooperation; and she was deeply suspicious of anything which might be thought to touch in any way on Northern Ireland's constitutional status. The argument that Northern nationalists felt 'alienated' from the institutions of law and order in the Province, and that measures were needed to end that alienation, had no appeal for her. Indeed, the mere word 'alienation' (which she regarded as Marxist) had the same rebarbative effect on her as 'magnanimity' had had in the aftermath of the Falklands campaign: she seemed to regard both as codewords signalling the substitution of sentiment for rational calculation. At the same time, she reluctantly recognised that the degree of visible security cooperation she was looking for was unlikely to seem politically feasible to an Irish Taoiseach without some gestures to nationalist opinion on the part of the British.

This was realistic as far as it went. Unfortunately, it led her (as she makes clear in *The Downing Street Years*) to see the whole negotiation as a distasteful process of 'bargaining about security', in which the Irish government was deliberately 'withholding full cooperation to catch criminals and save lives' in order to secure political gains. In calmer moments, I think she realised that as far as Garret FitzGerald himself was concerned this was a less than complete explanation of his motivation. But it was a conviction which reasserted itself again and again as the negotiation went ahead; and it consistently obscured for her the objective desirability of finding ways of reconciling Northern nationalists to the Northern Ireland State.

Despite this inauspicious prelude, the Summit went off smoothly. The Prime Minister and the Taoiseach spent the morning tête-à-tête, and I have no reason to doubt the general accuracy of Garret FitzGerald's published account of what passed between them (*All in a Life*, pp. 476–7). While the two prime ministers were alone together, Dick Spring (then Tánaiste) and Peter Barry, the Irish Foreign Minister, had a separate meeting with Geoffrey Howe and Jim Prior, in the course of which (according to Dr FitzGerald) the two British ministers not only explored the possibility of policing on either side of the border being jointly controlled (coordinated anti-terrorist patrolling being an important element, as we saw it, in better security cooperation), but also suggested that although 'joint sovereignty' was ruled out, 'there might be some possibility of joint authority', even without constitutional amendment on the Irish side. If this is correct, it did not, to the best of my recollection, emerge in the post mortem discussion after the Irish had left. But it must be remembered that all our exchanges, both ministerial and official, were at this stage entirely freewheeling and exploratory, with a good deal of thinking aloud; neither side could have been under any illusions that the other was in a position to put forward any firm positions; nor had terms like 'joint authority' or 'joint responsibility' taken on the clarity which they acquired once the Irish side began to use them as negotiating currency.

It has also been suggested that as early as September 1983, i.e., presumably in one of Michael Lillis's exploratory talks with me, the Irish were told explicitly that the proposal for Irish involvement in maintaining security and order in Northern Ireland would be negotiable in return for amendment of Articles 2 and 3 of the Constitution. I have no remembrance of saying this; and I find it difficult to imagine how I or any British official could have done so except conceivably in a purely speculative way.

What I think I did say was that unequivocal recognition of Northern Ireland's status as part of the United Kingdom by the Republic, embodied in a constitutional amendment, would in my personal opinion create a new situation in which all sorts of possibilities, including joint policing and joint courts, would become thinkable. Both these possibilities were in fact actively discussed later in the negotiations: the Irish, however, vigorously rejected the thought that joint policing might apply on both sides of the border.

In the course of their talk at Chequers, Dr FitzGerald explained to Mrs Thatcher the importance he attached to the New Ireland Forum, then in progress in Dublin, and suggested that, until its recommendations were forthcoming, private and informal contacts between Lillis and Goodall should continue. The Prime Minister, however, was adamant that she must be in a position to say truthfully that no secret talks were in progress about the future of Northern Ireland. So, to my disappointment the Lillis-Goodall channel was to be closed down.

My disappointment, however, was short-lived. As soon as Dr FitzGerald and his team had left after lunch, the Prime Minister invited a small group of us including Geoffrey Howe, Jim Prior, Robert Armstrong and me to a discussion round the fire. I cannot now remember the details, but what later became known among the negotiators as 'the basic equation' – according the Irish some form of political involvement in Northern Ireland in return for formal Irish recognition of the Union – was seriously canvassed without any fireworks on Mrs Thatcher's part; and Robert and I came away with a remit to put in hand the preparation of an interdepartmental paper examining all the various policy options as a basis for further discussion.

Although the exercise was intended to be exploratory rather than productive of firm recommendations, it amounted in effect to a radical review of British policy in relation to Northern Ireland, to be conducted with special reference to Dr FitzGerald's ideas. Recording this in *The Downing Street Years*, Margaret Thatcher describes her talk with Dr FitzGerald as 'modestly useful' and her meeting with us afterwards as 'from our side the origin of the later Anglo-Irish Agreement'. I wrote that night in my diary: 'The PM has plainly taken on board FitzGerald's presentation of his case'. (Two years later, shortly after the Agreement was signed, Garret FitzGerald told me that from his perspective this occasion had been 'the developing point' for the subsequent negotiations.)

The drafting of the discussion paper occupied a good deal of my time over the next six weeks, which included my first ever visit to Belfast and the news that Edgar Graham, the young unionist politician whom I had met at Balliol, had been shot dead near Queen's by the IRA. The murder of someone I had so recently met and talked to (and been tempted to find faintly absurd) not only shocked me: it brought home to me that unionist intransigence was in part a response to very real dangers and that, however unreasonable it might appear to an outsider, its expression required considerable personal courage.

In Belfast, I stayed at Stormont Castle and my contacts were limited to the GOC (General Bob Richardson, whom I had known in Berlin) and a selection of senior officials headed by Sir Ewart Bell, Head of the Northern Ireland Civil Service. A quick tour round the city gave me the impression of West Belfast and the area on either side of the Peace Line as unnatural and shocking sores on an otherwise comfortably British urban landscape. Officials disguised whatever suspicions they may have felt about me in a friendly welcome and readiness to discuss the situation without any apparent inhibitions. What was striking was the extent to which everything focussed on the UK. All statistical comparisons quoted were with the rest of the United Kingdom: comparisons with the Republic were simply not thought relevant enough to be available. As the Permanent Secretary of the Department of Education explained: 'Our duty is to ensure that our educational system at all levels meets the requirements of the UK'. The Republic was of minimal interest, systems being different and standards seen as lower.

Only in the Department of Agriculture was reference made to the need for any sort of practical cross-border arrangement, in the shape of an all-Ireland regime for animal health. At a discussion dinner to meet senior officials at Stormont there were no suggestions for political change except from George Quigley, then Permanent Secretary of the Department of Finance, who advocated devolving the government of Northern Ireland to a power-sharing administration with a £1 billion development grant from London by way of inducement. Security considerations apart, the Republic seemed to exist only on the periphery of people's professional awareness: Northern Ireland's outlet to the wider world was through the United Kingdom and in no sense through what was clearly thought of as the poor, small, second-class state to the South.

My draft discussion paper was approved at a meeting chaired by Robert

Armstrong and forwarded to the Prime Minister just before Christmas under a minute from Robert which said that we faced a choice between three possible lines of policy: integrating Northern Ireland into the United Kingdom; moving to meet some of the concerns of the minority community (and of Dr FitzGerald's government) while confirming the Union; or simply carrying on with direct rule in the hope of being able, sooner or later, to restore some form of devolved government. The unspoken message of this minute, which I helped to draft, was that the line of approach opened up by Garret FitzGerald's initiative was the only practicable alternative to sitting tight and doing nothing.

III

On 4 January 1984 the Prime Minister convened a meeting at Chequers of those privy to the full story so far: Geoffrey Howe, Jim Prior, Antony Acland (Permanent Under-Secretary at the Foreign Office), Robert Andrew (Permanent Under-Secretary at the Northern Ireland Office), Alan Goodison (Ambassador at Dublin), Philip Woodfield (a former Permanent Under-Secretary at both the NIO and the Home Office whom we had been allowed to take on as a source of expert advice), John Coles (Charles Powell's predecessor as Foreign Affairs Private Secretary at No 10) and me. Discussion took place in the Long Gallery round a log fire, which the Prime Minister kept restlessly getting up to poke and replenish.

As usual when confronted with a range of unwelcome alternatives, Mrs Thatcher tacked and veered from one point to another, interrupting Geoffrey Howe's attempts at ordered exposition and from time to time bringing things back to square one with an observation of startling primitiveness. Why could we not redraw the border to exclude predominantly Catholic areas and relieve ourselves of the expense of paying social security to people who did not want to belong to the United Kingdom anyway? It was pointed out that this would not solve the problem: Catholic and Protestant communities were too intermingled in border areas; and even if adjustments were made to the border, the main body of Catholics lived in West Belfast and would remain within Northern Ireland. In that case, why not a wall through the centre of Belfast like the Wall through the Centre of Berlin? (No one seemed to want to comment on this). Following this line of thought, the Prime Minister asked why arrangements could not be made to transfer those members of the minority community who did not wish to remain under British rule to the Republic. After all, she said, the Irish were used to large scale movements of population. Only recently there had been a population transfer of some kind. At this point the silence round the fire became transfused with simple bafflement. After a pause, I asked if she could possibly be thinking of Cromwell. 'Cromwell: of course.' 'Well, Prime Minister, Cromwell's policy was known as "To

Hell or Connacht" and it left a scar on Anglo-Irish relations which still hasn't healed'. The idea of a population transfer was not pursued.

Once the Prime Minister had purged herself of her irritation at the intractability of the problem by throwing out these more or less outrageous suggestions, it was quite quickly agreed that proposals were needed by way of response to the Irish ideas which would commit the Republic to accepting the Union while according the Irish a measure of involvement in policing and the administration of the criminal law. To be politically acceptable, however, as well as achieving Mrs Thatcher's objective of visibly improving cross-border security, these arrangements would have to be reciprocal, so that any Irish participation in policing and law enforcement north of the border would be matched, at least in principle, by British involvement in policing and anti-terrorist trials south of the border. At the same time there could be a revised local government structure which would produce nationalist majorities in some councils as well as unionist majorities in others. Proposals on these lines, if approved by ministers, could be used informally to sound out Irish reactions, on the basis of which a decision would be taken as to whether or not to open negotiations proper.

Over the next month these proposals were fleshed out in consultation with senior officials of the NIO and FCO and with a very helpful input from Philip Woodfield. As a former official head of both the NIO and the Home Office, Philip had invaluable practical experience of policing and administrative problems; he also had an admirably dry wit, and a creative imagination with which to balance the gloomier misgivings of his erstwhile NIO colleagues.

As part of the process of educating myself about the problems we were dealing with, I had lunch on 10 January 1984 with Sir John Hermon, the Chief Constable of Northern Ireland. I had heard him speak at the BIA conference and been impressed with his forceful and articulate answers to difficult questions; but I expected him to be dour and cautious in talking to me. In the event he was quite remarkably frank. In the long term, he thought the unification of Ireland in some form or other was inevitable, and he was strongly against any further integration of the province into the United Kingdom. Although he was very much opposed to joint policing – which he said would raise all the unionists' hackles and bring violent demonstrations on to the streets, he thought that the political situation in Northern Ireland was more fluid than for many years. With the right political leadership, it should be possible to strike a balance between the concerns of the nationalists, who could feel secure in the longer term but needed reassurance for the short term, and those of the unionists, who were secure in the short term but needed reassurance about the long term. He suggested 'a new Sunningdale', with perhaps a Northern Ireland version of the 'New Ireland Forum' then in progress in Dublin plus a referendum to reassure the unionists. This conversation confirmed me in my feeling that we were on the right lines in looking for ways of striking a new political and constitutional balance in Northern Ireland which would both consolidate the Union and enhance the status of Irish nationalism.

A month later I was in Dublin again for a meeting of the Coordinating Committee. The Irish were heavily preoccupied with their Forum, to which Garret FitzGerald understandably attached historic importance in the Irish domestic context, but which it was already apparent was unlikely to be seen in London as particularly constructive. (In the event, because of the modifications necessary to secure Fianna Fáil's agreement to the text and Mr Haughey's subsequent emphasis on the need for an Irish 'unitary state', the positive impact of the report on the British government was even more muted than I had expected). Michael Lillis gave me privately a copy of the 'principles' section of this document, which had just been agreed, and asked how I thought the Taoiseach should handle the presentation of the completed report in Britain. I suggested that he should send the Prime Minister an advance copy, with a personal message explaining what he thought was important in it, what might be disregarded, and what he thought it should lead to. Whether because of this advice, or simply because it was the obvious thing to do, this is what the Taoiseach in fact did when the report was finally agreed at the end of April.

Michael also asked me what message John Hume should aim to get across to Mrs Thatcher when he had his first substantive meeting with her the following week. I said that the impression he made on her could be crucial to the whole process: if she thought well of his sincerity and good sense, the meeting could be immensely helpful. If it went badly, it would be the reverse. I thought his objectives should be: to convince her that the SDLP were serious people, able to deliver what they undertook;

that they were implacably opposed to violence; and that any 'models' or possible solutions which might emerge from the completed Forum Report should be taken as strictly illustrative and not as exclusive of other possible ways forward. He should also do his best to explain to her, in language not offensive to British ears, just what the 'alienation' of the nationalist community amounted to and why it was in both our interests to end it. Michael asked if he should put Hume in touch with me, so that I could make these points to him personally; but this I declined.

On 10 February the Prime Minister held a meeting with the two Secretaries of State (Geoffrey Howe and Jim Prior), Robert Armstrong and myself to consider the proposals we had worked up in the light of the January meeting at Chequers. For once, her doubts about the process we were engaged in seemed to be in abeyance: it was evident that she had read the papers carefully and virtually made up her mind to go ahead. With the courtesy towards her officials which was always pronounced when she was in a good mood (and which one could not fail to respond to), she praised the quality of the papers we had prepared and the work that had gone into them and thanked me warmly at three different points in the discussion. This was interrupted in the middle by the news of Andropov's death, which immediately took her attention away from Ireland and on to the burning question of who should represent the government at the funeral. We came away, however, with a decision that our package of proposals was to be put in outline to the Cabinet and that, subject to Cabinet agreement, it should then be put to Dermot Nally by Robert Armstrong on a strictly personal and informal basis to see how the Irish reacted.

The crucial element on which all else was predicated was to be an unequivocal acceptance by the Irish of Northern Ireland's status as part of the United Kingdom, preferably involving amendment of Articles 2 and 3 of the Irish Constitution, or failing this by means of some form (unspecified) of legally binding declaration. If that could be assured, we would be ready to look at the possibility of joint policing within a band of territory on either side of the border, to be overseen by a joint Security Commission; progressive harmonisation of the criminal law in both jurisdictions; arrangements for associating judges from each jurisdiction with criminal or terrorist trials in the other and the establishment of a joint Law Commission; the introduction of measures to meet nationalist concerns in the North including repeal of the Flags and Emblems Act; and a new local government structure in Northern Ireland. It was to be made clear to the Irish that the whole package was strictly tentative and exploratory.

Cabinet approval for an approach on these lines was obtained without difficulty on 16 February. By an ironical, or possibly ominous, stroke of fate, Mrs Thatcher had lost her voice as a result of laryngitis. One or two doubts were raised, but given the Prime Minister's endorsement and the backing of the two Secretaries of State with primary responsibility for the issue, there was no real opposition. The argument that doing something was less dangerous than doing nothing won general assent. On 29 February Robert Armstrong and I travelled to Dublin to present the package to the Irish the following day.

IV

ROBERT AND I WERE received in the Taoiseach's Office behind Leinster House by an Irish team comprising Dermot Nally, Seán Donlon (Secretary of the Irish Department of Foreign Affairs), Michael Lillis and Brian McCarthy, an official from the Taoiseach's Office who, as far as I can remember, made no subsequent appearance at the negotiating table. The atmosphere was one of intense curiosity and some puzzlement, since (as they later explained to us) the Irish had not expected any significant movement from either side until the Forum Report had appeared.

Dermot and his colleagues listened with close attention to Robert's exposition, which emphasised the tentative nature of our ideas and the primary importance of a binding acceptance by the Republic of Northern Ireland's status as part of the United Kingdom. As the exposition proceeded, with its clear stress on security measures, the Irish showed signs of some dismay. Having had no preview of our thinking, Dermot Nally had to respond off the cuff. He expressed great interest but warned us that any suggestion of amending the Irish Constitution was politically sensitive in the highest degree. The Irish government would encounter fierce nationalist criticism if it backed joint security measures without any compensating political dividend. They hoped that our package could include a parliamentary dimension (the 'Parliamentary Tier' to which Mrs Thatcher was resistant but which eventually came into existence as 'The British-Irish Inter-Parliamentary Body' and that the European Human Rights Convention could be incorporated into Northern Ireland's domestic legislation.

By way of an alternative to amending Articles 2 and 3, Michael Lillis recalled the suggestion made at Sunningdale that the Republic's acceptance that Irish unification could come about only with the consent of the majority in the North might be embodied in a formal international agreement registered at the United Nations; and he strongly opposed the idea that joint policing should be reciprocal, even to the limited extent envisaged in our proposals. It was clear, however, that no authoritative Irish view could be given until the Taoiseach had been consulted. We therefore enjoyed a pleasant lunch in the Taoiseach's dining room and a quick visit to the National Gallery of Ireland before returning to London to await a considered Irish reaction.

This was not long in coming. Michael Lillis rang me on the Taoiseach's instructions the following day, which was a Friday, and arranged to come and see me in London on the Monday. He confirmed that the Irish had been considerably taken aback at being presented with detailed, if tentative, British proposals, bearing in mind the Prime Minister's stated wish to avoid secret talks. They were pleased with our acceptance of 'the basic equation' and wanted to explore further our thinking on joint law enforcement and harmonisation of the criminal law. But our package did not strike an acceptable balance: we could not expect the Irish government to enter into joint security arrangements without any share in political authority; and the idea of joint policing on both sides of the border was not a runner. The problem of how to make British security forces acceptable to the minority community in the North would not be solved by introducing such forces into the South, which had no need of them and where they would be deeply resented.

A few days later Peter Barry, in London for the St Patrick's Day reception at the Irish Embassy, had lunch with Geoffrey Howe, whom I described in my diary as 'unfailingly amiable and unostentatiously well-briefed'. According to Garret FitzGerald (*All in a Life*, p. 496), Barry was told by Howe that 'while joint sovereignty was not on, the British could contemplate joint authority, but would find "joint responsibility" more palatable'. Exactly what Geoffrey Howe said to give this impression, I cannot now remember; but once again the Irish seem either to have attached undue weight to a speculative remark or else to have given it a wider significance than was intended. Under our suggestions for joint policing along the border, the proposed Security Commission would in fact have exercised joint responsibility for those arrangements; but the Irish were of course thinking of shared political authority over the province in the wider sense subsequently put forward as one of the three 'models' in the Forum Report. Garret FitzGerald's own strong attachment to 'joint authority' as the best way forward no doubt contributed to the misunderstanding, if misunderstanding it was. At all events, the Irish conviction that joint authority might somehow be attainable remained the keystone of their negotiating position until the drastic 'Out, Out, Out' of Mrs Thatcher's notorious press conference the following November.

Shortly after this conversation with Geoffrey Howe, Peter Barry told Alan Goodison in Dublin in fairly blunt terms that our proposals were unacceptable because of their heavy emphasis on security; and that the Irish government would be putting counter-proposals to us once the Forum Report had appeared. None of this was encouraging from the point of view of Mrs Thatcher's preoccupation with the need for better security cooperation. Nor was it easy to avoid concluding, from the way Dermot Nally had reacted to Robert's presentation on 1 March, that the Irish were getting cold feet at the prospect of being taken up on their offer to amend Articles 2 and 3. What we did not realise was that – as revealed in his memoirs (*All in a Life*, p. 498) – Garret had not at this stage mentioned to his Cabinet colleagues any thought of Articles 2 and 3 being put on the negotiating table, let alone that this possibility had been floated with us as far back as the previous September.

On 13 March the Irish Ambassador, Noel Dorr, called on me to reinforce what Michael had said. Contact with Noel, who is one of the fairest-minded and most thoughtful people I have ever met, with a rare gift for understanding the other side's point of view, became one of the pleasures of the negotiations. On this occasion, which was my first introduction to his intellectually thorough and gently persistent style of exposition, he explained the risks for the cohesion of the Irish State in tackling the issues raised by our proposals for joint security operations on both sides of the border and the possible repeal of Articles 2 and 3. I replied that we had only been responding to proposals put forward by the Irish themselves; and that as long as Articles 2 and 3 remained part of the Irish Constitution, Irish governments would be perceived as sharing the same ultimate objective as the IRA.

Noel took this in good part and a couple of weeks later introduced me to John Hume in the margins of a talk by Hume at Chatham House about the New Ireland Forum. Hume's public performance had been a model of reasonableness but in private I found him less sympathetic and inclined to bluster when invited to say what the Irish government might offer the unionists by way of reassurance that they were not being pushed down the road to a united Ireland. The following day – at a reception to mark

Encounter's[3] first seminar – I was taken aside by Jim Prior, who wanted to air his thoughts about preparing the Prime Minister for a range of possible moves on Northern Ireland which might be made even if the Irish were unable to deliver on Articles 2 and 3. Of his own officials he said with a smile, 'My people are rightly very conscious of all the risks of doing anything. They don't want to go as far as I would, or perhaps as you would. But they're perhaps not so aware of the risks of doing nothing'.

The following week I again had a long session with Noel Dorr, this time over a quiet lunch at the Irish Embassy. After we had ranged over the various irritants in Anglo-Irish relations, historical and otherwise, and agreed on the many links which bind the British and Irish together in the same cultural universe, I urged Noel not to read our proposals as being exclusively concerned with security or as having been put forward in a take-it-or-leave-it spirit. On the contrary, they were intended as a basis for dialogue, and had been carefully devised to include the possibility of an all-Ireland dimension in the North if the Irish could find some explicit way of meeting unionist concerns about the future status of Northern Ireland. The Irish would surely do well to explore this possibility further. Noel took this well on board. He also floated the idea, to which the Irish reverted repeatedly, that we should try to agree first on a set of principles as a framework within which to work out the practical measures needed to achieve our joint objectives. This abstract method of proceeding had absolutely no attraction for Mrs Thatcher and little appeal to any of us on the British side, since we felt that the negotiating energy which we would exhaust in trying to reach agreement on principles would be more profitably channelled into reaching agreement on actual measures.

Garret FitzGerald's advance copy of the Forum Report reached the Prime Minister on 27 April, with its three 'models' for the future of Northern Ireland of a unitary Irish state, a federal or confederal state or 'joint authority' whereby the British and Irish governments would

3. As a result of the recommendation of the Anglo-Irish Joint Studies Group, Encounter was initiated in July 1983 by the UK and Irish Governments as an independent non-governmental organisation with the purpose to organise periodic conferences and seminars, with a wide range of representation, on economic, social, cultural and other matters of common concern with a view to promoting mutual understanding, useful co-operation and good relations. It held two conferences in 1984.

administer Northern Ireland jointly. While we were left in no doubt that the Irish government's preference was for the third of these models (which they argued could be consistent with continued British sovereignty), the Taoiseach placed great emphasis on the statement that 'all parties in the Forum also remain open to discuss other views which may contribute to political development', urging us to understand that the three models were meant to be illustrative rather than exclusive. When the Report was published in Dublin on 2 May, Mr Haughey, as Garret records in his book, tried to present it as endorsing exclusively the model of a unitary Irish state. No one in London, I think, took this as impugning in any way the Taoiseach's own good faith in seeking an accommodation acceptable to unionists as well as nationalists. It was nevertheless an unambiguous reminder that in doing so he was a very long way ahead of a large body of opinion in his own country.

V

At the beginning of May 1984, I spent two instructive days in Northern Ireland as the guest of Jack Hermon and the RUC. As well as a discussion dinner with Jack Hermon and two of his colleagues, my programme included visits to the RUC HQ at Knock, to embattled police stations at Derry, Strabane and Armagh, and then by helicopter to Crossmaglen, where the combined police and army garrison inhabited a massive concrete citadel like a Star Wars transmutation of a Beau Geste fort. The RUC Sergeant who escorted me was a Catholic. He told me ruefully that his father had been a policeman, but he had grown up on the Falls Road and been educated by the Christian Brothers – 'So I caught it from both sides'.

From this trip, I gained an abiding impression of the high quality, as human beings, of the senior RUC officers I met – high in terms of dedication and courage, but also in terms of balance: there was a remarkable absence of bitterness, and a policeman's readiness to take people as they are; 'extremist' was a term applied even-handedly to Sinn Féin/IRA and to Paisleyite loyalists. No one I spoke to disputed the truth of the contention (which Mrs Thatcher found it so hard to acknowledge) that the alienation of the nationalist community from the Northern Ireland state had grown stronger, and that Sinn Féin were within striking distance of taking over from the SDLP as the political representatives of Northern nationalism. At the same time there was a universal conviction that the police were a great deal more acceptable to the Catholic population than the UDR, and more acceptable also than the Army.

All the senior policemen I met made the point that the RUC constituted what little there was of 'cement' in a deeply divided society, since all parties had to come to them for clearance to organise their marches and demonstrations and needed their help with public order problems of all kinds. In Derry, Strabane and Armagh I was told of the readiness of SDLP leaders to consult the police privately, and of the cooperative attitude of the Catholic priests; and there was a general determination to keep the police on the streets, despite the risks, in order to enable them to be seen and spoken to and do their police business in a 'normal' way.

More surprising was a marked absence of criticism of the Garda Síochána. There was universal regret at the recent withdrawal to Dublin of the Garda's border Task Force; and it emerged that communications between the RUC Headquarters in Lisburn and the Garda HQ in Dublin were so slow as to be virtually still in the era of the cleft stick. But everyone agreed that at station level crossborder cooperation with the Garda was excellent, although it became more formal as one went higher. The tributes at Strabane and Crossmaglen were particularly warm. At Strabane, where there were said to be 130 wanted terrorists just across the border in the South, the RUC Chief Inspector flatly denied that the Republic constituted a 'safe haven', although he thought that the Garda were handicapped by lack of information and by being allowed to hold suspects for only two days (as against seven days in the North). Some thought it would be helpful if RUC officers could take part in the interrogation of suspects by the Garda in the South or favoured joint planning so that operations on either side of the border could be synchronised; but the Station Commander at Crossmaglen said that this in effect was already happening. It was apparent that although there was no cooperation between the British and Irish armies (because the Irish army was not allowed to communicate with its British counterpart), relations between the two police forces were a good deal better than was believed to be the case in London and (as the Irish negotiators subsequently confirmed) there was an encouraging degree of mutual professional respect between the RUC and the Garda.

Finally, there was a general acceptance, from the Chief Constable downwards, of the 'Irishness' of Ulstermen, and a general feeling that some sort of political initiative, whether in response to the New Ireland Forum or independently of it, would be welcome. The impressions I gained from this visit remained with me throughout the negotiations and made me more receptive than I otherwise might have been to subsequent Irish pressure for Army patrols to be accompanied by police personnel and to Irish criticism of the sectarian character of the UDR.

I came back to London via Dublin, crossing the border from North to South for the first time in my life, just in time for the arrival of Dermot Nally and his team on 11 May to present the Irish counter-proposals. These took the form of an outright bid for joint authority, in accordance with the Taoiseach's preferred option in the Forum Report. Although amendment of Articles 2 and 3 was not absolutely ruled out, the Irish preference was for a simple statement, to be registered with the United Nations, providing that there would be no change in the status of Northern Ireland without the consent of the majority. Formal sovereignty over Northern Ireland, together with responsibility for defence, foreign policy and finance, would remain with Britain; for the rest, the two governments would administer Northern Ireland jointly through a British and an Irish minister appointed for the purpose, under whom there would be an elected legislative assembly and executive. The security forces in Northern Ireland, both police and military, would be under joint command; there would be an all-Ireland Law Commission charged with harmonising the criminal law in both jurisdictions, leading to the establishment of an all-Ireland Court; and the people of Northern Ireland would be entitled to both British and Irish citizenship. The Irish side justified the far-reaching nature of these proposals by arguing that Irish security forces and judges could not be seen to be acting in support of continuing British control over Northern Ireland without some form of joint political structure there.

It is a reflection of the universal tendency of elected governments to view international negotiations through the prism of their own domestic political preoccupations that even Garret FitzGerald seems to have thought that a package on these lines might be a starter with Mrs Thatcher. In the event it nearly derailed the negotiations before they had seriously begun. In discussion with our Irish opposite numbers, Robert and I quickly sensed that the Irish were bidding high in the light of the Forum Report and in the expectation of hard bargaining to come. We left them in no doubt that their proposals went far beyond anything that British ministers had so far considered and would certainly not be acceptable as they stood. At the same time, we privately recognised the force of the argument that, in terms of Irish domestic politics, no Irish government, however well-disposed, could afford to give formal backing to British rule in Northern Ireland without being given any share of political responsibility for what was done there.

This was not, however, the light in which the Irish proposals were seen either by Northern Ireland Office officials or the Prime Minister. The

NIO argued with evident satisfaction that the Irish had set their sights so high that the chances of negotiating an acceptable compromise were nil and further discussion was unlikely to be profitable. Jim Prior maintained his view that the risks of doing nothing outweighed the risks of any attempt at political progress; but this did not necessarily envisage progress based on an agreement with the Irish. Robert's minute to the Prime Minister required even more careful drafting than usual: it concluded that although the Irish proposals were unacceptable and fraught with difficulties, there were elements in them on which it might be possible to build if we were willing to give the Irish a share of responsibility in limited areas.

The Prime Minister's reaction came at a meeting held immediately after Cabinet on 24 May. Her mood was not benevolent. The starkness of the Irish bid for joint authority savoured of effrontery and stung her into more than usually unguarded outbursts of irritation which, I noted in my diary, were the authentic echo of 'British ignorance, arrogance, contempt and dislike for Ireland down the ages'. However, I spoke up as well as I could; Geoffrey Howe did his patient best; and at the end of a bad-tempered discussion the show remained on the road. However unattractive the Prime Minister might sound when blowing off emotional steam, she was usually prepared to listen to a clearly and concisely deployed argument. More important, she realised that the fact that we were talking to the Irish about a possible political initiative was a protection against unwelcome pressure over Northern Ireland from the United States, from our European allies – and perhaps even from within the Conservative Party: Norman Lamont, whom I met at a dinner on 18 May, told me that opinion in the Party would favour a positive response to the Forum Report and possibly some Irish dimension in the north itself. Breaking off the talks would therefore have been a tactical mistake.

So, the Irish proposals were anathematised and their offer to recognise the Union in a statement, without amending their constitution, was seen as falling far short of what they had dangled before us earlier (which indeed it did). But the Prime Minister reluctantly accepted that if she wanted to take a political initiative in Northern Ireland which required Irish cooperation, then the Irish would have to be given a political role in the province of some kind. Making it abundantly clear that she disliked the whole business, she agreed that exploratory negotiations to arrive at a balanced package of proposals should continue; but it was unanimously agreed that a binding commitment by the Republic to recognise Northern Ireland's status as part of the United Kingdom should be an essential precondition of any Irish involvement in the North's affairs.

The day after this meeting, Jim Prior again saw Peter Barry in London and impressed on him our disappointment at the apparent Irish reluctance – contrary to the impression we had received from Michael Lillis – to offer to amend Articles 2 and 3. Barry expressed his own disappointment at our negative response to the Irish proposals; but he clearly took delivery of Jim Prior's message; and the Irish drew from it the not unreasonable conclusion that amendment of Articles 2 and 3 was a key British preoccupation. As we now know from *All in a Life* (pp. 498–9), it was at this point that Garret FitzGerald decided, in consultation with Dick Spring, Peter Barry and John Hume, that the time had come to be more forthcoming on Articles 2 and 3 and to drop the idea of joint command arrangements for the Northern Ireland security forces. As a result, when I visited Dublin for another meeting of the coordinating committee on 30 May, Peter Barry came down to the dining room at Iveagh House to see me. He said that, in the light of his conversation with Jim Prior, he had discussed the constitutional point further with the Taoiseach. It would be extremely difficult for the Irish government to secure an amendment of Articles 2 and 3. Nevertheless, he wanted us to know that, as part of a package which included a substantial political quid pro quo from the British side, the Taoiseach would be prepared to seek to amend the Irish Constitution. He did not suggest what this quid pro quo might be, but indicated that the Irish government's thinking was still very fluid. Armed with this important information, I returned to London and drafted a further minute for Robert to put to the Prime Minister reporting what Peter Barry had said. This commented that, although the Irish were looking for a substantial (and as yet unquantified) political quid pro quo for amending Articles 2 and 3, they had made a major move in response to what they perceived as a major British concern and had thereby changed the background against which we had hitherto been considering the Irish proposals.

At this point Philip Woodfield, in his capacity as Special Adviser, submitted a think piece which concluded that the Irish readiness to consider amending Articles 2 and 3 opened up possibilities for shared responsibility between London and Dublin, always provided that there could be agreement on a devolved administration in Northern Ireland (which would greatly reduce the scope for Irish government involvement). A few days later, Noel Dorr called on Robert Armstrong to confirm formally the Irish readiness to amend their constitution as part of 'a broad and balanced package'. At the same time, he acknowledged our difficulties with the Irish proposal for joint control of the security forces and emphasised instead the desirability of joint courts for the trial of terrorist offences.

The prospect of our having to take seriously the Irish offer of constitutional amendment (and consequently make some provision for Irish involvement in the affairs of the North), coming on top of the inflated expectations revealed by the Irish counter-proposals of 11 May, seriously alarmed the Northern Ireland Office. Robert Andrew lost no time in writing to Robert Armstrong questioning whether the Irish government would really be willing or able to amend their constitution, and seeking to scotch the idea that there might be any sharing of responsibility with the Irish other than on a strictly consultative basis. Using language designed to evoke a sharply unionist response from the Prime Minister, he suggested that ministers needed to decide whether professed Irish readiness to amend their constitution was enough to justify contemplating a 'potential infringement of British sovereignty over Northern Ireland': a 'num' question if ever there was one.

This was followed by a minute to the Prime Minister from Jim Prior, echoing Robert Andrew's doubts in less emotive terms and at the same time introducing the important concept of a two-stage approach. He suggested that in the first stage we could offer, in return for improved cross-border security arrangements, some minor reforms in Northern Ireland which we wanted to do anyway. If the Irish then showed serious interest in amending their constitution, we could go further and consider (for example) harmonising the criminal law in both jurisdictions, a strengthened political voice for the nationalist minority and measures to recognise the nationalist 'identity'. In no circumstances, however, should we contemplate sharing responsibility: the most the Irish could look for would be a right to be consulted, perhaps through a joint ministerial council, whereby they would be able to exercise 'influence rather than shared authority'. The unionists would find this difficult to accept, but might be brought to do so if the Irish had removed from their constitution the territorial claim to the North. Meanwhile we should continue to probe the Irish to see what was the minimum they would accept by way of political involvement in return for seeking to amend their constitution.

Although framed to sound as positive as possible, this approach struck me as being as unrealistic in its own way as the Irish ideas for shared authority. It was by now abundantly clear that the Irish government could not be expected to sell to its own electorate the idea of systematically closer collaboration with the British security forces without some corresponding political gain; and it seemed inconceivable that they would be enticed into a constitutional referendum, with all its domestic political risks, simply in return for an offer to consider the introduction of consultative arrangements if the referendum was successful. It was, nevertheless, an approach well calculated to appeal to Mrs Thatcher's preoccupation with improved security and mounting scepticism about the wisdom of the exercise on which we had embarked.

After Cabinet on 21 June, she discussed it at a meeting with the Foreign and Northern Ireland Secretaries in which Robert Armstrong and I participated. As she records in *The Downing Street Years*, Irish confirmation that they would be willing to hold a referendum to amend their constitution as part of a suitably substantial political package had alarmed rather than encouraged her, an instinctive feeling reinforced by the NIO's warnings about a possible infringement of British sovereignty. She had no difficulty with the principle of a two-stage approach; but it took some strenuous argument to establish the point that no improvement in cross-border security or in the attitude of the minority community was attainable without the cooperation of the Irish government and the involvement of the minority in the institutions of government in the North. Accepting the logic of this, the Prime Minister agreed that the balance of advantage lay in continuing the dialogue: but her reluctance was undisguised.

At the same time, Jim Prior's two stages were given more substance. It was envisaged that the first stage, as well as providing for enhanced cross-border security cooperation, might include some unspecified relaxations in the emergency legislation, repeal of the Flags and Emblems Act (which forbade public display of the Irish flag) and the establishment of an Irish consul in Belfast. The second stage, to be implemented only in the wake of a successful Irish constitutional referendum, might include strengthening the existing Intergovernmental Council to give the Irish some consultative say in Northern affairs; enhanced status for the Irish consul in Belfast; a joint Security Commission to implement a unified system of criminal justice in both parts of Ireland and joint policing arrangements along both sides of the border; a Law Commission to work towards harmonisation of the criminal law; allowing Irish citizens resident in the North to vote in elections there; an all-Ireland Economic Commission; a joint parliamentary body; and greater devolved powers for the Northern Ireland Assembly.

I saw little prospect of the Irish agreeing to amend their constitution on this heavily conditional basis. But at least it had the makings of a plausible negotiating package, which Robert Armstrong and I were mandated to work up into a set of proposals for ministers to consider. Meanwhile the Prime Minister would herself probe Dr FitzGerald's position on a constitutional referendum when she talked to him in the margins of the forthcoming European Council meeting at Fontainebleau on 26 June.

I have no knowledge of the mysterious indirect approach which Garret FitzGerald says he received at this juncture from Jim Prior (*All in a Life*, pp. 499–500): but it does not sound out of character. It was clear at the time that, although he was keener than his officials on seeking an agreement of some kind with Dublin, Jim Prior shared their scepticism both about the unacceptable price we would have to pay to achieve an Irish constitutional referendum and the unlikelihood of such a referendum succeeding. So, I assume that, as Garret seems to have guessed, Prior was hoping to explore with him the possibility of a scaled down package which would leave British sovereignty unimpaired and require no action on the Irish Constitution. Playing for higher stakes, the Taoiseach did not give him the opportunity to make his case. It is only fair to Jim Prior and the NIO to note that the eventual outcome of the negotiations was indeed a scaled down package which involved no change to the Irish Constitution. But the balance it struck between an enlarged 'Irish Dimension' and a more explicit Irish acceptance of the status quo in Northern Ireland was significantly different from anything envisaged by the NIO in June 1984.

The Prime Minister's brief encounter with the Taoiseach at Fontainebleau on 26 June did not advance matters much. Nor, however, did it derail them.

Given her dislike for the road on which she had embarked, this was in itself a positive outcome; and I was responsible for encouraging Garret (through Michael Lillis) to use every opportunity to argue his case with Mrs Thatcher face to face, since I knew that politicians are much readier to listen with understanding to one another than they are to officials trying to describe other people's political imperatives.

On this occasion, Garret was able to explain his thinking on replacing Articles 2 and 3 with an 'aspiration' to Irish unity by consent, which focussed Mrs Thatcher's mind on the unappetising but important question of what an amended Irish constitution might actually look like on this point. He also made his case for joint authority being distinct from joint sovereignty. This Mrs Thatcher firmly rejected as involving a derogation from British sovereignty. According to the British first-hand record of the conversation made at the time, she also made it clear that for the same reason none of the 'models' in the Forum Report could be a basis for progress. Garret FitzGerald's account makes no mention of this part of their conversation, perhaps because he did not take fully on board how categoric Mrs Thatcher's rejection of the options in the Forum Report was intended to be. This misunderstanding was to play its part later in sharpening the Irish sense of affront at the tone of Mrs Thatcher's press conference after the November Summit (see below). At the next Cabinet Meeting (for which I was on leave), it was agreed that we should continue to probe the Irish position through the Armstrong-Nally talks, on the basis of the proposals commissioned at the Prime Minister's meeting of 21 June.

VI

When I returned from leave at the beginning of July 1984, I had been transferred from the Cabinet Office back to the FCO as the Deputy Under-Secretary responsible for Intelligence and Defence matters; but, at Robert Armstrong's request, I retained responsibility for helping him with the Anglo-Irish negotiations. This meant that there was no reduction in my involvement or in my access to Robert; but the work load on matters other than Irish was a good deal heavier than it had been in the Cabinet Office. One advantage of the new arrangement, however, was that it brought me into a close working relationship with Geoffrey Howe and enabled me (I like to think) to give him the back-up he needed to play what proved to be a key role in keeping the Anglo-Irish show on the road until the Agreement was finally concluded. Geoffrey Howe's Welsh background gave him an innate sympathy with the Irish; and his judgements and calculations – as well as being weighed with sometimes exasperating care – were informed by a statesman's breadth of vision and sense of history. Attending meetings with him at No 10 on this and other matters over the next two and a half years familiarised me with his reflective and patiently exploratory approach to policy issues as well as making me a sometimes bemused witness of Mrs Thatcher's impatient and increasingly high-handed way of responding to it. In the middle of a battle across the table in the Cabinet Room, Geoffrey would sometimes scribble me a note: 'Are we winning?' We seldom were.

From my new desk in the FCO (where I occupied the handsome room originally designed for the Permanent Secretary of the old Colonial Office), the first task awaiting me on the Irish front was to finish preparing the papers for the meeting which Robert had arranged with Dermot Nally and Co in Dublin on 16 July. This involved obtaining the Prime Minister's approval for the line we were to take and also reaching prior agreement with the NIO on how the meeting should be handled. In the course of these preparations, I hit on the phrase 'institutionalised consultation' to describe what we might offer the Irish by way of involvement in Northern

Ireland affairs, and this became our standard negotiating shorthand with the Irish for the British alternative to 'joint authority'.

Among the ammunition we needed for the next round with the Irish was some illustrative wording to replace Articles 2 and 3, to which the NIO wanted to add an explicit provision that, in the absence of consent to Irish unity, the 'Irish nation recognises that the constitutional status of Northern Ireland as part of the United Kingdom must remain unchanged'. With Robert's support, I resisted this as being simply unrealistic: securing popular support for abandoning the 'territorial claim' inherent in Articles 2 and 3 would in itself be a major political hurdle for an Irish government; to ask them in addition to spell out in the constitution of the Irish state their acceptance of Northern Ireland's status as part of the United Kingdom would be to guarantee the failure of the whole enterprise. The NIO also expressed serious reservations about a joint parliamentary body and about having any form of resident Irish representation in Belfast – even though these developments were envisaged as taking place only in the event of a successful referendum to remove Articles 2 and 3.

It was common ground with the NIO that our aim should be to achieve a devolved, power-sharing government for Northern Ireland; and that if there were to be some Irish government involvement in Northern Ireland affairs on a consultative basis, the consultative arrangements would be limited to matters not within the responsibility of the devolved administration. But the NIO argued that the introduction of any Irish Dimension would nullify efforts to secure unionist agreement to power-sharing. There was evident force in this argument; but, as I argued in reply, it was equally true that if we failed to make provision for any Irish Dimension, the SDLP would continue to boycott the Assembly and refuse to take part in whatever power-sharing arrangements we might devise. If we were to make any progress at all, either on improving cross-border security cooperation or on winning the support of the nationalist community for the institutions of law and order in Northern Ireland, some form of Irish Dimension was inescapable. In the end, the NIO, with even greater reluctance than the Prime Minister, acquiesced in our going to Dublin to explore possible forms of Irish involvement in the North, provided it was made crystal clear that joint authority was ruled out.

Robert and I accordingly met Dermot Nally and his small team in

Dublin on 16 July and began the task of making clear to them that joint authority in any shape or form had to be excluded and of trying to persuade them that 'institutionalised consultation' could be made substantial enough to meet the conditions for amending their constitution. As we had been strongly encouraged to do both by the Taoiseach himself and in my informal conversations with Michael Lillis, we expressed interest in the paragraph in the Forum Report which recorded the Irish government's readiness to consider solutions other than the unitary, federal or confederal models which were unacceptable to us. We said that, provided the territorial claim contained in Articles 2 and 3 was formally and definitively waived, British ministers were prepared to consider 'a significant role' for the Irish government in the North, on the understanding that the final decision on all matters not devolved to a local administration must remain with the British government. The Irish side were doubtful whether such essentially consultative arrangements would meet the needs of their ministers or be sufficient to end the alienation of the nationalist community; but they did not reject the idea out of hand.

In answer to questions from the Irish side, we thought that the Irish government's right to be consulted might be exercised through an Irish representative resident in Belfast as well as bilaterally or through the machinery of the Anglo-Irish Intergovernmental Council; and that it could be enshrined in legislation and in a formal agreement. All this, while stopping short of 'joint authority', would in practical terms give the Irish government, for the first time, an effective say in Northern Ireland's affairs and provide the nationalist community with visible evidence that their interests were being protected. We also reminded the Irish that our proposal for a joint security commission was still on the table; and there was some exploratory and inconclusive discussion of ways of increasing the effectiveness of our security operations and making them more acceptable to the nationalist community.

At the end of this meeting, Robert reported to the Prime Minister that we thought we had convinced the Irish that joint authority was not on offer and had moved the dialogue on to a more realistic basis. This may have been true as far as Dermot Nally and his colleagues were concerned, but Irish ministers, and the Taoiseach himself, were not so easily disillusioned. Nally and his team met us in London on 30 July in the claustrophobic surroundings of a basement conference room in the Royal Horseguards Hotel to tell us that at first sight our approach appeared 'inadequate'. It would fail to satisfy the nationalists, while arousing unionist fears of creeping unification. To meet the Irish requirement for a settlement which would be both durable and sufficient to facilitate a successful referendum to amend the Irish Constitution, the Republic would have to be given a measure of 'substantial authority' in the North. We again rehearsed the case for 'institutionalised consultation' and pressed Nally to say whether he really thought that this would not be enough. Speaking very personally, Nally conceded that 'consultation was probably what it would come down to in the end': but the outcome would have to be presentable as consistent with the Forum Report.

At the same time, the Irish side put renewed emphasis on the need to reorganise the police and on the desirability of mixed courts (i.e., courts with at least one Irish judge) to try terrorist offences. On policing, they floated the idea of an unarmed force comprising Catholics and members of the Garda to police nationalist areas, an unarmed force drawn from the RUC to police unionist areas and a separate, armed force comprising members of the Garda as well as of the RUC to conduct anti-terrorist operations throughout the North, all three forces to be under the authority of the joint security commission which we had suggested. Although they stressed that these ideas were tentative, they were emphatic that visible changes in the arrangements for enforcing law and order in Northern Ireland were crucial to ending the alienation of the minority community.

In the light of this discussion, Robert Armstrong and I felt that there were real signs of give in the Irish resistance to 'institutionalised consultation'. Although their ideas about policing were far-fetched and unacceptable, they seemed to us to reflect a genuine and not unreasonable conviction that the nationalist community would never identify with a police force which was more than 90% Protestant, backed by the British Army, and by the UDR which was 97% Protestant. Political arrangements based on consultation and some movement on our side on the law and order front were therefore the key areas on which we judged that we now had to concentrate.

The Prime Minister found all this less than reassuring, and her doubts were reinforced by a minute from Jim Prior, in which he predictably dismissed the Irish ideas on policing as 'totally unrealistic'. Security was the most sensitive issue in Northern Ireland and impinged directly on sovereignty. There could be no question of tampering with it, beyond the suggestion we had already made for joint policing along a narrow border strip, nor should the police be brought under the control of a joint security commission. Our exploratory discussions should focus on fleshing out the possibilities for institutionalised consultation.

Accordingly, when the Taoiseach came to London in his capacity as President of the European Council on 3 September in a fairly buoyant mood, the Prime Minister firmly rejected the Irish ideas on policing and declined to contemplate any changes in either the RUC or the UDR. She stressed the magnitude of what we were offering in terms of giving the Irish a right to be consulted about Northern Ireland, reiterated the absolute unacceptability of 'joint authority' and expressed fears that whatever helped one community in Northern Ireland would arouse hatred in the other and thereby make the situation worse. She resisted the Taoiseach's wish to move the discussions forward at a faster pace (the familiar Irish desire to maintain 'momentum') and turned down as premature his suggestion that the Northern Ireland political parties might be brought into the discussion process.

On 10 September it was announced that Jim Prior (who had made little secret of his distaste for Mrs Thatcher and found her increasingly difficult to deal with) had resigned from the Cabinet and Douglas Hurd was promoted to be Northern Ireland Secretary in his place. As was to happen again later when Hurd was replaced by Tom King, the change of Secretary of State soon produced a hardening of the NIO's position on the negotiations, as senior NIO officials impressed on him their reasons for scepticism. In the immediate aftermath of the Thatcher-FitzGerald meeting, however, the negotiations entered a mildly euphoric phase.

At the annual BIA Conference at Cambridge on 15 September, Peter Barry gave an optimistic speech, raising expectations of an early joint UK-Irish initiative on the North. My impression that the Irish saw an agreement as being within reach was confirmed by a talk I had the same afternoon with Peter Sutherland (Attorney-General in Garret FitzGerald's government), whose approach to the negotiations struck me as well-informed and sensible. Then Michael Lillis (with whom I had been in regular contact during the summer) invited Morwenna and me to meet Garret FitzGerald and his wife, Joan, at dinner at the Lillis' house in Dublin on 18 September, the evening before our next negotiating session with the Irish. This was my first direct encounter with Garret, who arrived late from an all-day Cabinet meeting on the economy but then stayed talking animatedly and with great frankness about the negotiations until after 1 am, I wrote in my diary: '... a large, unassuming man, face papery in colour, no side, good sense of humour, discussed everything as an equal ... talking in quick machine-gun bursts, sudden gusts of hearty laughter. Realistic and perceptive on the prospects for an (agreed) initiative, realistic and a shade rueful about Mrs T'.

When Robert Armstrong and I met our Irish counterparts the next morning, it appeared that they had indeed accepted that joint authority was not to be had and were ready to explore with us the form and extent of the 'institutionalised consultation' they might expect in return for amending the Irish Constitution. They conceded that the last word on all the matters to which consultation might apply would remain with British ministers; but they argued that it would be impossible for an Irish government to carry a constitutional amendment to Articles 2 and 3 simply in return for something described as 'consultation', which on the face of it would impose no obligation on the British to take account of Irish views. So, while acknowledging that the reality would be 'consultative', they hoped that some stronger word could be found to describe the new arrangements, and one which would carry the implication that Irish views, while not decisive, would have a real influence on the eventual decision.

They accepted that foreign affairs, defence and finance would in any case remain with the British government, and hoped that consultation would apply to all other matters which were not devolved to an elected Northern Ireland government; and they explained their preliminary thinking on the content of a possible amendment to the Irish Constitution in which the alleged territorial claim would be replaced by an aspiration to Irish unity with the consent of the majority of the population of Northern Ireland.

At the same time, they continued to press for visible changes to the structures of law enforcement in the North. They welcomed our ideas for a joint security commission and all-Ireland law commission, but argued strongly that these would not be enough to end the alienation of the nationalist community; and although we seemed to be successful in persuading them that the changes which they proposed to the RUC were unrealistic, they continued to press hard for the establishment of mixed courts.

Although important differences of detail and emphasis remained and it was clear that ministers on both sides had yet to focus fully on what was emerging, Irish readiness to give up joint authority and accept consultation (in fact, if not in name) as the core of the proposed new arrangements seemed to mark a substantive advance. It was agreed there was now enough common ground to justify our aiming to produce together a tentative package of proposals for consideration by the Prime Minister and the Taoiseach at the next Anglo-Irish Summit, scheduled to take place in Dublin in November.

The Prime Minister's enthusiasm for the process, however, continued to wane. At two successive meetings with the Foreign and Northern Ireland Secretaries (on 5 and 10 October) she insisted that it was too early to start thinking in terms of an agreed package. The Irish, she thought, still had unrealistically high expectations and were trying to push ahead much too fast. She conceded that progress had been made in getting them to move away from joint authority, but this only made it easier for them to press for a package to be agreed at the Summit. She reluctantly accepted that consultation limited to security matters would not be enough for them but thought that a great deal more work needed to be done on how institutionalised consultation would work and on how the unionists were to be persuaded to accept an Irish Dimension.

I was present at only the first of these meetings, although I was heavily involved in the briefing for both. My main concern, in the face of Mrs Thatcher's sharpening misgivings, was that the negotiations should be allowed to continue. In my brief for Geoffrey Howe, and as far as I was able at the Prime Minister's meeting, I argued that the Irish had come a long way from their initial position and that, if it was accepted that to do nothing was more dangerous than to take a new initiative, the present exercise offered the best, and probably the only, hope of progress.

Mrs Thatcher's feeling that officials were moving ahead too fast under their own negotiating impetus was understandable and probably right. But it was clear that her doubts went deeper, and that the more feasible an Agreement with the Irish began to appear, the less she liked the idea. How far this dislike reflected her own instinctive mistrust of the Irish and how far it was fuelled by unionist arguments impressed on her privately by Ian Gow (her Parliamentary Private Secretary and trusted confidant), Enoch Powell and others, it was impossible for an official to judge; my impression is that these private contacts were an important influence on her throughout. At all events, although the argument that it was better to be seen to be engaged in a negotiation than to be doing nothing continued to carry the day, it did so only by a narrow margin: travelling (not very hopefully) was all very well, and helped to keep American pressures at bay; actually arriving would be quite another matter.

In the ministerial discussions the new Northern Ireland Secretary took a cautiously sceptical line: it would be possible to devise a workable basis for institutionalised consultation, but it was highly improbable that the Irish government would be able to deliver constitutional change; and we needed to think more about what could be offered to the unionists if we were not to exchange Catholic alienation for Protestant alienation. Douglas Hurd was keen to put the Northern political parties – and specifically the unionists – in the picture about the state of the negotiations, in order to avoid charges of bad faith if the Summit resulted in a degree of agreement with Dr FitzGerald for which they were unprepared; but Robert Armstrong argued successfully against this on the ground that disclosure at this stage of Dr FitzGerald's readiness to consider amending Articles 2 and 3 could wreck the negotiations and even bring down the Irish government.

On 12 October the measured diplomatic pace of our negotiations received a dramatic jolt in the shape of the bomb explosion at the Grand Hotel at Brighton, when the IRA narrowly failed to assassinate the Prime Minister and most of the British Cabinet. Nothing could have illustrated more vividly the reality of the antagonism we were trying to defuse than the singular brutality of the language with which the IRA claimed responsibility: 'Today we were unlucky but remember we only have to be lucky once'. In the light of her atavistic suspicions about Irish support for terrorism, Mrs Thatcher would have been only human if she had responded by withdrawing from the negotiating process which it was already clear that she disliked. In the event, however, although her scepticism continued to grow, the Brighton experience had no immediate impact on the Armstrong-Nally talks, the next round of which took place in London on 15 October.

Immediately beforehand I had forty minutes on Ireland with Geoffrey Howe, to all outward appearance unscathed by the appalling experience of Brighton, who (with an evident eye to the Prime Minister's doubts) stressed that the Anglo-Irish negotiations must not be rushed. For the meeting with the Irish which followed, the British team (hitherto confined to Robert Armstrong and myself) was expanded to include Robert Andrew and Tony Brennan from the Northern Ireland Office, Alan Goodison, our Ambassador at Dublin, also became a regular participant. Robert Andrew and Tony Brennan had been fully briefed and consulted throughout but they had not until then had a place at the negotiating table. Their arrival signalled Douglas Hurd's determination to gain some measure of control over what was going on as well as the Prime Minister's intensifying sensitivity to unionist concerns. While the NIO presence certainly provided a steady injection of realism into the British negotiating position, Robert Andrew's disposition to emphasise difficulties rather than try to find ways round them occasionally seemed to verge on sabotage.

Independently of the NIO contribution, the Armstrong-Nally meeting on this occasion revealed some important divergences of view. On 'institutionalised consultation', the Irish wanted formal, high profile arrangements based on a joint ministerial Commission for Northern Ireland. They envisaged the proposed joint security commission as giving them a say in the composition of the security forces, and emphasised the need for visible measures to win the confidence of the minority community in the police – if not by the creation of a separate police force for nationalist areas, then by restructuring the RUC so as to have nationalist areas policed by Catholic policemen. There was a lengthy discussion of the Irish proposal for mixed courts, on which Robert Armstrong and I were inclined to be sympathetic, while making it clear that there could be no considered British reaction until the judiciary, including the Lord Chief Justice of Northern Ireland, had been consulted. The NIO representatives emphasised the practical difficulty of finding enough suitable QCs in Northern Ireland to provide the additional judges which would be required.

At this meeting also, the question of devolution came into sharper focus. Both sides agreed that a devolved government for Northern Ireland was intrinsically desirable. The Irish suggested that it would constitute a powerful incentive to unionists to agree to participate in a devolved government if it was made clear that devolved matters would fall outside the scope of the 'institutionalised consultation' between the British and Irish governments. In other words, the more effectively the politicians of the two communities in Northern Ireland could agree to cooperate in governing it, the less room there would be for Southern involvement or interference. But the Irish envisaged the devolved government as being based on power-sharing between the two communities, whereas the British saw no early prospect of the unionists agreeing to take part in power-sharing arrangements on top of having to swallow the kind of Irish Dimension we were discussing.

Notwithstanding these disagreements, the atmosphere of the meeting was constructive and friendly, thanks in large part to the mutual confidence and liking between Robert Armstrong and Dermot Nally, both in their different ways strong on patience, tact and humour. It was agreed that it would be useful to try to produce, as a basis for discussion at the forthcoming Summit, a single working paper setting out those areas in which provisional agreement was close and those in which positions were still far apart. The day closed with a convivial dinner at Brooks's, at which there was an animated discussion of the right relationship between Britain and Ireland in the longer term. Both Dermot Nally and Noel Dorr believed that a much closer relationship, analogous in some ways to Home Rule, was a desirable possibility in the long run; Michel Lillis, heated with wine, forcefully disagreed and rehearsed some of Ireland's historic resentments against Britain in language which embarrassed the other members of the Irish team. Seán Donlon, who throughout the negotiations was the most outspoken advocate of nationalist concerns, poured oil on the waters with an eloquent tribute to the sustained and concentrated attention which the Irish Question was receiving from senior British officials to a degree unprecedented since the time of the Anglo-Irish Treaty.

In reporting this meeting to the Prime Minister, Robert Armstrong acknowledged that the Irish were pressing for greater changes than we could contemplate, although there was provisional agreement to some of the main elements in a possible package. He recommended that the Prime Minister should use the forthcoming Summit to impress on the Taoiseach the limits to which we could go as well as her commitment to the search for an agreement. The Taoiseach's response to the meeting was to urge us, through Alan Goodison in Dublin, to use the Summit to reach final agreement. If this could not be achieved, we should at least come close enough to a final agreement to enable the Irish to plan on holding their constitutional referendum before the local elections due to take place in Northern Ireland in May 1985.

The Prime Minister, for her part, commented that there was no question of reaching agreement at the Summit and that she remained concerned by the breadth of the gap between Irish expectations and what we could offer. Geoffrey Howe, meanwhile, impressed on me his wish to 'keep his hand on the process at every stage'; and I accordingly drafted for him a minute to the Prime Minister in which he endorsed Robert Armstrong's recommendations, weighed the pros and cons of the position reached in the negotiations and said he continued to believe that the process represented 'the least unpromising way forward on the Northern Ireland question'. Not for the last time, the effect of a reasoned and positive input from Geoffrey Howe was to prompt a rebuff: acknowledging the Foreign Secretary's minute, the Private Secretary at No 10 struck the most negative note we had yet received from the Prime Minister, observing that 'she is becoming very pessimistic about this exercise and doubts whether it can be taken further'.

VII

WITH THE PRIME MINISTER privately doubting whether the process should continue at all, and the Taoiseach apparently hoping for early agreement on a settlement, the omens for a harmonious discussion at the forthcoming Summit were hardly propitious. In the event, however, we did not have to wait until the Summit for an injection of acrimony. On 25 October, the new Secretary of State for Northern Ireland, Douglas Hurd, accompanied by Robert Andrew, paid an introductory visit to Dublin and had talks with Peter Barry, Michael Noonan and senior Irish officials. The NIO's own account of these talks at the time gave much the same idea of their content and impact on the Irish as does the account in Garret's book (p. 511).

Whether what Garret calls the 'negativism' displayed by Hurd and Andrew was deliberately intended to torpedo the negotiations was not clear to me at the time and is not clear to me now. Certainly, the NIO disliked the way the negotiations had developed. They resented (understandably) the initiative on Northern Ireland being taken from them by an unholy alliance between the Cabinet Secretary and an FCO official; and they mistrusted Robert Armstrong and myself as dangerous and unscrupulous enthusiasts for a Southern Irish dimension. Without necessarily aiming to precipitate an outright rupture, they set out to impress on the Irish that 'institutionalised consultation' on political matters was not seriously on offer and that it would be in the Irish government's own interests to settle for an agreement limited to security cooperation, saving itself the pain of an (inevitably unsuccessful) attempt to amend Articles 2 and 3.

Douglas Hurd had already shown that he was thinking on these lines; and he clearly sensed that it was what Mrs Thatcher herself really wanted. That the Irish had made it crystal clear that they were not interested in an agreement on these terms (and would not have been able to sell it to their own supporters, either in the South or in the SDLP if they had been) was apparently neither here nor there: if the Irish did not want such an agreement, the NIO would be happy to see the negotiations lapse.

Between them, Hurd and Andrew told their hosts that Irish ideas on how an Irish right to be consulted might be exercised went well beyond our understanding of what was meant by a consultative role; that there could be no question of restructuring the RUC or making changes to the judiciary; that even supposing that an agreed package could eventually be worked out, it was quite unrealistic to think that this could be done in time for the local elections in May 1985; and that replacing Articles 2 and 3 with an 'aspiration' to Irish unity would cut little ice with the unionists (or by implication the British government), since the claim had never been more than an aspiration in the first place. These points were put with particular force and clarity by Robert Andrew to Michael Lillis and his official colleagues.

Not surprisingly, the Irish reacted with dismay. Acknowledged differences of view between the two sides, which we had hitherto been exploring with an implicit mutual belief in the possibility of eventual compromise, were now spelled out to them with a starkness which suggested a calculated insensitivity to Irish concerns. They reacted by restating those concerns in terms which heightened the unacceptability of their ideas to British ears. This enabled Douglas Hurd to report to the Prime Minister that the gap between Irish expectations and what the British could offer looked too wide to bridge; and that unless this gap could be narrowed quickly it would be pointless to allow the negotiations to continue.

Irish dismay was not allayed by a further encounter between Michael Lillis and Robert Andrew on 30 October at a dinner at the Irish Embassy in London given by Noel and Caitriona Dorr in honour of Jim Prior to mark his departure from the NIO. Robert Armstrong, Robert Andrew and I were the only British officials present, along with a sprinkling of MPs and journalists. Jim Prior appeared avuncular and relaxed, keen to know how the Anglo-Irish 'process' was going. When I expressed regret at his departure, he said philosophically 'She wouldn't have let me do anything. If she'd backed me in 1982, that might have worked; but she didn't'. Meanwhile Michael Lillis was telling Robert Andrew that Irish ministers had been profoundly depressed by the Hurd visit. It appeared to them that Hurd did not believe in the current initiative and had been speaking with the backing of the Prime Minister. The Taoiseach was inclined to think that the current negotiations were doomed and that the impending Summit should be called off.

Lillis went on to accuse British ministers of having changed their position on several issues and to attribute this change to the negative advice of NIO officials – meaning Robert Andrew himself. Robert Andrew naturally bristled at this, protesting that the NIO was as anxious as anyone to find a solution to the Northern Ireland problem: but there was no point in pursuing schemes which would provoke an unmanageable unionist reaction or be rejected by senior police officers and judges. The British position had not changed. It might not be enough for the Irish, but it was all that was on offer. Hence Douglas Hurd's warnings to the Irish not to pitch their hopes too high.

Neither party to this exchange came away from it in a very friendly frame of mind. Reporting it to Robert Armstrong, Robert Andrew added a number of disobliging remarks about Michael Lillis, whom he described as not just strongly nationalist in outlook but untrustworthy, emotional, irrational and bent on driving wedges between the NIO on the one hand and the Cabinet Office and the FCO on the other by means of selective leaks to the press. When this reached me a day or two later, I put on record in reply that although Michael had made no secret of his strongly nationalist sympathies, I had never found him either irrational or untrustworthy and that he had, on the contrary, been a consistently accurate reflector of the Taoiseach's views.

More immediately, however, I had to deal with Michael Lillis himself, who carried me off after the dinner to his room in the Grosvenor House Hotel and unburdened himself about the damage done in Dublin to Irish confidence in the British government by the Hurd-Andrew foray and the threat which the NIO's hostility posed to the negotiations. It was impossible to give him an altogether reassuring reply, seeing that the Irish were indeed pitching their hopes too high in a number of respects and that Douglas Hurd and Robert Andrew, albeit with a somewhat unscrupulous brutality, had done no more than echo sentiments which we had all heard the Prime Minister express at one time or other in private discussion. I did, however, assure Michael that the line they had taken in Dublin had not been cleared with the Foreign Secretary: nor as far as I knew, had it been authorised explicitly by the Prime Minister who, whatever doubts she might have, remained committed to continuing the talks and to the desirability in principle of achieving a package agreement constructed around the 'basic equation'. I guess that it is this conversation which Garret refers to in his book (p. 512) as an 'authoritative' intimation that 'the Hurd-Andrew stance was unilateral and did not have the authority of either the Prime Minister or the Cabinet'.

The next Anglo-Irish Summit was now less than three weeks away; and its handling was to be discussed at a meeting between the Prime Minister and the two Secretaries of State on 1 November. It seemed to me that the negotiations were on the point of breaking down over a basic misperception by our side of what the Irish government could realistically be brought to accept. If this happened, a historic opportunity would have been thrown away to help reconcile the minority in Northern Ireland to the Union, to build bridges between North and South and to halt the advance of Sinn Féin. I put my analysis into a minute to Geoffrey Howe pointing out that the central concept of the package on which the Armstrong-Nally teams had been working was reciprocal: closer Irish cooperation on security and acceptance of the Union in return for a significant Irish dimension in the North to help end the alienation of the nationalist community there. If the elements on either side of this balance were scaled down too far, the whole package would come unstuck.

I argued that it was illusory to think that the Irish might be attracted by joint arrangements in the North confined to the security field (since they would simply be laying themselves open to the charge of collaborating with British 'repression' in Northern Ireland with no benefit at all to the nationalist community). To be viable in Dublin, any package would have to balance Irish acceptance of the Union with some visible measure of Irish political involvement in the North and be accompanied by moves to make the forces of law and order more acceptable to the minority. If we were not ready to contemplate going this far, we would have to give up the aim of a settlement dependent on Irish cooperation and opt instead for an internal settlement, with the adverse consequences this would have for the SDLP, for the standing of Dr FitzGerald's government and for cross-border security cooperation. I believe that Geoffrey Howe found this minute persuasive.

On the morning of 31 October came the news of Mrs Gandhi's

assassination; and the Prime Minister's meeting on Ireland was hurriedly brought forward to that afternoon so that she could fly to Delhi for the funeral the following day. We were accordingly bidden to her room in the House of Commons immediately after Prime Minister's Questions. These were an emotional high point in Mrs Thatcher's week. She prepared for them with enormous care and at the best of times they tended to leave her drained and on edge. On this occasion there was also the impact of the gunning down of Mrs Gandhi (with whom, as I discovered later, Mrs Thatcher had felt a strong affinity) coming on top of her own recent escape from assassination at the hands of the IRA. Mrs Thatcher appeared taut and strained, as though wrapped in a tightly stretched sheen of invisible nylon; the atmosphere was tense and rushed and the discussion even less orderly and more inconsequential than usual.

The prospect of having to go to Dublin for the Summit (the previous one having been at Chequers) was particularly unwelcome, prompting Mrs Thatcher to observe that the IRA 'will probably get me in the end, but I don't see why I should offer myself on a plate'. (In the event, in deference to her wishes, Garret FitzGerald agreed to come to Chequers again.) She then aired a series of arguments for using the Summit to bring the negotiations to an end: the element of reciprocity on which they had been based had disappeared, more and more difficulties kept emerging, Irish demands were increasingly unreasonable, was it really not possible to re-draw the border?

To my surprise and relief, Douglas Hurd softened the line he had taken in his minute and argued partly on tactical grounds against a premature rupture. There might still be the makings of a deal comprising a joint security commission, a resident Irish representative (preferably to be called a consul-general) in Belfast and consultation on a limited range of issues in return for the abandonment of the Irish territorial claim and SDLP cooperation in a devolved government. Something on these lines should be put to the Taoiseach at the Summit and if, as seemed likely, it was not enough for him, the negotiations could be plausibly broken off and our final offer made public to demonstrate to moderate nationalist opinion that we had done our best to meet their concerns.

The Prime Minister seized on the mention of a resident representative. 'Why should the Irish have such a thing?' I tried to deal with this point, only to be asked: 'How would you like it if there was a Russian representative in London who had to be consulted about everything?' 'Well, Prime Minister, 30% of the population of the United Kingdom aren't Russians.' 'I see. It's like the Sudeten problem.' Geoffrey Howe and Robert Armstrong both argued strongly for continuing the talks, the former emphasising (as he did at every point in the process when breakdown appeared likely) that the original argument that we could not afford to be doing nothing remained valid. A collapse of the talks would undermine the position both of moderate nationalists in the North and of Dr FitzGerald's government in the South. We should therefore continue in slow time to explore with the Irish in detail the various practical issues involved in a possible package.

After some further knockabout, the Prime Minister reluctantly accepted that the consensus was against bringing the negotiations to an end. 'Well,' (looking at Robert and me) 'you can go on talking.' But no decisions could be taken at the Summit except agreement to continue the exploratory negotiations. It must be made clear to the Irish that we had reached the absolute limit of what we could offer and that the SDLP must accept devolved government without power-sharing as part of the package. If the negotiations then broke down, we would at least have a publicly defensible position.

The two Roberts and I discussed the fallout from this meeting with the two Secretaries of State the following day and then proceeded to draft the promised working paper setting out the points of agreement and disagreement between the two sides subsequently known as 'the British Position Paper' for presentation to the Irish at the next Armstrong-Nally meeting.

This paper set out two 'central and reciprocal elements' on which an agreement would have to be based: action by the British government to accord the Irish government a right to contribute 'on a systematic and institutionalised basis' to the formulation of policy on security and other matters affecting the minority community and to introduce a measure of devolved government in Northern Ireland, balanced by action by the Irish government to replace the territorial claim in their constitution by an aspiration to unity dependent on majority consent and to encourage acceptance of devolved government. Joint sovereignty was again firmly ruled out, but there might be 'a formal obligation on the British government to consult and a right for the Irish government to be consulted' in respect of all matters 'within the executive responsibility of the Secretary of State for Northern Ireland'. The Irish by contrast wanted a formal obligation to reach agreement on matters which were the subject of consultation. Both sides accepted the need for a joint security commission, but the Irish wanted this to have an operational and policy-making role.

The reference to devolved government was as muted as the insistence of the NIO and the Prime Minister's ruling on the subject would allow, and was presented as part of the package rather than as a central condition. The paper was nevertheless authorised by the Prime Minister for presentation to the Irish with only two provisos: that any formal obligation to reach agreement must be 'absolutely excluded', and that an operational role for the joint security commission must be ruled out.

On the whole, I felt that the paper brought us within measurable distance of an agreement; and this was borne out by the tone of the next Armstrong-Nally meeting, which took place in Dublin on 2 and 3 November. Garret FitzGerald describes the British position at that meeting as 'disappointing' (*All in a Life*, p. 512), but our impression at the time was that the Irish side was relieved that our paper went as far as it did, and that it did not reflect the negative line taken by Douglas Hurd and Robert Andrew in Dublin the previous month. The Irish appeared to accept that the role they were being offered in Northern Ireland was essentially consultative, although they baulked at the word itself and hoped that some more positive term could be found such as 'contribute to the formulation of policy'. They continued to press for an effective say in security arrangements and for changes in the police (and particularly the UDR). But they recognised that it was unrealistic to expect that these and other outstanding differences could be decided at the forthcoming Summit. Overall, they gave us the clear impression that they badly wanted an agreement and accepted that they would have to be content with less than they had hoped for.

The main Irish concern was that devolved government should not be made an integral part of the package, since although they regarded devolution (on a power-sharing basis) as desirable, they did not believe that it would be feasible in the short term. They amended the way in which our paper described the Irish position on a number of points (because, as Garret delicately puts it, 'So as not to frighten off Margaret Thatcher our position had been understated' – i.e., by the Irish negotiators), but they were nevertheless prepared to take our paper and the accompanying draft communique as a basis on which to work. To be working on the basis of a common document is an important step forward in any negotiation. Robert Armstrong was therefore able to report the outcome of this meeting to the Prime Minister in cautiously optimistic terms.

Now, however, it was the turn of Irish officials to find that they had underestimated the suspicions of their own ministers and overestimated their readiness to acquiesce in British constraints. On the morning of 12 November, Michael Lillis came to see me in London to express the Irish government's dismay at what they interpreted as a fundamental shift in the British position, whereby we were making the entire package dependent on the establishment of a devolved government in Northern Ireland – something which, however desirable in itself, could not be achieved in advance and it was in any case not in our power to bring about, since it depended on the cooperation of the political parties in Northern Ireland. He returned in the afternoon accompanied by Noel Dorr. I had meanwhile alerted the NIO, and Tony Brennan joined me to help respond to the Irish démarche. Michael and Noel delivered a formal note summarising the Irish position on the various outstanding issues in uncompromising language, using terminology on joint authority and joint decision-making which we thought had been put aside. Devolved government based on majority rule (i.e., other than power-sharing) could be contemplated only in the context of Joint Authority; and, as for consultative arrangements, 'it was essential that the Irish nationalist role be that of equal participation in decision-making either at ministerial Commission level or at the level of devolved government'.

As is now clear from Garret FitzGerald's memoirs, the Irish thought that we were asking them to seek to amend their constitution on the basis of some consultative arrangement in Northern Ireland which would be no more than a cloak for majority rule under a new guise. In reality, our position on the relationship between the consultative arrangements under discussion and a hypothetical devolved government in Northern Ireland had not been worked out or agreed within Whitehall: everyone agreed that a devolved government would be desirable, with SDLP participation if possible or even (on the basis of Mrs Thatcher's obiter dictum at the end of her meeting on 31 October) without it if necessary; but how this should be fitted into the overall package had hardly been discussed. Indeed, apart from Jim Prior's embryonic suggestions for a two-stage approach, there had been no detailed discussion at all of the sequence in which the various elements in any agreed package should be implemented.

So, with helpful support from Tony Brennan, I assured Michael and Noel that the statement in our paper that devolved government was an integral part of our proposals was not intended to mean that none of the proposals under discussion could be implemented until a devolved government had been established. Meanwhile it was apparent from the tone and content of the Irish note that on a number of important issues the gaps between the two sides were wider than we had thought and only the Prime Minister and the Taoiseach could decide, in the light of discussion between them, whether and how those gaps might be bridged.

This Irish démarche made an inauspicious lead-in to the Prime Minister's meeting two days later with the two Secretaries of State and senior officials to brief herself for the Summit. She was predictably outraged by the assertive and uncompromising tone, as much as by the substance, of the Irish speaking note, to which she directed that an equally uncompromising reply should be prepared. It was doubtful whether the negotiations could continue: the Irish, in her view, were making demands which they knew to be unacceptable with a view to provoking a breakdown of the negotiations which they could then justify to their own domestic constituency on the grounds of British intransigence. So, as well as being uncompromising, our reply to the Irish démarche was to be in terms which we could, if necessary, use publicly to demonstrate the reasonableness of our proposals.

Robert Armstrong and I bore the first brunt of this assault. We pointed out that a breakdown would be a victory for the IRA and would seriously prejudice the prospects of closer cross-border cooperation with the Irish security forces. These arguments were reinforced (after a slow start) by Geoffrey Howe and Douglas Hurd. A breakdown would damage Garret FitzGerald's domestic position (which Mrs Thatcher had no wish to do), remove any hope of getting the SDLP to participate in a devolved government and be unhelpful vis-à-vis our relations with the United States. It was eventually agreed that a breakdown should, if possible, be avoided but that since the Irish were evidently getting cold feet about a constitutional referendum while still aspiring to joint authority, we had better think in terms of a more modest package of measures which would not require major concessions from either side. It was left that Mrs Thatcher would judge from her talks with the Taoiseach at the Summit whether the negotiations could usefully continue; but that, as well as (once again) ruling out joint authority, she would keep open the possibility of a consultative role of some kind for the Irish government in the North, Robert and I then retired to his room to discuss, over a much-needed whisky, the drafting of our reply to the Irish speaking note.

Between this meeting and the Summit, Geoffrey Howe saw Garret FitzGerald and Peter Barry in the margins of an EC meeting in Brussels. In a short conversation, both Irish ministers emphasised their concern to avoid a breakdown and their readiness to look for ways of reassuring unionist opinion, leading Geoffrey to minute the Prime Minister urging her to persevere with the negotiations.

VIII

THE SUMMIT BEGAN with a rather subdued dinner at Chequers on the evening of Sunday 18 November 1984, after which the Prime Minister took the Taoiseach off for a prolonged tête-à-tête in her study. While this was going on, the rest of us stood about in the hall – drinkless – waiting for the two leaders to emerge. When they finally did so, Mrs Thatcher looked round at us jauntily and said 'Well, have you all got drinks?' I said (with feeling) 'No, Prime Minister. Not yet'. At that point a servant approached her with a tray of drinks, which she waved away. 'No, no: my favourite churchman needs a drink. Mr Goodall is thirsty. Take it to him.' General laughter. The two sides then withdrew to be told by their respective principals what had transpired. The Taoiseach had argued that the time was ripe for amendment of Articles 2 and 3 of the Irish Constitution and that people in the South would accept this provided that reforms were made in the North to end the alienation of the minority. Mrs Thatcher had as usual taken exception to the word 'alienation' and been dismissive of the case for power-sharing. Her account of the conversation was aggressively negative. 'Not very encouraging,' observed Geoffrey Howe as we came out. Even Robert Armstrong admitted to being somewhat downcast.

I was, however, authorised to give Michael Lillis our reply to the offending Irish speaking note of 12 November, which I did immediately after breakfast next morning. Its contents are summarised in Garret's book (p. 515), in which he describes its tone as 'stiff' and its impact on the Irish side as 'thoroughly discouraging'. Had it fully reflected the mood in which Mrs Thatcher had commissioned it, it would have been a good deal stiffer and even more discouraging. As it was, it was less dismissive of Irish concerns than we had thought it likely, when we were drafting it, that Mrs Thatcher would agree to; and it went rather further to meet them than she went herself in her exchanges with Garret during the Summit.

On the critical issue of devolution as a precondition, which had so much upset Irish ministers, our reply made clear that although we regarded the introduction of devolved government ·as 'integral' to the proposed new arrangements, it was not a precondition for the implementation of any (underlined) of those arrangements, and it would have to be in a form which commanded the acceptance of both communities (thereby ruling out a reversion to Stormont-type majority rule). The minimalist effect of the emphasis on 'any' was the price paid for being allowed to waive devolution as a sine qua non of any agreement at all; but no attempt was made to spell out which of the proposed arrangements could take effect ahead of a devolved government and which would be dependent on its introduction – a development which the opposing views of the two communities in the North looked like relegating to the Greek Kalends.

For the rest, our note unequivocally declared joint authority in any form to be unacceptable and rejected the Irish claim that nationalists in the North were entitled to 'an equal role' in decision-making. It restated Mrs Thatcher's view that any new security arrangements should be reciprocal – i.e., should apply on both sides of the border, and it sounded a negative note (though not decisively so) on the possibility of changes in the structure of the RUC and the UDR. On the key question of institutionalised consultation, however, it reaffirmed without qualification the formulation used in 'the British Position Paper' presented to the Irish on 2 November, offering the Irish, in return for amending their constitution, a right 'to contribute, on a systematic and institutionalised basis, to the consideration by the United Kingdom government of a range of policy matters, including security, as a means of strengthening the confidence of the minority community in the institutions of government'.

With this language, now put to the Irish for the second time with the Prime Minister's personal endorsement, the British government formally offered the Irish government a 'right' to be consulted and to have their views taken into account, and conceded that the range of subjects to which this right would apply should extend beyond security to other matters affecting the confidence of the minority in the institutions of government. The importance of this offer – and of the fact that it had been left on the table despite Mrs Thatcher's hostile reaction to the Irish speaking note – seems to have been overlaid for the Irish at the time by the negative flavour of the Taoiseach's conversations with the Prime Minister during the Summit itself and the traumatic episode of their conflicting press conferences which followed. It was, however, this offer which was to bring about a fundamental change in the Anglo-Irish landscape and form the bedrock of the eventual Anglo-Irish Agreement – even though the condition on which it was predicated (that the Irish would amend their constitution) was not met.

The first part of the morning was taken up with a further meeting between the Prime Minister and the Taoiseach, this time with Robert Armstrong and notetakers present, but with the rest of us excluded. It was a grey, cold, foggy morning. Geoffrey Howe, Douglas Hurd, Dick Spring and Peter Barry, together with a little circle of deferential officials, sat by a crackling log fire in the library surrounded by row upon row of calf-bound volumes of eighteenth-century theology, white mist swirling at the windows. From a sense of duty, the four ministers began a desultory discussion of EC matters and then moved on to Northern Ireland, conscious all the time that the substantive discussion was happening next door. I noted in my diary: 'Howe obliquely positive, Hurd obliquely negative, Barry courteous, Spring restive'. The two leaders broke for coffee and once again debriefed themselves to their respective teams. Once again Mrs Thatcher gave us a combative and indignant account of what had passed. The tête-à-tête then resumed and seemed to go slightly better, after which we were all admitted to a plenary session in which much of the ground covered in private was gone over again.

Garret's account (*All in a Life*, pp. 517–521) correctly gives the flavour of Mrs Thatcher's eclectic and discontinuous style of argument. In essence the discussion followed familiar lines. Mrs Thatcher was sceptical of the Irish government's ability to carry a referendum to amend the constitution. She thought that the legitimate grievances of the Catholic minority in Northern Ireland had been removed by the measures already taken to end discrimination there: other minority concerns could be met by the establishment of a joint Anglo-Irish security commission in which Irish government representatives could act as advocates for nationalist anxieties about the security forces and the administration of justice. Subject to expert examination, she saw no difficulty in principle with measures to harmonise the criminal law as between the two jurisdictions or even (provided the Northern Ireland judiciary were agreeable) to mixed courts for the trial of terrorist cases; but a consultative political structure was a different matter, and very difficult to separate from joint authority, which was totally unacceptable.

Douglas Hurd intervened to point out that 'institutionalised consultation' would be admissible only if the Irish amended Articles 2 and 3 of their constitution, and even that was unlikely to carry much conviction with unionists: so, it would be much better to settle for a joint security commission, without the need for constitutional amendment. Peter Barry pointed out tartly that he had been given to understand that we attached enormous importance to the revision of Articles 2 and 3. As for a joint security commission, to be of any value it would have to have a degree of executive authority over, for example, senior appointments in the police.

The Taoiseach meanwhile pressed the case for ending nationalist alienation with his usual flow of rapid (and to English ears, not always intelligible) eloquence. Unless agreement on suitable measures could be reached between the two governments, representation of the minority's interests would pass from the SDLP to Sinn Féin. A united Ireland was no longer a serious prospect (his own account renders this as 'not now likely in the short term'), so that amendment of Articles 2 and 3 was politically feasible provided only that the legitimate concerns of the Northern nationalists could be met. All they wanted was to be allowed to live in peace and to express their own national identity as the unionists did. This included being policed by members of their own community instead of being bullied by security forces drawn almost entirely from the other community, being able to fly their own (Irish) flag, and having confidence in the impartiality of the courts.

Mrs Thatcher said his ideas on policing sounded as if he wanted to establish a Republican enclave in the centre of Belfast. As for discrimination, the sorts of constraints complained of were the lot of minorities in all countries from Sudeten Germans to Sikhs. She could accept the need for a joint security commission to deal with law and order grievances. She saw no insuperable problems about a joint law commission to harmonise the criminal law or about making changes to the courts; and she recognised that devolved government would have to be on a basis acceptable to both communities. But a joint political framework was too difficult: giving Irish ministers a role in the North smacked of joint authority, which was simply 'unacceptable'.

To this Garret replied that Northern Ireland was essentially a political not a security problem. A joint security commission without a political dimension was impossible. He was not wanting to challenge British sovereignty over Northern Ireland, but a middle way had to be found between a consultative role for the Irish government, which was not enough, and joint authority.

The discussion was interrupted by lunch, where I found myself sitting between Seán Donlon and Peter Barry, who wondered whether he had been too blunt in dismissing the possibility of having a joint security commission without a political dimension. Since both the Prime Minister and Douglas Hurd still seemed as attached to this idea as did the Irish to the equally unrealistic goal of joint authority, I said 'not blunt enough'. At this point Robert Armstrong and Dermot Nally brought to the table the draft joint communique on which they had been working. Mrs Thatcher held it up in front of her and proceeded to read the text aloud, rather slowly and in a tone of mocking distaste. 'At a meeting of the Anglo-Irish Intergovernmental Council,' she began 'What on earth is that?' 'You invented it, Margaret', said Garret between gritted teeth. It was a moment at which everyone round the table felt acutely uncomfortable. Peter Barry said audibly to me 'I'm not going to sit and listen to this' and made to walk out, but I put a restraining hand on his arm and he stayed in his seat.

Dermot and Robert were sent away to have another try and Mrs Thatcher, having relieved her nerves in a characteristically outrageous way, became relaxed and reasonable. Back in the library after lunch, the discussion with the Taoiseach about press handling became almost cordial. The Prime Minister declined to agree to a further meeting early in the New Year, saying that timing must depend on progress in the negotiations (thus implying her commitment to reaching an eventual agreement). She spoke warmly of the mutual good will between the Taoiseach and herself and of her feeling that they had for the first time got seriously to grips with the subject. The Taoiseach acknowledged that the British proposals were a step forward, although they were not enough to achieve a lasting solution; to which Mrs Thatcher said that an enduring settlement was worth going for but it had to be a realistic one. Rather oddly, she referred to the difficulty of having to work through 'people we can't trust', to which Garret replied jocularly 'I hope you mean Northern Ireland politicians and not our civil servants'. At that Mrs Thatcher sat up very straight, looked hard in our direction and said: 'I think our civil servants are (with great emphasis) remarkable'. Pause. 'And they are so patient'. I said, 'Prime Minister, that's the nicest thing you've said this weekend'.

The meeting ended in mid-afternoon with warm farewells all round. The Prime Minister and the Taoiseach went off to give their separate press conferences and I drove back to London with Geoffrey Howe in a long column of official cars which swept through traffic lights and along the side of the Serpentine under police escort. As soon as I got back to my desk, Alan Goodison and I sat down to draft the statement and 'Notes for Supplementaries' for the Prime Minister to use in reporting on the Summit to the House of Commons; and at about a quarter to eight I walked across with them to No 10 to deliver the drafts to the Private Secretary.

To my surprise, I found the Prime Minister herself in the Private Secretaries' outer office, propped up against a desk, apparently relaxed and disposed for conversation. 'Poor Dr FitzGerald', she observed, with real affection in her voice. 'I'm afraid he went away disappointed. I didn't want to disappoint him. But WHY was he disappointed? He knew that I wouldn't be able to agree to joint authority'. I said that, as well as having his own domestic imperatives to contend with, the Taoiseach was genuinely convinced that nationalists in Northern Ireland could never come to terms with being within the United Kingdom unless their sense of Irishness was given institutional and political expression; and I explained that when he spoke of 'alienation' he was not appealing to some Marxist concept, but was describing the inevitable reaction of people who perceived the institutions of the state as weighted against them and the forces of law and order in particular – the courts, the police and above all the UDR – as manned overwhelmingly by members of the opposing community.

Mrs Thatcher gave this exposition her full attention, nodding thoughtfully and interjecting an occasional question. Then her eye lit on a newspaper lying on the floor, which happened to be the (Communist) *Morning Star* (previously *The Daily Worker*). She swooped down on it indignantly and waved it under my nose. 'What can you do (she demanded) when the Archbishop of Canterbury is praised on the front page of the *Morning Star*?' I realised that our colloquy on Northern Ireland was at an end. As I walked back to the Foreign Office, I reflected on Mrs Thatcher's evident regard for Garret FitzGerald and congratulated myself on having, for the first time in my experience, seen her show some understanding of the causes of continuing nationalist resentment.

The next morning, I spent an hour with her in her study going through the draft statement. Although at the start she was agitated and strident after a difficult meeting with Geoffrey Howe on the Foreign Office budget, she calmed down as we proceeded, reading out each paragraph aloud, and once again seemed concerned to be as helpful to the Taoiseach as she could.

Only when I returned to the Office did I learn that the separate press conferences given by Mrs Thatcher and Dr FitzGerald the previous afternoon had conveyed conflicting impressions of the state of play, with the Taoiseach apparently unsighted about some of the Prime Minister's comments. The Irish media had focussed in particular on the Prime Minister's response when asked about the three 'models' for the future of Northern Ireland put forward in the Forum Report, each of which she had robustly dismissed with the comment 'That's out'.

Not until the following morning, however, did the full extent of Irish outrage and of the embarrassment caused to the Taoiseach, become apparent. Always inclined to inflate the magnitude of British misdemeanours and put the most malign interpretation available on the actions of British ministers, the Irish media, egged on by Mr Haughey and Fianna Fáil, proclaimed that the Forum Report had been deliberately rubbished and the Taoiseach resoundingly humiliated. The Taoiseach reacted by telling a private (but well-reported) meeting of his own Fine Gael party that the Prime Minister's remarks had been 'gratuitously offensive'; and we found ourselves in the middle of a major Anglo-Irish row of which our fragile negotiating process looked like being a casualty.

On 22 November Noel Dorr called on Robert Armstrong with an oral message from Garret FitzGerald to the Prime Minister to explain that the relatively satisfactory outcome of the Summit itself had been negated by subsequent developments, specifically the tone and substance of the Prime Minister's remarks at her press conference, in which she had appeared to dismiss the notion of 'alienation' on the part of the nationalist community and to reject the whole of the Forum Report; and a later press conference by Douglas Hurd in Northern Ireland at which he had revealed discussion at Chequers of the possibility of a joint security commission and implied that nothing further could be contemplated. All this had enabled Mr Haughey to claim that he had been right all along about the impossibility of doing a deal with the British and about the unreality of the Taoiseach's ideas. The Taoiseach underlined this message the next day in a personal letter to Mrs Thatcher making the same points and stressing that her dismissal of the reality of 'alienation' had been particularly damaging. He hoped that she could find a way of acknowledging the reality of this phenomenon, since her dismissal of it had 'suggested to our public opinion that there is little or no point in the Irish government making any efforts to find a common approach with yours'.

I had no direct encounter with the Prime Minister in the immediate aftermath of these communications, although it fell to me (after some hectic consultations with Robert Armstrong and the NIO) to produce the first draft of her reply. I knew, however, that she had never intended to undermine the Taoiseach's position in the way she had done, nor (on the basis of my conversation with her the previous Sunday evening) did I think that she was as impervious to understanding the reality of alienation as she had appeared to be at her press conference. Robert Armstrong reported that she was dismayed and even a little abashed at the damage her remarks had done: characteristically, however, she was in no mood to apologise outright.

Michael Lillis flew over to London early on 28 November to impress on me the harm which had been done to the Taoiseach's standing and the strength of the anger and resentment felt in Dublin; but there was nothing further I could do to influence the terms of the Prime Minister's reply to the Taoiseach, which issued the next day. In it, she said that as she had been specifically asked about the three 'models', she had been bound to reaffirm (as had been made clear at the time by Mr Prior in the House of Commons) that they were unacceptable to the British government. If she had been asked about the Forum Report as a whole, she would have endorsed Mr Prior's reference to the helpful elements in it. And although she thought the term 'alienation' 'liable to exacerbate the problem it purports to describe', she recognised that 'there are members of the minority community in Northern Ireland who do not have confidence in the system of authority and law and order and who look to the Republic'. She committed herself to continuing 'our joint search for ways of promoting lasting peace and stability in Northern Ireland' and promised before long to indicate 'the areas which we believe that it would be fruitful to explore further'.

By Mrs Thatcher's standards this was an emollient letter. Its effect was reinforced a few days later in a short personal conversation with Dr FitzGerald in the margins of a European Council meeting in Dublin on

3 December. In the course of retracing some of the ground covered in their exchange of letters, Mrs Thatcher wryly remarked that it was clear that one had to develop an extra sensitivity in commenting on Irish problems, to which the Taoiseach could only agree. She declined to commit herself to saying anything positive about alienation, but said she would try to be helpful at her press conference at the end of the European Council. This she did by describing her conversation with the Taoiseach as having been very successful, both of them being united inter alia in recognising the need for a new political framework in Northern Ireland as mentioned 'in other parts of the Forum Report'. Albeit ruefully, the Taoiseach seems in his memoirs to acknowledge that she had kept her word.

From 28 November to 5 December I was away in Ottawa and Washington talking to the Canadians and the Americans about intelligence matters. By the time I returned on 5 December, the immediate furore over the Prime Minister's post-Chequers press conference had subsided but it was clear that the Anglo-Irish landscape on which the dust was settling had changed. Although relations between the Prime Minister and the Taoiseach had been patched up, the little there had been of mutual confidence between them had not been restored. Mr Haughey and Fianna Fáil had had a field day at the Taoiseach's expense. The personal chemistry between the official negotiators was unimpaired, but it was clear that Irish ministers were bruised, angry and apprehensive. Noel Dorr gave me a copy, written out in his own hand, of Auden's poem [from In Time of War] about a diplomatic negotiation:

Across the lawns and cultured flowers drifted
The conversation of the highly trained ...

Far off, no matter what good they intended,
The armies waited for a verbal error
With all the instruments for causing pain
And on the issue of their charm depended
A land laid waste, with all its young men slain,
Its women weeping, and its towns in terror.

On 17 December 1984 the Armstrong-Nally group had its last meeting of the year in London. On the British side we were without fresh instructions. The Irish side could do no more than stress the 'nuclear change' which the Chequers affair had wrought in Irish opinion, ending any hope of a bipartisan approach on Northern Ireland between Dr FitzGerald's government and Fianna Fáil and highlighting the inadequacy of a purely consultative role for the Irish government in the North. The 'triumphalist' reaction of the unionists to the whole affair had further polarised opinion in the North and intensified nationalist support for the men of violence. Robert Andrew rehearsed once again the NIO's preference for a joint security commission and the Irish once again explained why this was totally unacceptable unless accompanied by joint political arrangements. Both sides confirmed that they remained committed to continuing the negotiation, and Dermot Nally said that the Taoiseach had not altogether given up hope of achieving a package which would enable him to amend Articles 2 and 3 of the Irish Constitution; but it was clear to us all that a chapter in the negotiations had come to an end and that when they resumed it would be on a basis of diminished confidence and reduced expectations all round.

IX

ALTHOUGH THE PRIME MINISTER had taken some trouble to mend her fences with the Taoiseach, her enthusiasm for the negotiating process remained as low as ever. On the outcome of the 17 December meeting, she commented tartly that 'the Irish want more than we can give and always will' and doubted whether we would find a way forward. However, she agreed that an options paper should be prepared for ministerial consideration in mid-January. This was to examine three issues: the scope for a limited bargain, excluding amendment of Articles 2 and 3 of the Irish Constitution; whether it was possible to construct a political framework in Northern Ireland which would enable the Irish government to accept such a limited bargain; and how the negotiations might be terminated with minimum damage to Anglo-Irish relations if (as she clearly continued to believe and half to hope) it proved impossible to reach agreement.

The process began with a meeting on 4 January 1985 between Geoffrey Howe and Douglas Hurd which reflected the continuing differences of view and emphasis between the NIO and the Cabinet Office/FCO combination. Although the two Secretaries of State agreed on the need for an Irish Dimension of some sort in the North, Hurd's view of the form this might take was firmly minimalist. He downplayed the value of obtaining amendments to the Irish Constitution and stressed the impossibility of fudging the distinction between consultation and joint decision-making. Geoffrey Howe and I thought that a comprehensive agreement including constitutional amendment was still worth trying for; and I emphasised again my conviction that the Irish would not enter into any agreement which was purely consultative and confined in essence to security.

Geoffrey Howe, in an eminently characteristic phrase, foresaw 'creeping cataclysm' in Ireland if the negotiations failed; but Douglas Hurd ('all rational complacency' as I noted afterwards) was inclined to dismiss the risk of increased nationalist support for Sinn Féin, which he thought had levelled off and was unlikely to be affected for good or ill either by the failure of the negotiations or by the introduction of an Irish Dimension. Nor did he see any possibility of agreement being reached with the Irish (as the Taoiseach hoped) in time to influence the Northern Ireland local elections, due in May. I made one or two attempts to narrow the gap between Irish history and English detachment, but Douglas Hurd's urbane rationality was, as usual, not easy to penetrate.

It was agreed that the options paper should offer two models, one for a limited agreement focused on security, with consultation on a narrow range of issues; and the other for a more comprehensive agreement posited on amendment of the Irish Constitution and a correspondingly greater degree of Irish involvement in decision-making. Producing a draft which did justice to the case for both models without coming down too firmly in favour of either proved predictably difficult. At a fraught meeting with Robert Armstrong and Robert Andrew on 11 January, it was clear that the NIO, feeling that they had the Prime Minister on their side, were drawing back from any significant Irish involvement in the North at all, and were ready to dissociate themselves from the paper altogether. In the end, however, we reached agreement on a paper in which the NIO case for a limited agreement was matched by the FCO case (endorsed by Robert Armstrong) for a more ambitious one.

The paper outlined two models, 'a' and 'b'. Model 'a' , advanced by the NIO, envisaged a standing committee of the Anglo-Irish governmental Council (AIGC) in the form of a Joint Security Commission comprising the Northern Ireland Secretary and an Irish minister, together with their senior security advisers, which might meet in either Belfast or Dublin to review cross-border security cooperation and which could also meet in a different configuration to discuss measures to recognise the Irish identity of the minority community and public appointments in the gift of the Northern Ireland Secretary. There could also be a body to consider the scope for harmonising the criminal law and the Irish proposal for joint courts to try criminal offences. All these arrangements would be purely consultative. In return, the Irish would be asked to offer some form of unconditional recognition of Northern Ireland's status as part of the United Kingdom (without amending their constitution) and to enter into commitments to improve cross-border security cooperation.

Model 'b', advanced by the FCO, consisted of model 'a' plus arrangements to give the Irish a role in decision-making in the North on such matters as came within the purview of the Northern Ireland Secretary but were not devolved to a local administration – essentially the offer contained in the

'British Position Paper' which we had put to the Irish with ministerial agreement on 2 November 1984. Although the arrangements envisaged were to be consultative, in deference to Irish sensitivities the word itself was to be avoided. Both models included provision for a devolved local administration, model 'b' envisaging that if such an administration could be established much of the Irish involvement in decision-making would lapse. Thus, the crucial difference between the two models lay in the range of subjects on which the Irish were to be offered the right to express their views through some form of joint ministerial body, and the extent to which the essentially consultative nature of this right was to be made explicit or finessed.

The NIO argued that the Irish were unlikely to be able to deliver the proposed amendments to their constitution, and even if they did it would not compensate for the degree of unionist outrage which model 'b' would provoke. The FCO counter-argument was that removal of the territorial claim on the North enshrined in the Irish Constitution would be a valuable prize and that model 'a' would not only fail to achieve it but would be rejected by the Irish government outright (a judgement endorsed by Robert Armstrong). My private belief was that although model 'b' was unlikely to be enough to secure amendment of the Irish Constitution, it would at least keep the negotiations going; whereas putting forward model 'a' would probably lead to their collapse.

As was clearly foreseeable, Mrs Thatcher took against model 'b' straight away, commenting through her Private Secretary that it would commit us to governing the North jointly with the Irish Republic. When we came to discuss it with her on 16 January, however, although she strongly backed the NIO point of view, her style was somewhat less hectic than usual, and she allowed all of us to have our say. The argument that model 'b' would create more difficulties with the unionists than amendment of Articles 2 and 3 would assuage, was persuasive in one direction; but the argument that an unalloyed model 'a' could lead to the Irish breaking off the negotiations proved equally persuasive in the other. We were, therefore, instructed to prepare proposals based on model 'a' but incorporating elements of model 'b', including provision for the proposed joint body to deal with human rights issues as well as security. It was recognised that this would probably not be enough to induce the Irish to hold a referendum on Articles 2 and 3; but we were not to suggest to them that we no longer expected them to do so: that decision should be left to them.

In the reformulation of model 'a' authorised by this discussion, we refrained from describing the arrangements as 'consultative'; and Robert Armstrong succeeded in obtaining the Prime Minister's approval both for this omission and for making it clear to the Irish that the proposals were not being put forward on a 'take it or leave it' basis but that we were open to comments and counterproposals. We were thus able to go into the next Armstrong-Nally meeting in Dublin on 21 January with some degree of negotiating flexibility.

Dermot Nally and his team took half an hour to study the new British Paper and then responded with some cautious and probing comments. Although tinged with disappointment at what they saw as the 'shallowness' of what we were offering, their reaction seemed to be one of relief that we were still in business, and even some satisfaction. They appeared to be more concerned to widen the range of subjects to which the consultative arrangements would apply than with strengthening their decision-making character; and although Nally said they were under instructions to seek a 'deeper solution', he acknowledged that our proposals were a basis for progress. For our part we were able to point out that the topics proposed for consideration by the joint body went well beyond security, that other topics could be added by agreement; and that although provision was made for a devolved local administration in Northern Ireland, we had fully met the Irish concern that the proposed arrangements should not be dependent on devolution being achieved.

Michael Lillis told me after lunch that his colleagues seemed 'a bit seduced by it' but that the concentration on security was politically too dangerous to be acceptable. The Taoiseach meanwhile saw Robert Armstrong on his own and gave much the same message: he would have preferred to explore the 'deeper' options which had been discernible in the British Paper of 4 November 1983; and he emphasised once again that he would not be able to sell an agreement which appeared to tie the Irish government into British security policies without giving them a 'sufficient involvement' in other matters. But despite the 'Out, Out, Out' debacle, he believed that Irish public opinion would welcome an agreement and he still hoped that one could be reached in time for the Northern Ireland local elections in May. Robert Armstrong and I agreed on our return to London that the blend of relief and disappointment with which the Irish had received our paper suggested that it had at least been substantial enough to get them hooked. A couple of days later this seemed to be confirmed when I heard from Mary Holland [journalist] that John Hume had told her enthusiastically (but not entirely soberly) that what was on offer was 'better than anything since 1974' (i.e., Sunningdale).

On 4 February, Peter Barry came to London for talks with Geoffrey Howe and Douglas Hurd. I remember the occasion chiefly for the fact that, leaving it (not unnaturally) to the two Secretaries of State to sustain the dialogue with the Irish Foreign Minister, I was passed a note from Geoffrey Howe which read 'You are not under a vow of silence!'. Barry made it clear that the definitive Irish response to our proposals must await the next Armstrong-Nally meeting; but he suggested that our offer was 'too little and too concentrated on security' while acknowledging that it was, from our perspective, 'a historic piece of paper'.

The next Armstrong-Nally meeting took place in London a few days later, on 8 February, when the Irish presented us with a counter-proposal in the shape of an amended and enlarged version of our own paper. In this they abandoned the language of joint authority and accepted that the Irish government's role would be limited to 'putting forward views and proposals'; but they proposed to widen the scope of the joint body by including economic and social matters among the topics it could consider, along with the modalities of devolution; and they wanted the establishment of a joint Anglo-Irish parliamentary body as counterpart to the intergovernmental arrangements. At the same time Dermot Nally told Robert Armstrong privately that these proposals would not be sufficient to enable the Irish government to carry a referendum amending Articles 2 and 3; instead, they would be prepared to consider some form of solemn reaffirmation of the Sunningdale Declaration.[4] Some further, mostly

4. In the Sunningdale communique of December 1973, the British and Irish governments made separate, parallel statements on the status of Northern Ireland, the Irish declaring that 'there could be no change in the status of Northern Ireland until a majority of the people in Northern Ireland desired a change', and the British declaring that 'the present status of Northern Ireland is that it is part of the United Kingdom ,' but that if in the future a majority of the people of Northern Ireland should wish to join a united Ireland 'the British government would support that wish.' The intention was that these declarations should be included in a formal international agreement, but the Sunningdale settlement collapsed before that could happen.

helpful, modifications of the paper were supplied three days later by Michael Lillis and Noel Dorr, on instructions from the Taoiseach.

When Geoffrey Howe and Douglas Hurd discussed the state of play with the Prime Minister on 14 February, her mind was more on a recent fracas in the House of Commons over the Ponting affair[5] than on Ireland and she seemed rattled and on edge. She conceded that the Irish had moved some way to meet us and were showing greater realism on the question of joint decision-making but noted somewhat sourly that they had withdrawn their offer of a constitutional referendum (which, of course, she had never fully believed in). Douglas Hurd reverted to his negative mode, arguing that the inclusion of economic and social matters, the diminished focus on security and the idea of the Irish government speaking for the nationalist community on devolution would all make an agreement harder to sell to the unionists. The Prime Minister accordingly called for 'a very careful assessment' of the Irish proposals, to be conducted without haste.

This meant that we were without fresh instructions for the next Armstrong-Nally meeting, which took place on 19 February in the luxurious surroundings of Barrettstown Castle in Co Kildare, a Victorian Gothic country house lavishly – and colourfully – restored and furnished by Elizabeth Arden and at this time being used by the Irish government as a guest house. In this hospitable and secluded atmosphere, warmed with coffee and Irish whiskey before a large peat fire, our discussions were notably friendly and relaxed; and Noel Dorr and I ended the evening with a midnight walk in the park after which we made ourselves tea in the kitchen.

Although neither side had new proposals to put on the table, the meeting was not without its importance. If I remember rightly, it was at Barrettstown that there emerged the Irish emphasis on the need to supplement the main structural elements of any agreement with additional measures to convince the Northern nationalist community that the new arrangements would make a real difference to their situation. If Northern nationalists were to be denied the reassurance of the 'deeper' solution, which would have given the Republic a share of executive authority in the North, the Irish argued that it became even more important to tackle not only perceived economic

5. *Editor's Note* Clive Ponting (1946–2020) was a senior British civil servant and historian best known for having leaked documents about the sinking of the Argentine warship, the *General Belgrano*, in the Falklands War in 1982.

and social discrimination in the North (hence their wish to bring social and economic matters within the remit of the proposed joint body), but also to reform other features of the regime with which nationalists were unable to identify. These included the Flags and Emblems Act, which prohibited the public flying of the Republic's flag; the overwhelmingly Protestant UDR; the almost equally Protestant RUC (although the RUC were acknowledged even by the Irish to be more acceptable to nationalists than the UDR or the Army); and the Courts.

From my arms control past in the Vienna MBFR negotiations, I suggested the term 'associated' or 'confidence building' measures (CBMs) for what the Irish were talking about and they seized on this as exactly expressing what they meant. As a result, although Mrs Thatcher never reconciled herself to the term, 'confidence building measures' was adopted on both sides to describe what became a central issue in the concluding stages of the negotiations.

One CBM to which the Taoiseach was personally attached was the idea of mixed courts for the trial of terrorist offences – i.e., a judge from the South sitting alongside two judges from the North, or vice versa. Intimidation of juries in the North had led to the establishment of the so-called 'Diplock courts', whereby terrorist cases were tried before a single judge sitting without a jury (whereas in the South they were tried – also without a jury – by a panel of three judges). The Irish had put forward the idea of mixed courts from the start and the Taoiseach had floated the idea with the Prime Minister at Chequers without being rebuffed. At Barrettstown we agreed to give it sympathetic consideration, while again stressing that the Law Officers and the Lord Chief Justice of Northern Ireland (Lord Lowry) would first have to be consulted. Before this could happen, however, Dr FitzGerald himself encountered Lord Lowry at a rugby international in Dublin on 4 March and put the idea to him direct.

This particular instance of informal intimacy in cross-border relations proved unfortunate. Although Lord Lowry must have known that the idea was in the air, he had apparently not realised that it was being seriously canvassed in the negotiations. Taken aback and indignant, he minuted to the Prime Minister that he was strongly opposed to it on both constitutional and practical grounds and would 'feel bound to resign' rather than participate in such courts. His opposition was endorsed by the Lord Chancellor

(Lord Hailsham); and we were obliged to make it clear to the Irish that although the idea might be considered it was very unlikely to prove a runner.

The tone and content of the discussions at Barrettstown led us to judge that the outlines of an Agreement were now in sight, if ministers still wanted one. There could be a consultative role for the Irish in Northern Ireland affairs on a range of issues of concern to the nationalist community, to be exercised through a joint or coordinating body, plus some 'confidence building-measures'; all to be balanced by closer cross-border security cooperation and a solemn affirmation by the Republic of the constitutional status of Northern Ireland. In the reporting minute to the Prime Minister which I helped to draft, Robert Armstrong suggested that, as substantive political decisions were now required on whether and how this outline was to be fleshed out, a wider group of ministers should be brought into the picture and a sub-committee of the Defence and Oversea Policy Committee of the Cabinet established for this purpose.

To this the Prime Minister agreed. First, however, she convened a meeting with the two Secretaries of State for 8 March, in preparation for which they each put in their own comments on the state of play. Douglas Hurd thought that an Agreement would still be worth having, provided we could obtain a satisfactory return for conceding a substantial role in Northern affairs to the Irish; but he saw serious difficulty about widening the range of subjects to be dealt with by the joint body, particularly the inclusion of economic and social matters. Geoffrey Howe, who judged (I thought correctly) that the moment had arrived when it would be helpful for him to assume a more direct role in the negotiating process, minuted that the talks had got about as far as they could at official level, and that the next step should be for Douglas Hurd and himself to go to Dublin to explore with Peter Barry and Dick Spring the possibility of reaching an acceptable Agreement within the parameters which officials had established.

The Prime Minister's meeting on 8 March, however, found her at her most unreasonable, stabbing and underlining with her pen, indulging all her prejudices, disliking the whole thing and interrupting anyone who attempted to develop a continuous line of argument. I defined it to myself at the time as the technique of indiscriminate destruction from which at the end some substantial fragments are grudgingly allowed to be retrieved. Robert Armstrong tried to cope first, then Douglas Hurd and Geoffrey

Howe. Towards the end I put in a word or two edgeways myself; but for most of the time I sat back and listened with a mixture of amusement and distaste.

I think that this got through to the Prime Minister, because she suddenly turned on me with a disarming smile and said 'Mr Goodall: wouldn't you like to go and be an Ambassador somewhere else – a long way away?' Returning sharply to earth, I said 'Where would you suggest, Prime Minister?' 'Indonesia, perhaps'. Afterwards I asked Robert why he thought she had suggested Indonesia. He replied 'It was the greenest place she could think of'.

On substance, Mrs Thatcher endorsed Douglas Hurd's view that there could be no question of allowing the proposed joint body to discuss economic and social issues, which would significantly widen the Irish government's role: only cross border issues should be discussed. The drafting of any Agreement should take account of unionist sensitivities at every point: the joint body should not be called a 'co-ordinating committee', since this implied equality of status on the part of the two participating governments; nor did she like 'joint', for the same reason. Indeed, an Agreement which included the establishment of any joint body without a more substantial quid pro quo from the Irish than was at present on offer would antagonise the unionists and look as if we were giving the Irish a substantial role in the North without getting anything worthwhile in return.

Not for the first time, the Prime Minister appeared to be working herself up to the point of turning away from the whole process. Once again, however, her sense of reality prevailed over her prejudices. Insofar as her tangential interruptions allowed, we argued variously that an Agreement would be the surest way of securing improved security cooperation from the Republic; that it offered the best hope of persuading the SDLP to accept a devolved administration; that it would be well received in the United States; and that the collapse of the negotiations would have a negative effect all round.

So, it was eventually agreed that the two Secretaries of State should be allowed to meet their opposite numbers in Dublin; but their remit was defined in terms which recalled Lady Catherine De Bourgh taking no leave of Elizabeth Bennet and sending no compliments to her mother. They were to explain that the proposed joint body could not be allowed to discuss economic and social matters, other than cross-border issues;

no undertaking should be given about the timing of a future Anglo-Irish Summit; and no encouragement given to the idea of an Anglo-Irish Parliamentary entity, which would only raise Irish expectations and heighten unionist suspicions. The draft text relating to the joint body should be brought back into line with the original model 'a'; and it should be impressed on the Irish that we would require firm commitments on the constitutional status of the North and on the SDLP's willingness to play a full part in moves towards devolution. As the meeting closed on this uncompromising note, I said 'I think I'll take you up on Indonesia, Prime Minister'. Even Mrs Thatcher laughed.

Walking back from No 10 to the Foreign Office, Geoffrey Howe not surprisingly showed signs of wear and tear and both of us were somewhat cast down at the prospect of trying to maintain a constructive dialogue with the Irish on the basis of the restrictive remit now imposed on us. The gloom was lifted a little, however, when we received a minute from the Prime Minister's Private Secretary explaining that the tone of her remarks at the meeting was not to be taken as indicating that she wished to end the negotiations or had lost interest in reaching an Agreement. A conversation which she had had on 5 March with Enoch Powell had sharpened her sensitivities about unionist feelings; but she remained committed to the search for an Agreement broadly on the lines of the paper we had given the Irish on 21 January.

X

WE NOW HAD TO PREPARE for the Dublin ministerial meeting. This involved drafting a joint minute to the Prime Minister from the two Secretaries of State, defining their proposed objectives: no easy task given the continuing pessimism of the Northern Ireland Office about the whole enterprise. Robert Andrew quoted the Prime Minister in support of the contention that the introduction of an Irish dimension in the North would be a disincentive to the SDLP to cooperate in any internal, devolved form of government there. When I asked him whether he subscribed to the corollary, viz. that the absence of an Irish dimension would make it more likely that the SDLP would cooperate in an internal, devolved settlement, he admitted that he didn't.

The drafting of the minute coincided with the preparation of a major speech to the Royal United Services Institute by Geoffrey Howe, in which I was heavily involved, on the subject of President Reagan's 'Strategic Defence Initiative' (SDI), better known as 'Star Wars'. This was a particularly delicate job, as the Whitehall view of SDI (which Geoffrey Howe and I shared) was decidedly sceptical, while Mrs Thatcher, true to her friendship with Reagan, had firmly endorsed it. Geoffrey Howe's criticisms therefore had to be both oblique and interrogative. Inevitably, however, the speech (delivered on 15 March) was correctly seen as taking a different view from that of Margaret Thatcher and as being sceptical rather than supportive. The resulting row with the Prime Minister did nothing to increase her receptiveness to recommendations emanating from the Foreign Secretary about Ireland.

As it eventually issued, the joint minute gave priority to the lowering of Irish expectations. The Irish were to be told that we remained keen to reach an agreement on the lines under discussion between officials, but that it must not go beyond what unionists could be expected to acquiesce in. Consultation could be extended to economic and social matters only if the Irish were prepared to amend their constitution, or at least find an unequivocal way of acknowledging the Union which would be proof against challenge in the Irish Courts. The achievement of devolved government in the North was not a precondition for an agreement, but we would expect the Irish government to seek to persuade the SDLP to cooperate in the introduction of devolved arrangements. Meanwhile it would not be practicable (as the Irish hoped) to finalise an agreement in time for the Northern Ireland local elections, due in May.

The Prime Minister's endorsement of these objectives was accompanied by a stern warning not to give any ground on extending consultation to economic and social matters until she had satisfied herself of the value of whatever concession the Irish might offer in return. The overall flavour of the instructions thus agreed, together with the tone of the discussion which led up to them, made me think that the Irish would be left wondering whether we still stood by our proposals of 21 January in their entirety, let alone whether we had taken any account of the points they had made in response. So, I minuted Geoffrey Howe urging the need to reassure the Irish that we continued to regard our January proposals and the Irish response to them as the basis on which we were negotiating, and to explain that our main difficulties were over the inclusion of economic and social matters and the wording to be used about mixed courts, i.e., how strongly to frame any commitment to consider their introduction. (By this time, I was personally persuaded that a visible change in the system whereby justice was administered in the North could be crucial in winning the support of the nationalist community for an agreement).

Geoffrey Howe, Robert Armstrong and I flew to Dublin on 22 March from Norholt, meeting Douglas Hurd and Robert Andrew at Baldonnell, the Irish military airport now renamed 'Casement'. (When informed of this, Geoffrey Howe drily remarked: 'Ah: Roger and out – or perhaps Roger and Out, Out, Out'.) The talks began with ministers (Howe, Hurd, Barry and Spring) meeting for an hour on their own, being joined by the Taoiseach for lunch. Officials meanwhile had their own exceptionally good lunch in Seán Donlon's office, for which Michael Lillis had chosen the wine. In making this clear, Michael impressed on the rest of us several times that he had himself given up alcohol for Lent – prompting Noel Dorr to remark gently: 'How true it is that the martyrs are those who have to live with the saints'.

The ministerial discussions resumed after lunch, without the Taoiseach, but with officials present. Douglas Hurd and Geoffrey Howe argued the merits of the British proposals of 21 January and insisted that it would be impossible for the British government to move beyond them, e.g. by extending consultation to cover economic and social matters, unless the Irish government was willing to tackle the constitutional issue – although Geoffrey Howe indicated that this did not necessarily mean formally amending Articles 2 and 3. Peter Barry said that, even with the changes suggested by the Irish side, the British proposals of 21 January would not be a sufficient basis for amending the Irish Constitution: for that, the Irish government would require to be given not just a right to be consulted, but 'an effective role in decision making' in the North. Simply extending consultation to cover economic and social matters would not be enough. Instead, however, they would be willing to consider a revived Sunningdale formula, which could be incorporated into an international agreement registered with the UN.

Barry and Spring also pressed hard for 'confidence-building measures', notably reform of the RUC and the UDR, stressing the need for visible changes to the structures of law and order in the North in order to convince the nationalist community that the agreement would make a real difference to their lives. The NIO were adamantly against any interference at Irish behest with the RUC, which they believed would make its already difficult task impossible and arouse unionist fury; with less justification (as it seemed to me) they were equally adamant against interfering with the UDR. So, Geoffrey Howe acknowledged the desirability in principle of some confidence-building measures into the agreement but said it was difficult in practice to identify measures which could be taken straight away.

The NIO interpreted this essentially inconclusive meeting as demonstrating that the gap between the British and Irish positions was too wide to bridge; that the Irish failed to understand legitimate British concerns; and that they were determined to press 'quite unacceptable demands'. I commented to Geoffrey Howe that the NIO wish to report on the meeting to the Prime Minister in these stark terms suggested that they wanted the negotiations to fail. My own reading of the meeting was that the real gap between the two sides had been reduced to manageable proportions; and that provided we no longer wanted to insist on the Irish amending their constitution, agreement on something close to our proposals of 21 January should be attainable.

Geoffrey Howe minuted the Prime Minister in judiciously downbeat terms, to the effect that there was still a significant gap between the two sides, but that if the Irish could find an effective way of meeting us on the constitutional point, we might be able to accommodate them on economic and social matters. Meanwhile, the Irish needed to be 'brought down to earth' about the sort of confidence-building measures we could contemplate. He suggested that when the Prime Minister saw the Taoiseach in the margins of the impending European Council at Brussels, she should impress on him that there could be no question of giving the Irish a 'decision-making role' in the North in return for amending the Irish constitution, and that without some 'legally secure' undertaking on the status of Northern Ireland, economic and social issues (other than cross-border ones) would have to be excluded from the consultative arrangements. Nor could we contemplate confidence-building measures which might undermine the effectiveness of the security forces or produce a unionist backlash.

The Brussels meeting, which took place on 30 March, produced no new developments. Garret FitzGerald (*All in a Life*, p. 538) calls it a 'marking time kind of meeting', which included discussion of the Irish proposal for an 'Ireland Fund', to be funded by the US government and the European community; and some exchanges about confidence-building measures, in which he again pressed the case for joint courts. On all this, Mrs Thatcher was discouraging without being categorically negative. The British record of the conversation additionally records the Prime Minister as stressing the need for the SDLP to engage in serious discussions about devolution and the importance of a firm Irish statement about the constitutional position of Northern Ireland – to which the Taoiseach replied by adverting to the possible use of the Sunningdale formula.

XI

On 24 April there took place the first meeting of the wider ministerial group monitoring the negotiations which had been recommended by Robert Armstrong at the beginning of March. Since this was a formally constituted Cabinet subcommittee (known as OD(I)), and I was no longer a Cabinet Office official (my place there having by this time been taken by Christopher Mallaby, who from this point onwards was an important contributor to the negotiating process), I was not present. I was also away from the Office (at a conference in Bavaria about nuclear deterrence) in the run-up to the meeting, and so missed taking part in some of the preparations for it.

The two Secretaries of State presented a joint paper setting out revised British proposals based on those we had put to the Irish on 21 January; but, in deference to the Prime Minister's wishes, the strictly consultative nature of the role envisaged for the Irish was made explicit (a reversion to the old 'model "a"'), as was the fact that the agreement would involve no infringement of British sovereignty over Northern Ireland. Although strictly speaking these changes were presentational rather than substantive, from the Irish point of view (as soon became clear) they greatly reduced the attractiveness of the package which the Taoiseach would have to sell to his electorate. The passage on mixed courts, on which we had been reasonably forthcoming in January, also had to be watered down to take account of Lord Lowry's opposition.

In the sub-committee discussion, Douglas Hurd was recorded as advocating our proposals mainly as the price of obtaining improved cross-border security cooperation from the Irish government, while Geoffrey Howe stressed that an agreement would be worthwhile for its own sake. The Prime Minister accepted that the proposals held out the prospect of improved security cooperation from the Irish, as well as greater cooperation from the nationalist community within Northern Ireland and a firm recognition of the border by the Irish government. Success would be judged on the reaction of the unionists and on whether the agreement was sufficient to persuade the SDLP to join the Northern Ireland Assembly.

On this basis, the proposals, as amended, were approved for presentation to the Irish at the next Armstrong-Nally meeting. This took place five days later at Chevening, the Foreign Secretary's official country residence in the Kent countryside. Robert Armstrong and I drove down together in the afternoon, and the Irish joined us in time for drinks before dinner – Philip Earl of Chesterfield (by Gainsborough) looking down on our proceedings from the drawing room wall with a weary, knowing, ironical eye.

On their arrival, we gave the Irish copies of our revised proposals to study overnight; but there was no opportunity for them to look at them before dinner, at which discussion concentrated on the pros and cons of confidence-building measures. In a private talk with me, however, Dermot Nally revealed his own deep misgivings about what we were about, and his fears of the hostility that would be aroused in the Republic at the spectacle of the Taoiseach doing a deal with the British which would be seen as calculated to strengthen the British position in the North. He recalled that when he was a boy in South Dublin at the outbreak of the War, most of his neighbours wanted the Germans to win: a thought which came as a shock – although he also reminded me that some 44,000 men from the South had fought in the British armed forces.

Next morning after breakfast the Irish team held a meeting on their own to discuss the British paper and then joined us to give their reaction. Dermot Nally described this as 'deep disappointment' and it soon became clear that there were undercurrents of real dismay and anger on the Irish side. Predictably, their dismay focussed on the changes British ministers had made to the operative paragraph which eventually became Article 2 (b) of the Agreement. The reintroduction of 'consultative' to describe the role to be given to the Irish government was particularly unwelcome, as was the omission of a phrase (to which Mrs Thatcher had taken exception) that, within the proposed joint inter-governmental body or 'Standing Committee' (as we were calling it for negotiating purposes), 'every effort would be made to resolve any differences'. They objected also to our refusal to commit ourselves to the establishment of mixed courts, and to the exclusion of economic and social issues from the Standing Committee's purview.

All in all, the Irish thought that we had reneged on areas of agreement reached earlier, and indeed gone back from the proposals we had put to them in January. Robert Armstrong drew on all his drafting skills to find a form of words which might stand some chance of being accepted by Mrs Thatcher while meeting Irish concerns on the role of the Standing Committee, dropping 'consultative' and restoring 'every effort'. Thereafter the atmosphere gradually returned to normal and there was a useful discussion of possible 'confidence-building measures' relating to the RUC and the UDR as well as of Irish accession to the European Convention on the Suppression of Terrorism. The Irish also confirmed their readiness to give a formal and binding assurance on the constitutional status of Northern Ireland – though without altogether dispelling the imprecision (which persisted into the Agreement itself) as to just what that status was. Nevertheless, we ended the meeting with Irish hints of bad faith on the British side still hanging in the air; and both Robert Armstrong and I felt that unless we could be authorised to restore the operative paragraph to broadly its original form, there was a real risk of Irish ministers walking away from the negotiations and blaming us for the breakdown.

Robert minuted in this sense to the Prime Minister, asking for authority to put to the Irish the compromise formula he had devised; and I suggested to Geoffrey Howe a supporting minute from him to the Prime Minister, which he approved and sent. I argued that the wording we had put forward in January had been studied and accepted by Irish ministers on the understanding that it had the approval of the Prime Minister and both Secretaries of State (which it had); that as modified by the Cabinet sub-committee, the flavour of the paragraph had, from an Irish point of view, been radically altered; and that in my judgement this was a make-or-break point in the negotiations. Shortly afterwards, and somewhat to my surprise, Douglas Hurd also minuted to the Prime Minister to the effect that the revised Armstrong formula met our basic requirement (that the British government retained sole executive authority in Northern Ireland). So 'it would not be sensible to allow its wording to become the rock on which the Anglo-Irish talks founder', nor would we be 'on good ground in resisting a return to wording closer to the text we ourselves offered on 21 January'.

The Prime Minister, however, was characteristically tenacious of her point. She did not like 'every effort' because she thought it could imply giving in to Irish wishes against our better judgement; and she was insistent on making it explicit that the British government 'would retain full responsibility for decisions'. After further exchanges, she was persuaded to accept 'determined efforts' with 'every effort' as a fallback. In the event, when we next met the Irish in Dublin on 15 May and presented them with the revised text, they professed themselves relieved and reassured and had no problem with 'determined' (which is what appeared in the final Agreement).

Among the issues settled at this meeting (to which Tony Brennan of the NIO made the constructive contribution noted by Garret FitzGerald, *All in a Life*, p. 544) was the formula expressing Irish acceptance of the constitutional status of Northern Ireland. The Irish having made it clear that the Agreement as it was shaping up was not 'substantial' enough to enable the Taoiseach to carry amendments to Articles 2 and 3 of the Irish Constitution, it was necessary to find language which would leave no doubt of the Republic's acceptance of the legitimacy of the Union (as long as a majority of the Northern Ireland wanted it) without inviting constitutional challenge in the Irish Supreme Court.

Both Dermot Nally and Robert Armstrong, with Sunningdale experience behind them, had been round this course before. Dermot argued his case with metaphysical zeal and persuasiveness and Robert brought all his ingenuity to bear. The resulting formula was something of a hybrid between assertion and commitment. In particular, the use of 'would' rather than 'could' in the sentence '... affirm that any change in the status of Northern Ireland would only come about with the consent of a majority ...', which echoed the wording of the Haughey/Thatcher communique of 21 May 1980, carried the flavour of a factual statement (rather than a commitment susceptible of being found inconsistent with the Irish Constitution). The formula also fell short of making Northern Ireland's status as part of the United Kingdom explicit; but it was stronger than the Sunningdale formula in that both governments employed the same wording on status, and both governments formally recognised that the 'present wish' of 'a majority' (there were strong Irish objections to 'the majority') of the people of Northern Ireland was for no change.

I did not take much part in this particular discussion; but my clear understanding of Dermot's argument at the time was that the formula arrived at was intended by the Irish side not only to reduce the risk of the Agreement being challenged in the Irish Supreme Court as unconstitutional, but also to have the effect of neutralising Articles 2 and 3 without requiring their actual amendment. In the event, of course, it did not escape constitutional challenge, and the resultant Supreme Court judgement included a ruling that the description of the national territory in Article 2 was a 'constitutional imperative'. It thus became possible for unionist opponents of the Agreement to argue that, instead of neutralising the Republic's territorial claim on the North, the Agreement gave it new life; and an important element in 'the basic equation' – Irish acceptance of Northern Ireland's status as part of the United Kingdom – was thereby significantly weakened.

After reading my report of this meeting, Geoffrey Howe told me that he wanted to 'catch the tide while it was there' and clinch an Agreement quickly. I drafted a speaking note for him to use with his colleagues and on 23 May our draft text, as it had emerged from our latest discussions with the Irish, was approved by the cabinet sub-committee with only minor amendments. Less helpfully, ministers thought that the Agreement should include a review clause, the purpose of which would be to enable the British government to terminate the work of the joint Standing Committee without releasing the Irish government from its commitment to respect the constitutional status of Northern Ireland. Both Robert Armstrong and I regarded this requirement with scepticism. It hardly seemed realistic to invite the Irish to agree to be held to that part of the Agreement which gave them most difficulty, while giving us discretion to set aside the part which mattered most to them; nor did we think we could put forward such a suggestion without reviving all the Irish suspicions of British bad faith which we had just allayed. Robert put these points in slightly more tactful language to the Prime Minister; Geoffrey Howe sent a supporting minute which I drafted for him; and the idea was mercifully modified. At Douglas Hurd's suggestion, we proposed a clause which would allow either party to seek a review of the working of the proposed joint Standing Committee 'to see whether any changes in the scope and nature of its activities are desirable'. The Irish too saw advantage in this and a clause to this effect (Article 2) was adopted.

On 11 June I gave Noel Dorr the text of the draft Agreement with our latest suggested amendments. He read it with his usual care and said that his own personal reaction was positive. This was confirmed at the next

Armstrong-Nally meeting in Dublin on 14 June, when the Irish told us that although their ministers had not had time to consider our proposals collectively, their initial reactions were favourable. They made it clear that they still had requirements in the field of confidence-building measures (now referred to more neutrally as 'associated measures' – another term borrowed from the MBFR negotiations in Vienna) without which the Irish government would find it impossible to sign up. But we came away from Dublin with the feeling that the salient and most difficult issues had been resolved. Constitutional amendment on the part of the Republic had faded from the agenda, but a less ambitious agreement on the lines of the British proposals of 21 January, was now within reach.

XII

As THE NEGOTIATIONS entered what looked like being the home straight, the pace of official activity increased, as did the degree of ministerial and political involvement. On 30 May Douglas Hurd had met Peter Barry in London; on 12 June the Taoiseach and Geoffrey Howe had met in Lisbon, in the margins of the ceremonies marking Portugal's accession to the European Community; and on 29 June there was to be a critically important meeting between the Prime Minister and the Taoiseach during the European Summit at Milan.

In his meeting with Peter Barry in London, Douglas Hurd warned him that we would shortly need to give unionist leaders some authoritative briefing about the course of the negotiations so as assuage their feeling that they were being kept in the dark – in marked contrast to the way in which the Irish government were consulting the SDLP at every stage. On 20 June, with the Prime Minister's agreement, he had separate meetings with Ian Paisley and James Molyneaux, and saw them again together on the following day. These meetings were not expected to be satisfactory, nor were they.

According to the NIO account, Douglas Hurd emphasised that although the talks with the Irish were confidential, they were taking place within parameters clearly and publicly set out in the communique issued after the Anglo-Irish summit at Chequers in 1984. There would be no derogation from British sovereignty in Northern Ireland, no executive role for the Republic there and no breach of the constitutional guarantee. The aim was to find ways of enabling the SDLP to take a more positive attitude towards the institutions of government in Northern Ireland and to improve cross-border security cooperation. To achieve this aim, it was necessary to talk to the Irish government and listen to what they had to say. Paisley disagreed: the right way to deal with Dublin was to treat it as an unfriendly government which was seeking to destroy Northern Ireland as part of the United Kingdom. The right way to improve cross-border security was to seal the border. Jim Molyneaux was less outspoken, but equally sceptical.

He contended that the constitutional guarantee would be infringed if judges from the South were involved in administering law in the North.

Later, on 26 July, Douglas Hurd had a further meeting with Molyneaux, who was accompanied on this occasion by Enoch Powell, and offered them a more detailed briefing on the state of the talks 'on a Privy Councillor basis' (which meant that they would have had to treat it as strictly for their own information). Again, according to the NIO account, Mr Molyneaux was attracted by the idea, but Enoch Powell was not. The offer of a Privy Councillor briefing was left on the table, but was not taken up.

Before the Prime Minister's meeting with the Taoiseach in Milan took place, I had myself to go to Dublin on 24 June to talk to Seán Donlon and Michael Lillis about another of Garret's ideas – the establishment of an International Fund for Northern Ireland, with American and EC backing. The international flavour of this idea did not appeal to Mrs Thatcher, and the proposal did not find its way into the Agreement, although the Fund was established shortly afterwards. My discussions with Seán and Michael on this subject were nevertheless entirely amicable. They also raised an issue which was about to loom large in the weeks leading up to signature of the Agreement, namely the role and location of the secretariat needed to service the joint Standing Committee.

At the end of my talk with them, I was invited to accompany Alan Goodison to an interview with Garret himself. The purpose of the interview was for Alan to reply, on instructions, to some Irish representations about the Northern Ireland Police Authority. I cannot now remember the details, except that the British response was to be negative. The Taoiseach did not look well; he was a bad colour, with dark bags under his eyes and (as Michael Lillis told me afterwards) had been grieving for the death of his cousin and close friend, Alexis FitzGerald. He listened in silence and with increasing coldness as Alan spoke to his instructions, and then commented sharply and angrily that he had been deliberately misled. This led him on to speak of the depth of Irish cynicism about British trustworthiness. 'I know,' he said, speaking with an indignant flood of rapid, half-swallowed words, 'that British ministers think that their word is their bond. But if I were to give Mrs Thatcher a full-frontal view of what Irish nationalism thinks of a British minister's word, she'd be more shocked than if I gave her a full-frontal view of something else.'

Having delivered himself of this memorable outburst, the Taoiseach allowed us to calm him down and explain the reasons for the British position. He then dwelt heavily on the importance of the Agreement being accompanied by 'associated measures' which would convince the SDLP of the genuineness of British good intentions towards the nationalist community and the practical value of the Agreement itself. As he finished, I said to him that the biggest contribution he could make to Anglo-Irish relations – and to the success of our negotiations – would be to find language acceptable to the Prime Minister with which to convince her, when they met at Milan, of the reality of nationalist mistrust and the need for associated measures in order to allay it.

The importance of associated measures was impressed on me again in London the next day by John Hume, whom I came across him talking to Margaret van Hattem of the *Financial Times* at a dinner party given by Richard Ryan of the Irish Embassy. Hume was cautiously positive about the Agreement that was taking shape, the historic significance of which he acknowledged; but he stressed that it would not achieve its purpose without accompanying measures to render the institutions of law and order in Northern Ireland – the courts and the security forces – acceptable to the minority community. On the morning after this conversation I flew to Washington for talks with the National Security Council and the State Department about international terrorism and arms control issues; and in a private conversation with Admiral Poindexter (then Deputy Head of the NSC), I briefed him in fairly general terms about the state of play in our negotiations with the Irish and what we now reckoned to be the good prospects for reaching an Agreement.

As we now know from *All in a Life*, the Irish government and the SDLP were by this stage seriously worried that the British side was failing to register the critical importance of associated measures, especially for the SDLP, who needed to be able to point to tangible improvements in the position of the nationalist community on the ground if they were to endorse the Agreement without exposing flank to Sinn Féin. Garret had already pressed Geoffrey Howe on associated measures at Lisbon; together with the location of the Secretariat, they were now to become the main focus of discussion in the penultimate phase of the negotiations.

The measures which the Irish most wanted to see were the introduction of joint courts for the trial of terrorist offences (an idea which Garret had made very much his own); reform of the RUC and the UDR so as to dilute the overwhelmingly unionist complexion of both and reduce the role of the latter as far as possible; a review of prison sentences; and repeal of the Flags and Emblems Act. I thought the logic behind these proposals entirely convincing as far as it went: if Northern Ireland nationalists were to be persuaded to identify with the institutions of government in a Northern Ireland which was to remain an integral part of the United Kingdom, they had to be able to see real changes for the better in the way in which those institutions operated.

But Mrs Thatcher's reluctance to be drawn too far down this road was not irrational either. All the measures suggested were bound to be anathema to unionists. By carrying the negotiations with the Irish as far as she had, the Prime Minister had already demonstrated her resolve to face down unionist hostility to the extent she judged necessary to achieve a deal with Dublin. Prejudice apart, there were limits beyond which it would not be prudent to go, bearing in mind that there could be no long-term settlement in Northern Ireland without unionist acquiescence. Changing the character of the RUC in particular, as well as risking the collapse of its morale, would be interpreted outside the nationalist community as a victory for terrorism, and by unionists as a real threat to their own security.

Moreover, in his impassioned arguments with Mrs Thatcher, Garret FitzGerald was always so convinced of his own and his party's abhorrence of terrorism and loathing of the IRA that he never quite understood how, in the eyes of many British people as well as the Prime Minister, Irish nationalism as a whole was tainted with the terrorist brush, with the South being seen as a source of support and sympathy for IRA activity and Irish governments as sharing essentially the same Republican objectives as Sinn Féin. Garret emphasised that the Republic spent proportionately more on security than the United Kingdom; but it did not seem to strike him that a decision by the Irish government to withdraw the Garda's anti-terrorist Task Force from the southern side of the border in order (as we were told) to cope with a rising tide of car thefts in Dublin might appear incompatible with assurances that the Irish took the terrorist threat to the people of Northern Ireland as seriously as we did. There was always something of a dialogue of the deaf about discussions between Garret and Margaret Thatcher.

At Milan, however, they were able to do some serious talking. Since I was not present, I can add no personal glosses to the brief account given by Mrs Thatcher in *The Downing Street Years* (pp. 401–2) or the much longer one in Garret's *All in a Life*. What is clear from both, and also from the official record, is that when Garret had made his pitch on mixed courts and reform of the RUC and the UDR without much initial success, he then went into rhetorical top gear ('at this point Dr FitzGerald became very agitated'); and that although Mrs Thatcher continued to resist most of his suggestions, his advocacy had its effect.

The Prime Minister insisted that she could not go further than 'consider the possibility' of mixed courts and gave no encouragement on the likelihood of radical changes to the RUC or the UDR. But without accepting the concept of either associated or confidence-building measures, she nevertheless took the point that the various provisions of the Agreement, including those relating to the administration of justice and the security forces, would need to be put into visible effect without undue delay; and she offered the phrase 'prompt implementation' as the objective. Garret FitzGerald, for his part, said that a Garda task force would be sent back to the border and that the Irish government would ratify the European Convention on the Suppression of Terrorism (ECST), which it had hitherto professed itself unable to do. (The importance of this offer, which became an important issue in the concluding stage of the negotiations, was that the ECST excepted all terrorist acts from the category of 'political' crimes, thereby rendering them extraditable.)

It would seem that both leaders realised that the negotiations had passed the point of no return, and that it would be better to have an Agreement on the terms available, less than satisfactory though these might be to either side, than to admit failure and call the project off. At the end of the conversation, both felt sufficiently confident to start discussing the timing and location of the signature ceremony.

As soon as we received the record of the Milan meeting, we set to work to compile a menu of measures which we could put to the Irish as candidates for 'prompt implementation'. Robert Armstrong suggested to the Prime Minister that signature of the Agreement should be accompanied by a public statement that the joint Standing Committee would hold its first meeting within a few days and would consider a stated agenda of topics, including some of those of most concern to the Irish. These might include a code of conduct for the security forces, improved training for part-time members of the UDR, filling the outstanding vacancies on the Northern Ireland Police Authority, repeal of the Flags and Emblems Act and the establishment of machinery to consider harmonisation of the criminal law and judicial cooperation. Mrs Thatcher was more or less content with this list, with the exception of repeal of the Flags and Emblems Act. In return for all this, the Irish were to be asked to announce the redeployment of the Garda Task Force to the border and their readiness to accede to the ECST.

Further meetings of the Armstrong-Nally Group followed in quick succession, in Dublin on 9 July, in London on 15 July and at Barrettstown Castle in the Republic on 22 July, at all of which good progress was made. On 9 July, subject to one or two minor amendments, the Irish indicated that they were broadly content with the draft text of the Agreement as it now stood, but were reserved about the downgrading of 'associated measures' to 'prompt' (or 'rapid') implementation, and did not find our list of measures adequate. They were under firm instructions from the Taoiseach to press for an assurance that mixed courts would be established within a defined period of time; and they warned us that there was a risk of a split within the SDLP, where Seamus Mallon would not be satisfied with measures to reform the UDR and bring its part-time members under better professional control, but wanted to insist on its outright disbandment (something which the Taoiseach had told the Prime Minister he was not asking for).

The Cabinet sub-committee met again on 15 July (with the Prime Minister in the chair as usual) and agreed that our aim should be to sign an Agreement (on the lines which were now clear) at the end of September, after it had been debated in Parliament; and that meanwhile there should be further discussion with the Irish about measures for 'prompt implementation'. There could, however, be no question of our accepting a commitment to establish joint or mixed courts, as distinct from agreeing to examine the possibility. In his memoirs, Garret makes much of a letter to the Prime Minister from the members of the Northern Ireland Judiciary, confirming that they would abide by the will of Parliament on this issue. But this did not really address Mrs Thatcher's objections which, as I understood them, were based partly on the strong opposition of the Lord Chief Justice of Northern Ireland, backed equally forcefully by the Lord Chancellor, Lord Hailsham; and by the belief that (as Jim Molyneux had argued to Douglas Hurd) the admission of Irish judges to the Northern Ireland courts would be an infringement of the 'constitutional guarantee' that Northern Ireland would remain part of the United Kingdom. Douglas Hurd told his colleagues that there was considerable tension in Northern Ireland because of the Anglo-Irish talks and the secrecy surrounding them; but he still believed that unionist reaction to the Agreement would be containable.

At the Armstrong-Nally meeting that evening and the following morning in London, the Irish suggested a couple of amendments to the text which British ministers had just approved (neither of which found favour with the Prime Minister) and continued to press for a firm commitment on mixed courts. They accepted our 'prompt implementation' approach, and agreed that the communique issued at the time the Agreement was signed should go into detail about the matters to be considered at the first meeting of the joint Standing Committee (which they suggested should be called the 'Intergovernmental Commission'). This discussion was continued at Barrettstown.

Meanwhile the Prime Minister and the two Secretaries of State had agreed that the conclusions of the Cabinet sub-committee needed to be approved by the whole Cabinet, where it was discussed on 25 July. The problem of mixed courts was debated at some length, and constitutional as well as political reasons were apparently advanced (presumably by the Lord Chancellor as well as some others) against having any mention of the possibility in the Agreement at all; but it was thought that the Irish, and the Taoiseach personally, would be unlikely to conclude an Agreement which did not include a British undertaking at least to consider the possibility, without commitment.

The Cabinet also discussed likely unionist reactions. It was recognised that these might be severe; and that there was great resentment that unionist leaders were not being consulted by the British government as the SDLP were by the Irish. But it was doubted whether there would be a sustained campaign of violent protest. (It was immediately after this discussion that Douglas Hurd made the offer of a Privy Councillor briefing to Jim

Molyneaux and Enoch Powell.) The Cabinet decided that on balance the risks were worth taking; and that an Agreement (which was considered to offer security advantages) was preferable to simply continuing with direct rule and the containment of terrorism without any prospect of change or sign of hope. It was agreed that the negotiations should continue, on the understanding that the Agreement would be brought back to Cabinet for final approval before signature.

XIII

Reform of the UDR being one of the central planks in the Irish demand for associated measures, and Irish complaints about the discriminatory way in which the UDR operated against nationalists having to my ears more than a ring of truth, I thought it would be useful to go and see for myself what the UDR was like and what it was doing. By good luck, the Brigadier commanding the UDR, Roger Preston, and his wife Polly were old friends of ours; and in my National Service days Roger and I had been subalterns together in the KOYLI.[6] Roger and Polly readily invited my wife and myself to spend a long weekend with them, and Roger offered to give me a full briefing and introduce me to UDR units on the ground. Field Marshal Edwin Bramall, the Chief of the Defence Staff, was happy for me to go and asked me to give him my impressions on my return. So, on 26 July, after Geoffrey Howe's farewell lunch for Archbishop Bruno Heim, the departing Papal Pro-Nuncio in London, my wife and I flew to Aldergrove where we were met by Roger and taken off to his house at Lisburn.

The Ulster Defence Regiment (UDR) had been established in 1970 in place of the 'B Specials', a part-time special constabulary with a bad reputation for brutality and discrimination against Catholics, composed almost exclusively of Ulster Protestants. The intention was to recruit in its place a non-sectarian, partly half-time territorial force commanded at senior level by British officers seconded from the Regular Army, and with a small leavening of regular NCOs. Its role was to assist the Regular Army in guarding installations, patrolling, and manning vehicle checkpoints. It was not to be used in covert, plain clothes operations, or in crowd control or riot situations; nor did it operate in certain strongly republican areas of West Belfast, Londonderry and South Armagh.

Despite best endeavours, however, it had proved even more difficult to recruit Northern Ireland Catholics into the UDR than into the RUC. I was told that although at the outset Catholics had comprised 18% of the force,

6. *Editor's Note* The King's Own Yorkshire Light Infantry – according to OUP's *Who Was Who*, Goodall served as a 2nd Lieutenant 1955–56.

by 1985 the proportion was down to 2.7%. Intimidation was such that local Catholics joined at the risk of their lives; and such Catholics as there were in it were almost all English and to be found among the regular officers. To serve in the UDR at all required courage, since its members were particular targets of IRA attack; but an uncomfortable number of serving or former UDR soldiers had either been convicted of, or were awaiting trial for, serious offences. The part-time officers and other ranks were nearly all Protestants, some of the NCOs were ex-B Specials, and the ethos at company and battalion level was overwhelmingly Protestant and unionist. For all these reasons, the nationalist community regarded the UDR as a hostile force.

At the same time, the UDR, comprising at this date nine battalions and over 6,000 men, had come to be an indispensable element in the maintenance of internal security, complementing the Regular Army and releasing Regular units for more active roles. It had been expanded more than once, and had an 'established' strength almost double its actual size. Recognising the impracticability of requiring its total disbandment (which would have necessitated a proportionate increase in the number of regular British Army personnel serving in the Province), the Irish government was pressing us to dispense with the U's part-time component (well over 50% of the total) and to introduce more regular officers and NCOs at all levels of command.

I spent the next two and a half days travelling round the Province visiting UDR units and talking to regular and part-time members of the Regiment, both on the job and socially. I was given a comprehensive and straightforward briefing by Roger and his Chief of Staff (a regular major) and separate briefings by the Commanding Officers of 6 UDR at Omagh and 8 UDR at Dungannon. I visited 4 UDR on a field firing range at Gortin, drove around through Clogher, with its bleakly classical little cathedral, Portadown (the streets still heavy with bunting and Orange banners from the 12th) and Craigavon; and later went to Aughnacloy and along the border through Caledon to Armagh. In the course of these journeys, I spent some time with UDR patrols engaged on 'route-clearing operations' (searching for explosives and detonating explosives) and on a vehicle road-block and narrowly escaped becoming entangled in an IRA funeral, which made my escort, a part-time captain who in private life was a bank official in Lisburn, extremely nervous. My wife and I also had a large and vinous lunch at the Officers' Mess in Dungannon, where I was buttonholed by two part-time UDR officers in succession.

Both the (English) commanding officers who briefed me gave the impression of being thoroughly professional, objective in their judgements, on top of their job, deeply conscious of the risks their part-time soldiers ran and proud of their performance. Not surprisingly, however, they saw their task in straight, anti-terrorist terms, with community relations as an important but entirely subsidiary consideration.

On the firing range, a number of the NCOs and soldiers were middle-aged, ex-B Specials. A large, lugubrious man with a walrus moustache held out his hand to me and wished me welcome in Ulster. 'We hear you're from the Foreign Office: we hope you haven't come to make a foreign country of us'. Two of the men were farmers from isolated farms near the border, worried about their future in the event of a nationalist take-over. One of them had been shot at by the Catholic farmer next door. All their neighbours were Catholics – 'two-faced people you can't trust'. On patrol, a cheerful, bright-eyed Colour Sergeant asked 'Why should the Free State have a say in our affairs?' A corporal on the same patrol had been attacked in his home by the IRA and wondered whether the risks he was running were worth it. 'What was it all for?' I said it was 'for' the defeat of terrorism. Privately, I hoped I was right.

Over lunch at Dungannon, I was assailed by both the part-time officers who sat next to me, full of suspicion that the government, and the FCO in particular, were selling out to the Republic. One of them had prepared a typed memorandum which he gave me. It began 'As the senior native officer who has lived and worked most of 58 years in this area' ... and went on to warn that 'the Protestant tribe is currently like a wasp's nest that has been upset... very confused and potentially dangerous'. This state of affairs had been brought about by the participation of Sinn Féin in local government, continuing terrorist murders, a feeling that 'the war was being lost' but 'above all by the morale-sapping uncertainty of the prolonged Anglo-Irish talks'. It ended: 'A Dublin voice (i.e., in the affairs of the North) could easily be to Northern Ireland what animal fat on bullets was in India'.

Strong though their feelings were, both officers and soldiers were friendly and our discussions remained amicable. I thought they were likeable people: tough and suspicious, but also brave, committed and honest; and their indignation and anxieties were understandable. But there was a startling colour-blindness to the other half of the picture: the feeling of their Catholic neighbours that the province was being run by, and in the interests of, the rival tribe. Nor could I help noticing a certain zest with which the patrols had stopped and questioned passing motorists. Despite the professionalism with which the UDR was commanded and sought to operate, it had the feeling of one half of a divided society armed to defend itself against the other half. I came away confirmed in my view that, by relying so heavily on the UDR, we were trying to maintain security on the cheap; and that the price was being paid in heightened divisiveness and intercommunal resentment.

In the light of my discussions with Roger Preston and other senior UDR officers, it seemed to me that there were four small, but useful, steps which could be taken without too much pain to improve matters: the established strength of the part-time component of the Regiment should be cut back to something like its actual strength, as a clear indication that it was not going to be expanded; a code of conduct should be promulgated for all the security forces, and not just the RUC (as was then under discussion in the negotiations); the power of summary arrest should be confined to NCOs in charge of sections, instead of being exercised by any soldier in uniform; and there should be further limitations on the areas into which the UDR would be deployed.

The next morning, I put these points to the GOC, Sir Robert Pascoe, a quietly spoken Greenjacket. At first rather unforthcoming, he thawed as we talked. He did not seem surprised either by my general conclusion or by my suggestions, all of which he agreed were starters; and he was emphatic that there needed to be an Anglo-Irish Agreement. Field Marshal Bramall, the CDS, whom I saw a couple of days later in London, was equally receptive and promised to give these ideas a fair wind.

I rounded off my stay in Northern Ireland with discussions over lunch with Tony Stephens, the senior NIO official at Stormont, followed by visits to 7/10 UDR in Belfast City and to the Castle Street checkpoint. There I had the odd experience of being walked round Castle Street among the shoppers and strollers flanked by two armed soldiers, with two more behind and two more in front taking up firing positions as I went along.

Almost as soon as I returned to London, I was off to Chevening for another Armstrong-Nally meeting, at which a good deal of progress was made in drafting the communique. The Irish showed a lively interest in my impressions of the UDR, especially Seán Donlon, who had a long tale of complaints about the way in which he had himself been treated by the UDR at checkpoints. I did my best to be both honest and discreet, but I did not disguise my feeling that the UDR was a divisive element on the scene.

Both sides at this meeting indicated that their ministers thought the Agreement which was emerging looked broadly acceptable, but wanted to see the complete package before reaching a decision. Robert Armstrong explained that the Agreement would have to be debated in the House of Commons before any steps could be taken to implement it; and that as the Prime Minister did not want to recall Parliament prematurely for that purpose, this pointed to signature at a Summit meeting at the end of October, closely followed by a Parliamentary debate and then the first meeting of the joint Standing Committee to begin implementation. Irish ministers were still hoping that signature could take place early in September. More substantively, they still needed a firm British undertaking on joint courts and on other associated measures, without which they said the Taoiseach would have difficulty in defending the Agreement in the Dáil or in persuading the SDLP to support it. They stressed that measures to reduce the role of the UDR were particularly important from this point of view.

Reporting from Dublin after this meeting, Alan Goodison thought that the Taoiseach was personally committed to signing an Agreement with us, but could not do so without the support of his Cabinet and the SDLP. For this to be forthcoming, the Agreement would need to contain more measures likely to have an immediate impact on the lives of the minority. Notwithstanding this important proviso (with which I agreed), we went into the holiday month of August with the strong feeling that an Agreement was now all but in the bag.

XIV

As business resumed towards the end of the month, the Prime Minister convened a small meeting on 30 August to discuss the final stages of the negotiation, including possible ways of meeting the Irish wish to strengthen the 'associated measures'. We met in her study at No 10. Douglas Hurd, Robert Armstrong, Christopher Mallaby and Nigel Wicks (the Prime Minister's new Private Secretary) were there; and I represented Geoffrey Howe, who was away. Mrs Thatcher, whom we knew to be in the throes of a Cabinet reshuffle, looked pale but was in full vigour. Throughout the discussion, she treated Douglas Hurd with unusual consideration, repeatedly asking his opinion and calling him by his Christian name.

On mixed courts, she reiterated the Lord Chancellor's view that these would constitute an infringement of sovereignty, and made it clear that she did not believe we could ever accept them. But she recognised the importance of the issue for the Taoiseach, and acknowledged that some way needed to be found of meeting his concern. It had already been accepted that there should be an article in the Agreement referring to the importance of public confidence in the administration of justice. Mrs Thatcher now agreed that this article might also provide for the proposed Standing Committee to consider 'ways of giving practical expression to this aim' (i.e., sustaining public confidence in the administration of justice) 'including the possibility of mixed courts in both jurisdictions for the trial of certain offences'. This was an important concession, although one destined in due course to lead to Irish accusations of bad faith.[7]

There was a lengthy discussion of the UDR, in which I explained as firmly as I could why I thought Irish resentment was understandable, and put forward my suggestions for reducing the Regiment's role. The Prime Minister accused me only half-humorously of arguing in defence of terrorism: 'you're supposed to be on our side'. But she listened all the same,

7. After the Agreement had been concluded, we not only refused to have mixed courts but also turned down a subsequent Irish suggestion that the Diplock procedure should be amended so as to have three British judges sitting in terrorist trials instead of one.

and I felt I had made my point. Douglas Hurd, however, was strongly opposed to making any offer on the UDR beyond saying that there was no present intention of increasing its size and that we would be reviewing its establishment levels and possibly its deployment. I thought this would not be enough.

After further argument, it was agreed that we could tell the Irish that British ministers recognised Irish nationalist sensitivities about the UDR (which was an equally sensitive issue for unionists); and that initial training for part-time members of the Regiment would be extended, with more regular NCOs being seconded to it for that purpose. This was not much, but it was something; and since the Prime Minister was clearly not in a mood to gainsay Douglas Hurd, I had to be content with that.

Douglas Hurd was also concerned to establish that there would be unequivocal support for the Agreement from the SDLP; and was worried that the Irish envisaged an active, 'crisis management' role for the proposed joint Secretariat. But neither he nor Mrs Thatcher questioned the need for a permanent Secretariat or revived objections to it being based in Belfast. So, after the meeting, I was able to report to Geoffrey Howe that both Mrs Thatcher and Douglas Hurd seemed committed to securing an Agreement on the lines under discussion, and that Douglas Hurd thought the unionist reaction should be containable – provided no further concessions were made to the Irish.

Two days later, the outcome of the Cabinet reshuffle was announced. Douglas Hurd became Home Secretary in place of Leon Brittan; and Tom King, with no previous experience either of the Province or of the current negotiations with the Irish, became Secretary of State for Northern Ireland. The reason for the unusual courtesy with which Hurd had been treated by the Prime Minister at her meeting was now clear. I noted that night in my diary that 'the NIO move seems unsettling just at the present juncture, with the Anglo-Irish talks coming to a head – the Irish will be dismayed at the departure of Hurd after a year (proof of their contention that British governments don't take Northern Ireland seriously): and King doesn't strike me as being as a man of either bottom or leadership. But at least he will sustain the impression that policy on Northern Ireland will be made by the PM'. (Insofar as this judgement impugned Tom King's courage, I now think it less than fair.)

Geoffrey Howe, on his return, echoed my dismay at this sudden change and expressed surprise at Hurd's promotion to the Home Office. He observed drily that at a ministerial meeting on 4 September, Hurd had acted the part of 'the man on the Clapham omnibus'. 'Anyone less like the man on the Clapham omnibus it would be difficult to imagine'.

The results of the Prime Minister's meeting of 30 August were discussed with the Irish at Armstrong-Nally meetings in Dublin on 3 September and in London on 12/13 September. By this time a good deal of well-informed speculation about the Agreement was appearing in the British press, and the Irish expressed dismay at the way in which the role foreseen for the Irish government was being described as 'consultative'. Dermot Nally said it would be suicide for the Irish government to enter into an Agreement in which its role was described in these terms and stressed that some alternative to 'consultative' must be found. He also stressed the importance of a firm British undertaking on mixed courts and of more ambitious measures to limit the role of the UDR. Michael Lillis came to my flat on the evening of 11 September to reinforce these points and discuss the state of play over a late-night whiskey.

For much of September I was preoccupied with the climax of the lengthy covert operation involving Oleg Gordievsky, the acting Head of the KGB Station in London, who had been successfully smuggled out of the Soviet Union and granted asylum in the United Kingdom. On the morning of 12 September, it fell to me to summon the Soviet Chargé d'Affaires (a friend and close colleague of Gordievsky's), communicate the news to him and require the withdrawal from London of 25 Soviet officials whom Gordievsky had identified as spies. While this uncomfortable and dramatic interview was taking place, the Prime Minister held a quick meeting with the two Secretaries of State to consider how the Irish demands should be handled. As a result, we were instructed to tell them that we would much prefer to omit all mention of mixed courts, about which we had very serious reservations; and that in no circumstances could we go beyond the cautious formula already offered. On the UDR, we could give an assurance that the Catholic population would, by the end of October, be able to see that a higher proportion of UDR patrols than hitherto were being accompanied by the RUC.

In response, Nally welcomed our move on the UDR, while insisting that it was not enough; and said he had no discretion to abate the Taoiseach's insistence on an undertaking that mixed courts would be established within a stated period of time. The discussion then turned to the role and status of the proposed joint Secretariat. The Irish – and the SDLP in particular – saw this as a key feature of the new arrangements, both symbolically (by virtue of its being located on Northern Ireland soil) and practically (because it would be the official channel through which they would be making their 'views and proposals' known to the British). They, therefore, wanted to give it a high profile, and to ensure that it should be headed on both sides by senior officials of weight. For precisely the opposite reasons, the NIO wanted to downplay its role and status to the maximum extent possible.

The issue of location had (as I thought) already been settled at the meeting between the Prime Minister and Douglas Hurd which I had attended on 30 August; and it had also been accepted that the Secretariat would necessarily have a continuous function and would need to be staffed at a level consistent with its responsibilities. Robert Andrew, however, as well as contributing more than his usual share of qualifications and hesitations to the rest of the discussion ('Robert Andrew particularly costive', I noted in my diary), back-pedalled so persistently on the Secretariat that the Irish were treated to a lengthy argument between members of the British team about the role and status of the Secretariat. As this became increasingly protracted and acrimonious, Robert Armstrong cut Robert Andrew short and told the Irish roundly that if we got the Agreement it would be our intention to make it work.

Robert Armstrong's brisk exercise of the guillotine on Robert Andrew cleared the air with the Irish; and despite the continuing points of difference, it was agreed to aim for signature of the Agreement towards the end of October. The Prime Minister being adamantly opposed to signature anywhere in the Republic, it was suggested that the ceremony might take place at Hillsborough.

The aftermath of the Gordievsky affair – including how to handle the Soviet retaliation – continued to preoccupy me for the next few days, during which Tom King, accompanied by Robert Andrew, went to Dublin for an introductory meeting with Peter Barry. In what was almost a re-run of Douglas Hurd's unhelpful introductory visit to Dublin a year earlier, Tom King took the opportunity to pour as much cold water as possible on Irish expectations. He was strongly discouraging on mixed courts (without quite ruling them out as a very remote possibility) and changes in the UDR. He reminded Barry and the Taoiseach of the strength of unionist fears, stressed that the Secretariat must not be too high powered or interventionist and suggested that, in presenting the Agreement to our publics, its significance must not be overplayed.

From the NIO report on the visit, the Irish seemed at the time to have taken these caveats philosophically enough, only reminding Tom King that nationalist fears also had to be respected and that nationalists would need to see that things really did change as a result of the Agreement. Not surprisingly, however, at the next Armstrong-Nally meeting, which took place in Dublin on 22/23 September, the Irish again urged the need for further restrictions on UDR deployments in nationalist areas if SDLP support for the Agreement was to be forthcoming; and they pressed us hard on the need for a visible and influential role for the Secretariat (on which the Taoiseach had determined that Michael Lillis should be the Irish representative) and for it to be in situ in Belfast from the start.

According to Garret's account, the NIO suggestion at this meeting that the Secretariat should start off in London, and only move to Belfast after the first couple of meetings of the Standing Committee had taken place, came 'as a bombshell'. The Irish certainly left us in no doubt that this would be unacceptable to their ministers. More worrying from our point of view, however, was the hardening of the Irish position on mixed courts. On this, they said that Tom King had given the Taoiseach and Peter Barry the impression that mixed courts were simply a non-starter, and that he personally was opposed to them. This had reinforced the Taoiseach's doubts about the value of the proposed reference in the Agreement to mixed courts as 'a possibility'. Unless we could give them a better offer on mixed courts, they would have to withdraw their own offer to accede to the European Convention on the Suppression of Terrorism.

Notwithstanding these remaining difficulties, I came away from Dublin convinced (as I noted in my diary) that the Irish had 'clearly made up their minds to have the Agreement and settle for as much (or as little) as they can get on joint courts, UDR etc.'. When the results of the meeting were reported to the Prime Minister (along with the suggestion that the Standing Committee should be called the 'Intergovernmental Standing Conference'), she reacted with predictable asperity to the Irish threat to withdraw their commitment to accede to the European Convention – not unreasonably, since this put a question mark against the increased security cooperation between Dublin and London which, in her view, was to be the main quid pro quo for giving Dublin a role in Northern Ireland's affairs. We were, therefore, to make it plain to the Irish that we would see this as a breach of faith. Nor did she like the title 'Intergovernmental Standing Conference'. She did, however, confirm her earlier consent to the Secretariat being located in Belfast from shortly after the signing of the Agreement.

XV

TWO DAYS LATER, on 25 September, Robert Armstrong held a meeting with Robert Andrew, Clive Whitmore (PUS at the Ministry of Defence) and me, to discuss the UDR, which I noted as being 'modestly fruitful'. As a result, we were able to tell the Irish at a subsequent Armstrong-Nally meeting that the training of the part-time members of the UDR would be lengthened and that UDR attachments on patrol would as often as possible be accompanied by an RUC officer. There was also to be a Code of Conduct promulgated for the RUC. We were not, however, able to offer any further restrictions on the areas into which the UDR might be deployed.

Geoffrey Howe, meanwhile, was away in Ottawa; and on the following day, 27 September, I flew to Bonn for anti-terrorist discussions with the Germans. In the course of these, I received an agitated telephone call from Colin Budd, Geoffrey Howe's Assistant Private Secretary in London, to say that there was a long minute from Tom King to the Prime Minister raising a catalogue of doubts about the Agreement, which required an urgent response from the Foreign Secretary. I finished my talks with the Germans, flew back to London that night, and spent the next morning drafting a minute for Geoffrey to send to the Prime Minister.

In his own minute, of which we had been given no warning, Tom King paid lip service to the desirability in principle of reaching an Agreement with the Irish, but saw the one now in prospect as 'offering considerably more to the Irish than it does to us. It will certainly be so perceived by the unionists'. The Irish were to be given an 'unprecedented role' in the internal affairs of part of the United Kingdom as representatives of the nationalist community there, while there would be no corresponding representation for unionists, since the British government had to be even-handed as between the two communities. Unionist opposition to it meant that the Agreement would infringe the undertaking that arrangements for the internal government of Northern Ireland must command widespread consent; and the role envisaged for the Irish government had unacceptably 'executive' overtones.

He was particularly unhappy about the 'wide gulf' between Irish and British perceptions of the role of the Secretariat, with the Irish wanting to make it into a high-powered body able to take decisions on its own. (Robert Andrew had been noticeably dismayed at the news that Michael Lillis was to be the Irish representative on the Secretariat.) Moreover to 'locate the Irish element of a permanent Secretariat in Belfast from the outset would be asking for trouble'. The Intergovernmental Conference should hold its first meetings in London, and the secretaries should remain in London and Dublin between meetings. He wished to discuss these misgivings with Peter Barry before the Agreement was finalised, and accordingly asked for the Cabinet discussion of it scheduled for 3 October to be postponed.

Here indeed was a bombshell, which it was impossible not to think had been timed to coincide with Geoffrey Howe's absence abroad. Robert Andrew, whose hand was clearly discernible in the drafting, rang me with a mild apology during the afternoon. I had no doubt that if Tom King was given free rein to put all these points to Peter Barry, the Irish would conclude that we were reopening the whole negotiation with a view to scuppering the Agreement altogether. So, in the reply I prepared for Geoffrey Howe (and which Colin Budd and I telegraphed to Ottawa that evening), Geoffrey expressed willingness to look at the textual points raised, but warned against giving the Irish reason to doubt our good faith or our determination to strike a bargain. He pointed out that we had succeeded in the negotiations in moving the Irish from all their initial positions and bringing them to accept our basic requirements. If we now proposed substantive and unexpected changes and requested postponement of signature, the Irish would probably withdraw from the negotiations and the Agreement would be lost. This would be seen at home and abroad as a major missed opportunity resulting from a last-minute switch of policy on our part. He agreed that we should press the Irish to sign the European anti-terrorist convention; but thought that all were agreed that Belfast was the right place for the Secretariat.

This minute, strengthened by some personal touches of his own, Geoffrey telegraphed to the Prime Minister from New York on 28 September. Mrs Thatcher said that she would wish to discuss the exchange of minutes with the two Secretaries of State concerned as soon as possible after Geoffrey Howe was back in England. Meanwhile, at the Armstrong-Nally meeting due to take place in London on 29/30 September, we were to press the Irish hard on the ECST, rejecting any comparison with the British position on mixed courts; float the various (relatively minor) textual points raised by Tom King; and warn the Irish that further ministerial discussion would be needed before the Agreement could be finalised.

In the event, the Armstrong-Nally meeting went better than we had feared, despite starting on a Sunday evening and in the claustrophobic surroundings of the basement of the Royal Horseguards Hotel. The briefing meeting of the British team immediately beforehand was somewhat tense, given the unresolved differences of view between our respective Secretaries of State and the part Robert Andrew had clearly played in crafting – if not prompting – Tom King's minute to the Prime Minister; but the discussions with the Irish, lubricated by another excellent lunch next day in the private dining room at Brooks's, were, as Michael Lillis reluctantly observed, 'not too bad'.

Our proposed textual amendments produced no serious problems. On the ECST, the Irish argued that they wanted to accede to it, but that without some movement on our part on mixed courts (which Tom King had convinced them that we had no intention of agreeing to in the foreseeable future), the Taoiseach would not be able to get accession through the Dáil. If we could not do more than offer to consider the possibility of mixed courts, they could not do more than offer to consider accession. They accepted that the Secretariat should be primarily a channel for communication between the two governments rather than a decision-making body, but they insisted that at least some elements of it should be present on the ground in Belfast from the start, otherwise unionists would do everything to prevent its arrival. It was also agreed that the Standing Committee should be known as 'The Intergovernmental Conference'.

I was not present at the Prime Minister's meeting with the two Secretaries of State, which took place on 2 October. I gathered from Robert Armstrong that she had been in her hectoring and tangential mode, both confusing and dominating the discussion. The conclusion, however (despite Tom King's expressed misgivings), was that the consequences of failing to conclude an Agreement now outweighed the risks of having one. It was agreed that there must be a statement of Irish willingness to accede to the

ECST, on which Mrs Thatcher would send the Taoiseach a personal message; that wording should be introduced into Article 2 of the draft agreement to spell out the retention of national sovereignty (' ... each [government] retains responsibility for the decisions and administration of government within its own jurisdiction'); and that Tom King's anxieties about the Secretariat could be eased by not describing it as 'permanent' and by defining its function as being to 'service' the Conference and 'enable it to carry out its duties'. It was also agreed that the two Secretaries of State should arrange to meet Peter Barry to discuss how the Agreement and the Secretariat should work in practice.

None of this looked likely to pose any serious threat to the successful conclusion of negotiations; nor did the Prime Minister's subsequent message to the Taoiseach. In this she pointed out that, whereas the Irish had volunteered the commitment to accede to the ECST, which was now an important element in the balance of the package, we had all along made clear our difficulties over mixed courts. (This was not quite true, since she had not rejected the idea when it was first raised by the Taoiseach at Chequers in November 1984; but we had repeatedly rehearsed the difficulties ever since the Taoiseach's unfortunate conversation with Lord Lowry the previous March). She urged the Irish to keep their component of the Secretariat small, and 'perhaps' not leave it continuously in Belfast 'at any rate until the new arrangements have settled down'. This was language calculated rather to placate Tom King than to persuade the Taoiseach to change his mind.

On 7 October, Peter Barry and Dick Spring, accompanied by the Irish official team of Dermot Nally, Seán Donlon, Michael Lillis and Noel Dorr, came to London to talk through the outstanding points of difficulty with Geoffrey Howe and Tom King, who were accompanied by Robert Armstrong, Robert Andrew and me. Geoffrey Howe emphasised the Prime Minister's commitment to conclude an Agreement, provided the balance was right. The two main issues to be resolved were Irish accession to the ECST and the arrangements under which the Secretariat would operate.

Dick Spring, gloomier but more authoritative than on previous occasions, complained that, as a result of leaks and speculation, the main lines of what was agreed were now in the public domain and unionist opposition was gathering momentum. The sooner the Agreement could be concluded the better. Peter Barry said that the Irish government wanted to accede to the ECST but were inhibited by nationalist lack of confidence in the Northern Ireland Courts. Accession could not be got through the Dáil without some prior, visible change in the judicial system in Northern Ireland – i.e., mixed courts, or at the very least some rectification of the imbalance between Protestants and Catholics in the Northern Ireland judiciary. After some argument, I suggested that the British acceptance of an obligation to consider the possibility of mixed courts (without introducing them) could be matched by the Irish government declaring its intention to accede to the ECST (as distinct from immediately acceding to it). Tom King clearly did not like this suggestion, but Geoffrey Howe allowed it to stand; and the Irish side welcomed it.

Tom King then concentrated his fire on the Secretariat, emphasising that its function would be strictly limited to servicing the ministerial Conference, not to take decisions or act as a complaints bureau. He accepted that Belfast would in principle be the right place for it, but given the risk of hostile demonstrations, he thought that the Conference should hold its first meeting in London and that the Secretariat should develop gradually thereafter. Spring and Barry strongly rebutted this idea. Unless the first meeting of the Conference were in Belfast, unionist opposition might prevent it meeting there at all. Postponement would only exacerbate unionist hostility. As for the Secretariat, they accepted that its functions should be limited to servicing the Conference; but they insisted that a visible Irish presence in Belfast from the outset was absolutely essential if the nationalist community were to be persuaded that the agreement was going to make a real difference.

I just had time to dictate a record of this inconclusive discussion (in the shape of a minute to the Prime Minister from Geoffrey Howe) before rushing off to catch a plane to Dublin for the follow-up Armstrong-Nally meeting which began that evening with a dinner at Iveagh House, and continued for most of the next day. At this meeting we went over much of the same ground again, though in a less fraught atmosphere. On the ECST, the Irish said that although actual accession was impossible without changes to the system of justice in Northern Ireland, the Taoiseach could go as far as saying that the Irish government intended to accede to the Convention as soon as possible – provided it was understood that this commitment would not in practice be honoured without some visible changes in the Northern Ireland judicial system. We also seemed to edge nearer to agreement on the size, role and location of the Secretariat; and the Irish took delivery of our modest concessions on the UDR, while still pressing hard for restrictions on its deployment.

The Armstrong-Nally discussions continued in London on 13/14 October, when further progress was made on the text of the agreement. On Article 2, we yielded to Irish insistence that the Intergovernmental Conference should be concerned with relations between 'the two parts of the island of Ireland' rather than 'the Republic of Ireland and Northern Ireland'; but the Irish in turn reluctantly gave way on the inclusion of 'decisions and' in the final sentence of Article 2(b), stating that each government would retain 'responsibility for the decisions and administration of government within its own jurisdiction'.

The status of the Secretariat continued to give difficulty. The Irish wanted to describe it as 'permanent', which was anathema to the NIO, but eventually agreed to refer to their ministers Robert Armstrong's ingenious suggestion of 'on a continuing basis'. The other outstanding problem turned on the link between mixed courts and Irish accession to the ECST. From an Irish point of view, the value of the undertaking in Article 8 that the Conference should consider 'the possibility' of mixed courts had been undermined by the warnings we had given both privately and publicly that we would be very unlikely to agree to them. This was an issue of great importance to the Taoiseach personally; and unless the Irish could be satisfied that there was a real British commitment to take the possibility seriously, they could not offer to accede to the ECST. A subsidiary point of disagreement was the title of the Intergovernmental Conference. 'Conference' was already a compromise between the Irish preference for 'Commission' (which Mrs Thatcher thought smacked too much of joint authority) and the British preference for 'Committee', which the Irish said was something of a derisory term in Ireland. Mrs Thatcher, however, was still holding out for it. But neither of these unresolved issues looked likely to delay the rapid advance towards a completed agreement.

Immediately after this meeting, on 15 October, the Taoiseach telephoned the Prime Minister to fix a date for signing the Agreement; and it was agreed that, subject to the approval of their respective Cabinets, signature should take place on 15 November at a summit meeting in Northern Ireland, the exact location still to be determined. (Hillsborough was decided on only at the last moment, after Garret FitzGerald had turned down Mrs Thatcher's suggestion of RAF Aldergrove). Officials still had plenty of work to do in resolving the remaining difficulties and in drafting the joint communique which was to complement the Agreement itself; but with the date for signature fixed, the text all but negotiated and the main issues of principle settled, it looked as though we were at last opening the final chapter in the negotiations. Tom King, however, thought otherwise.

XVI

THE AGREEMENT WAS NOW due to be reviewed and (as we hoped and assumed) approved by Cabinet on 31 October; and for this purpose, it was to be circulated to ministers under cover of a joint memorandum by the two Secretaries of State, commending it to their colleagues. The NIO asked to produce the first draft of this memorandum; and with some misgivings on my part, but in the expectation that the draft would be produced in plenty of time for discussion and amendment, this was agreed. Meanwhile, on 17 October, Tom King saw Noel Dorr and told him flatly that he (King) did not favour the continuous presence of a joint British-Irish secretariat in Belfast from the outset because it would be a target for those who wanted to wreck the Agreement: to which Noel replied that this was a point of principle for the Irish government. Then on 23 October, a week before the Agreement was due to be taken by Cabinet, Robert Andrew wrote to Robert Armstrong at Tom King's request proposing a quiverful of amendments to the text.

The most substantive proposals were to remove any mention of mixed courts, even as a possibility; and to expand the wording of the two clauses in Article 2 dealing with the remit of the Conference, so as to make it explicit that this remit would apply in principle to both parts of Ireland, and not just to Northern Ireland. He also required the deletion of 'permanent' in relation to the Secretariat.

After consulting Geoffrey Howe, I wrote to Robert Armstrong saying that the minor amendments were acceptable but that we should be wary of proposing too many alterations at such a late stage. As to mixed courts, this had all along been a central issue for the Irish government and for the Taoiseach personally. We had with great difficulty brought the Irish to accept that we could not commit ourselves in advance to the establishment of mixed courts. But we had sought to impress on them that our position was genuinely open and that (although we continued to see great difficulties about it) the possibility of mixed courts was not ruled out. The wording of the text on this point had been approved by the Prime Minister. If we were now to go back on these assurances and require the removal of this provision, Geoffrey Howe was in no doubt that it would be seen by the Irish as a major change in the balance of the Agreement, call in question our good faith and once again put the negotiation at risk. On 28 October Robert Armstrong minuted to the Prime Minister to the same effect.

On 29 October, two days before the Agreement was due to be considered by the Cabinet, Tom King and Geoffrey Howe met the Prime Minister to discuss Tom King's proposed amendments. Robert Armstrong told me immediately after the meeting that Tom King had conceded defeat on the inclusion of the reference to mixed courts, with the proviso that the Irish were to be warned that the Prime Minister, in presenting the Agreement to Parliament and the press, would spell out the difficulties. It had also been agreed that the Secretariat should be in Belfast from the start; and Mrs Thatcher had accepted 'Intergovernmental Conference' as the title of the joint ministerial body. This left the question of an Irish commitment to accede to the ECST as the only major issue still outstanding from the British point of view.

It then emerged, however, that Tom King was closeted with his officials 'trying to decide what had been decided'; and that he was still sitting on the draft joint memorandum for Cabinet which neither the FCO nor the Cabinet Office had yet seen. Whitehall rules required that papers for Cabinet had to be circulated two days in advance. This meant that the joint memorandum had to be approved and signed by the two Secretaries of State by close of play that evening at the very latest. Unless it made clear that they both regarded the Agreement in a positive light and were recommending it to their colleagues, there was a danger that the doubters in Cabinet (of whom the Lord Chancellor was certainly one) would reopen issues of principle and the Agreement would be lost. Given Tom King's track record, it seemed likely that he would want to give the memorandum a decidedly hesitant flavour, and that some last-minute horse-trading between the two departments would be required to achieve wording which both Secretaries of State could accept. Robert Armstrong and his team were due to leave that afternoon for another Armstrong-Nally meeting in Dublin; but it was therefore decided, with Robert Armstrong's encouragement, that I should remain behind in London to agree the memorandum with the NIO, joining our colleagues in Dublin the following morning; and Tony Brennan of the NIO arranged to do the same.

I spent the afternoon anxiously waiting for the NIO to disgorge the draft, for which we had now been waiting for more than a week. After repeated telephone calls, it eventually reached me at 5.30 pm., but even then, not in a form finally approved by Tom King, who was said to be still working on it. Long, defensive and balancing one consideration against another, its overall impact was negative. Time was now running out. I walked it along to the Secretary of State's room and put it in front of Geoffrey Howe, who promptly went off the deep end: it was far too long, reopened arguments which had already been settled, needed positive conclusions, and in short must be redrafted ab initio. I said that I entirely agreed, but that it was no use making all these criticisms to me: officials could only draft on whatever basis was agreed between ministers. Urgent telephone calls between Private Secretaries ensued. While these were going on, I returned to my office to find that Tony Brennan had arrived bearing the version finally approved by Tom King, who (he explained) had now left his office for the evening, during which he had a dinner engagement. The memorandum had therefore been typed fair, ready for distribution by the Cabinet Office, and all that was required was for the Foreign Secretary to approve it and append his signature.

Tony Brennan and I (although our approach to the Irish question differed) liked and respected one another and normally got on well. On this occasion, however, it seemed to me that the NIO had deliberately exploited the time factor to ensure that the memorandum fully reflected their own longstanding doubts, in a last-ditch effort to prevent the Agreement as it now stood from being approved by Cabinet. (With hindsight, I suspect it was Tom King's indecisiveness rather than any Machiavellian calculation on the part of his officials, which had held the draft up past its eleventh hour.) I told Tony roundly that the draft was completely unacceptable, and that Geoffrey Howe had instructed me to have it radically redrafted. Tony replied that this was impossible, as there was by now (nearly 7.00 pm) no time to prepare a new draft, no one available in the NIO to type it, and no possibility of clearing any redraft with Tom King, who had gone out to dinner. I said that my PA was on hand; that I would dictate a fresh draft myself straight away, with or without NIO cooperation; and that it would be for the NIO to find a way of clearing it with their Secretary of State.

In the meantime, Geoffrey Howe had managed to arrange for a reluctant

Tom King to meet him in his (Geoffrey's) room in the House of Commons at 10.00 pm to settle matters. With Tony Brennan sitting silently thunderous in my office, I then dictated a completely new memorandum which Brenda Wheeler, my long-suffering PA, just finished typing by 9.55 pm. Armed with this, and accompanied by Tony Brennan, I then walked across to the House of Commons, where Geoffrey Howe was waiting to read it.

Ten minutes or so later, audibly huffing and puffing and elegantly attired in a dinner jacket, Tom King arrived to join us. He read through the new memorandum and immediately began to demur. When he reverted yet again to the undesirability of including in the Agreement any reference to mixed courts, Geoffrey Howe suddenly lost his temper: the reference to mixed courts had been expressly agreed with the Prime Minister; and it was now far too late to reopen this or any of the other issues which had been exhaustively discussed and agreed. This unexpected and unwonted display of exasperation on Geoffrey Howe's part proved remarkably effective. Tom King backed off at once, and the redrafted memorandum was agreed virtually without alteration. I went home very tired but feeling, I must admit, that I had done the state some service.

Early next morning Tony Brennan and I flew together to Dublin, drowning our differences in a champagne breakfast on the plane. The Armstrong-Nally meeting began with the Irish (who apparently had a difficult ministerial meeting behind them) displaying cold feet about the references in the Agreement to Northern Ireland's 'status'. But there was no disposition on our part to listen to misgivings on that score, and the discussion moved on to resolve most of the remaining drafting points. Over lunch, we discussed how to handle the Bishops in relation to the presentation of the Agreement – a subject on which everyone round the table, both British and Irish, had something to say.

I had supper in Dublin, and back in London the next morning I had twenty minutes with Geoffrey Howe briefing him for the Cabinet discussion. At 1.00 pm Geoffrey's Private Secretary, Len Appleyard, phoned me to say that Geoffrey had returned from Cabinet and given the thumbs up sign. The Cabinet had decided that, 'on balance' the government should conclude the Agreement essentially in its existing form, with such improvements as might be secured from the Irish in the concluding stage of the negotiations; and that it should be presented to the public as a 'modest but useful step forward'. With considerable relief, I left London to join the family for a long weekend in Yorkshire.

Tom King, however, had still not given up. On 5 November, he minuted to the Prime Minister suggesting that he should make another approach to Peter Barry to see if he could be got to agree to dropping the reference to mixed courts from the Agreement and to accept that, on security grounds, the Secretariat should not be located in Belfast at the start and the Conference should hold its first meeting elsewhere. He also wished to remove 'ambiguities' in the Secretariat's role in the light of the Irish intention to appoint Michael Lillis as their representative (Michael having acquired bogeyman status in the eyes of the NIO). He proposed to impress on Peter Barry that, once the Agreement had been concluded, we would have to say without equivocation that Northern Ireland was part of the United Kingdom and would remain so for as long as the majority so wished; to emphasise that we wanted to see a visible improvement in cross-border security cooperation and a sustained increase in the resources which the Irish were devoting to counter-terrorism; to press for Irish accession to the ECST instead of just making a statement of intention to accede; and to encourage the Irish government to put pressure on the SDLP to end their boycott of the Northern Ireland Assembly.

The Prime Minister replied promptly, and a shade tartly, through her Private Secretary, that as the Cabinet had decided to accept the Agreement essentially in its present form, the extent to which we could reopen issues or press them to the point of dispute with the Irish government was limited. The points about mixed courts and the ECST should therefore be pursued 'with great caution' and not be presented as make or break demands. Nor did she see any need to tell Peter Barry that Northern Ireland would remain part of the United Kingdom, since this was 'self-evident'. But she had no objection to Tom King 'pursuing' the points about improved security cooperation, signature of the ECST and the location of the Secretariat and the Conference.

These points were aired in an Armstrong-Nally meeting in London on the afternoon of 5 November, and necessitated another journey to London by Messrs Spring and Barry the following day. The Armstrong-Nally meeting was difficult going. It appeared that the Irish were now getting cold feet. They thought that our repeated and publicly expressed reservations about mixed courts were depriving the reference to them in the Agreement of any value. They resented the implication that they were not trying hard enough to counter terrorism on their side of the border; and they were seriously concerned at the idea that the first meetings of the Conference should not be in Belfast and that the Secretariat should not be established there from the outset, which they said would make it impossible to get SDLP endorsement of the Agreement. Christopher Mallaby and I continued discussion of these points over a working dinner with Dermot Nally, Seán Donlon and Noel Dorr at the Irish Embassy which went on till after midnight.

The next day brought the meeting with Irish ministers – the second within the month occasioned by Tom King's rearguard resistance to those features of the Agreement which he was persuaded would be most objectionable to unionists. First of all, however, the British side – Geoffrey Howe, Tom King, Robert Armstrong, Robert Andrew and I – met in the Foreign Secretary's room to discuss tactics. Geoffrey drew attention to the Prime Minister's reminder that the Cabinet had accepted the Agreement as it stood and that the Irish were not to be pushed too hard to make changes. Tom King thrashed about from one point to another. The Irish had suggested that the ECST was no longer open for signature, but since this was incorrect, they should be pressed to commit themselves to early signature. Since they were unhappy about the reservations we had expressed on mixed courts, they might be persuaded to drop the reference altogether. Robert Armstrong pointed out that the issue of mixed courts had been settled. If we reopened the argument the Irish would have counter demands of their own and the Agreement would be put at risk. Tom King protested that he was not asking for the removal of the reference to mixed courts but only suggesting that the Irish themselves might be having second thoughts about including it.

Tom King then complained that the references to the 'status of Northern Ireland' in Article 1 of the Agreement were a retreat from the wording of the communique issued after the 1984 Chequers summit, which had spoken of 'constitutional status'. I said that the 1984 communique was simply a statement of Irish government policy, whereas the Agreement, as a legal document, had to be consistent with the Irish Constitution. The argument then shifted to the location of the Secretariat, with Tom King asking why it needed to be settled before the Agreement was signed.

By this time the Irish ministers had arrived and the substantive meeting began. With Tom King in the lead, it was not a very orderly affair, nor did the Irish ministers, who were clearly pained by both the tone and content of the discussion, manage to put their points across very forcefully. Tom King led off with his views on status. The majority community had to be given the clearest possible reassurance about this. The formula in the Agreement was less than the Taoiseach had felt able to say in the 1984 Chequers communique. As this would make Article 1 less of a selling point for unionists, we would have to put more emphasis on the improvements which the Agreement would bring on cross-border security cooperation; and we would be pressing the Irish hard on this. Peter Barry objected to the implication that the Irish were not doing enough on security.

There followed a messy and not very good-tempered argument about the location of the first meeting of the Conference and the siting of the Secretariat. Tom King emphasised the security threat to the Irish representatives on the Secretariat from loyalist paramilitaries, and raised again the question of the Secretariat's functions. Peter Barry confirmed that its function would be to service the Conference and not act as a complaints bureau for nationalists. But unless there was an Irish presence in Belfast from the beginning, the Agreement would not be seen as having any tangible benefit for the nationalist community. Tom King reserved his position on where the first meeting of the Conference should be, while accepting in principle that it should be in Belfast. Security considerations pointed to the Secretariat being sited at Stormont, but Tom King thought that this would be symbolically offensive to unionists.

Geoffrey Howe said that it was our intention to have the first meeting of the Conference in Belfast and to have the Secretariat located there, and that this was the basis on which we should plan. He mentioned the desirability of the Irish agreeing to early signature of the ECST, but Tom King veered off on to the need for the SDLP to enter the Assembly. Peter Barry said the SDLP could split if the Irish government pressed them too hard on this. They might be willing to re-join the Assembly eventually, but only in exchange for power-sharing. With undercurrents of dissatisfaction on both sides, the discussion ended with the conclusion that the text of the Agreement should remain as it was but that a further Armstrong-Nally meeting would be needed to tie up the practical arrangements.

That evening Christopher Mallaby and I gave Michael Lillis and Noel Dorr dinner at the Oxford and Cambridge Club. Michael was decidedly gloomy. The Irish had the impression that Tom King would use security considerations as an excuse for delaying the establishment of the Secretariat in Belfast indefinitely. It was difficult to understand how, only a few days before signature of the Agreement, the NIO were still unable to identify suitable premises to house the Secretariat, although this had been a subject of discussion for months. This was a key issue for the Irish and Messrs Barry and Spring would be reporting to their colleagues in Dublin in 'pretty pessimistic' terms.

This conversation convinced me that having the Secretariat located in Belfast really was critical for the Irish, and in particular for the attitude which the SDLP would adopt towards the Agreement. I was less than certain, however, that Messrs Barry and Spring had put this message across, or that it would get through to the Prime Minister, who was in any case inclined to sympathise with Tom King's reservations. I did not myself believe that having the Secretariat in Belfast would add significantly to the hostility with which it was already clear that the Agreement would be greeted by unionists. So, I had a private word with Michael at the end of the evening and suggested to him that if this was the make or break issue, he had represented it to be, the only way to convince Mrs Thatcher would be for the Taoiseach to send her a personal message to that effect.

XVII

THE TAOISEACH'S MESSAGE to the Prime Minister arrived on 8 November. He expressed his belief that 'all misunderstandings have now been eliminated' but went on to express 'very serious concern' about the location of the Conference and the Secretariat. It was 'essential both for credibility and effectiveness that the Conference meet in Belfast from the beginning and that its Secretariat be established there on a continuing basis, in or near where the Conference is to meet'. The difficulties on grounds of security and unionist hostility had to be faced: delays or hesitations 'would only serve to make the implementation of these elements more difficult as time went on'. He confirmed that Michael Lillis would be appointed to head the Irish component of the Secretariat, and that he would have two other senior officials to support him; and concluded that 'it is only right that I should let you know in complete frankness that, so far as we are concerned, it is essential that clear understandings are reached now in relation to the matters addressed above, and are implemented in full from the beginning'.

The Prime Minister summoned Geoffrey Howe and Tom King to discuss this message with her that afternoon, and I saw Geoffrey beforehand and briefed him on the background history of the Secretariat and the dispute over its location. Mrs Thatcher predictably took exception to the firm tone of the message. She feared that Garret's remarks about the Conference and the Secretariat, and his determination to send Michael Lillis to Belfast to head it (despite our declared preference for it to operate at a lower level), foreshadowed an Irish intention to use it as an instrument of pressure on us and a means of claiming greater influence on Northern Ireland affairs than the Agreement gave them. She endorsed Tom King's opposition to siting the Secretariat at Stormont, and Tom King said that he 'would be looking at alternative sites' (this only six days before the Agreement was due to be signed!). Geoffrey Howe agreed that Stormont was unsuitable, but pointed out that attention had focussed on Stormont mainly because of the stress we had laid on the security risks; so, it was now up to us to find a suitable secure location somewhere close by.

After further argument, it was agreed that the Irish should be told that the first meeting of the Conference could take place in Belfast, subject to an assessment of the security considerations at the time. An appropriate, secure location would be found for the Secretariat reasonably close to Stormont; and until that was ready ad hoc arrangements would be made to accommodate such members of the Secretariat as needed to be in Belfast. At the same time, we were to stress the Secretariat's limited role and emphasise that Lillis's 'normal point of contact' would be his (more junior) British opposite number and that he (Lillis) would not have an 'automatic' right of access to senior NIO officials.

In these somewhat grudging terms the Taoiseach's two essential points were to be met. The news was conveyed to Garret FitzGerald in a message from Mrs Thatcher which was the subject of further internecine negotiation within Whitehall. Robert Armstrong discussed his first draft with me over the telephone two nights later and Tom King intervened the next day, so that the final draft reached Mrs Thatcher only shortly before she had to make an important speech at the Guildhall that night. Having spelt out the provisos about the Conference and the Secretariat in courteous language, she allowed the message to conclude on an upbeat note: '... we are embarking on something entirely new and exciting in the hopes and possibilities it contains for making life better for all the people of Northern Ireland. We both know that it is not going to be all plain sailing. I am sure that as the new arrangements bed down during the coming months we shall need on both sides patience and forbearance, as well as the understanding and good will that have been brought up during these long months of negotiation. They will be forthcoming on our side, I can assure you'.

The Armstrong-Nally group meanwhile had been preparing briefing for the Prime Minister and the Taoiseach in the shape of a question and answer paper, with a view to ensuring as far as possible that both heads of government would take the same line in answer to press and parliamentary questions about the Agreement and its implications. This tricky task was by now well advanced. But there were contentious issues of substance still to be settled, and the results incorporated into the text of the joint communique due to be issued when the Agreement was signed.

With the Agreement itself virtually finalised, the communique text had become the main focus of the concluding phase of the negotiations.

Following the Prime Minister's offer of 'prompt implementation' as a way of dealing with the Irish demands for 'confidence-building measures', it had been agreed that the communique should spell out those issues arising from the Agreement which the Intergovernmental Conference would tackle urgently. In this way the communique became in effect an extension of the Agreement as well as a commentary on it. Wording had to be found to reflect both the Irish requirement for early and visible changes in the way the police and the UDR operated and the British requirement for improved cross-border security cooperation. There remained too the crucial problem of how to reconcile the Taoiseach's continued insistence on firming up the British commitment on mixed courts with the Prime Minister's insistence on firming up the Irish commitment on the ECST.

These problems preoccupied us up to the last moment. I came home from the Office on 9 November promising myself a quiet evening and an early bed, only to be rung up at 10.30 pm by Michael Lillis, who was spending the night in London on his way back from a meeting in Brussels and wanted to learn the Prime Minister's response to the Taoiseach's message. He came round by taxi, talked to Robert Armstrong on the telephone and then sat up discussing the outstanding issues over whiskey and a cigar until about 12.30 am, I told him that it looked as if British ministers had finally decided to have the Agreement – provided that Irish ministers would have it as it stood. To this Michael replied: 'Of course we're going to have it: you know that'. I got to bed full of whiskey and absolutely exhausted.

Notwithstanding Michael's assurance, the final Armstrong-Nally meeting prior to signature of the Agreement had something of a cliff-hanging quality. We met on the upper floor of Iveagh House (the Irish Department of Foreign Affairs) in Dublin on the evening of 12 November. With a break for supper (and a vigorous argument with Michael Lillis about the Irish understanding of what was meant by 'the status of Northern Ireland' in Article 1), we worked steadily through the texts of the question and answer paper and the communique until only the wording on mixed courts and the ECST remained unsettled. Then at 10.30 pm word was received that the Taoiseach was downstairs. The Irish team withdrew to consult him, leaving the British side alone, wondering whether there was to be a last-minute hitch.

After nearly an hour, the Irish came back to tell us that the Taoiseach had finally agreed (paragraph 7 of the communique) to declare his intention of acceding to the ECST 'as soon as possible', provided that this was stated to be 'against the background' that both sides were 'committed to work for early progress' in 'seeking measures which would give substantial expression to the aim of underlining the importance of public confidence in the administration of justice'. This tortured formulation was understood by both sides to be code for British readiness to address the need for some visible change in the conduct of terrorist trials in Northern Ireland, including at least the possibility of mixed courts. But the wording was sufficiently opaque to avoid any firm British commitment on mixed courts, while satisfying the Irish that their commitment to accede to the ECST was linked to, if not wholly conditional upon, changes of some kind being made to the Northern Ireland courts to make them more acceptable to nationalists.

The atmosphere then became euphoric, tinged with exhaustion. Dermot Nally said a few words of appreciation to Robert and the British team, and Andy Ward (the Secretary of the Irish Department of Justice) thanked me in an aside for all that I had done, not least (he said) for having always made it unequivocally clear what were the points of real importance to the British side. It was after 1.00 am when we finally broke up. I stayed the night with Michael Lillis at his house in Rathmines, where he told me that the Taoiseach had had a 'very emotional' meeting the previous evening with the SDLP, at which Seamus Mallon had endorsed the Agreement and paid a warm tribute to the Taoiseach, tears had been shed and the Irish National Anthem sung. So perhaps the previous few hours had not been quite so cliff-hanging as they had seemed.

The next morning Michael's wife Jane (whose father, an Irish doctor living in Lincolnshire, had attended Éamon de Valera on his release from Lincoln Gaol), drove me to Dublin Airport. I returned to the Foreign Office at mid-day, bearing the news that the Anglo-Irish Agreement was complete. During the afternoon I began to feel a gathering sense of achievement as I thought of all the emotional and other efforts of the past two years having led finally to what Peter Ricketts, one of Geoffrey Howe's Assistant Private Secretaries, predicted would be one of the historic landmarks of the Thatcher Administration. To have seen a great diplomatic enterprise through from its first beginnings to completion is a rare experience in the peripatetic career of a diplomat. Moreover, as I wrote that night in my diary, to have loved Ireland (and cared about its relationship with England) and to have found myself in a position to contribute to improving that relationship ('especially at the start, and by helping to keep the process from foundering when people thought it would, or perhaps wanted it to') had been a blessing and a privilege. I had no illusions about the difficulties, friction and violence which lay ahead; but I believed that the Agreement could gradually drain some of the bitterness out of the British-Irish relationship and create the basic geometry for an eventual settlement.

Conclusion

Two days later, on Friday 15 November, I was included in the Prime Minister's party for the signature of the Agreement at Hillsborough Castle. Robert Armstrong collected me from home and I breakfasted on the Prime Minister's plane with Geoffrey Howe, who was generous in his praise and thanks for my contribution to the negotiations. It was a brilliant morning as we came over Northern Ireland, the sky a clear blue, the small fields almost emerald, the golden autumnal trees casting long morning shadows and frost still lying in silver patches where the sun had not yet melted it.

From Aldergrove we were taken in two RAF helicopters to Hillsborough, where we landed in the grounds of the Castle, the former residence of the Governors-General and latterly of the Secretaries of State for Northern Ireland, which I had never seen. It proved to be a massive, pale grey, handsome eighteenth-century mansion fronting the main street of the elegant little Georgian town across a courtyard closed off by heavy wrought-iron gates. Outside the gates a crowd of discontented unionists was gathering, headed by Ian Paisley, whose stentorian shouts of anger and disapproval occasionally penetrated to the proceedings inside.

Within the house, all was stateliness and comfort – 'mahogany living' in the most dignified gubernatorial style, large portraits of Carson, the Duke of Abercorn, George V and other symbols of the Union. The Irish arrived a few minutes after us with much friendly hand-clasping bringing with them an atmosphere of nervous cheerfulness. After some mingling over coffee, Mrs Thatcher and Garret FitzGerald withdrew with Robert Armstrong and Dermot Nally to rehearse together some of the trickier questions expected at the forthcoming press conference; the other ministers, British and Irish, went together into Tom King's study, and Michael Lillis and I went into the Throne Room, where Michael showed me privately the text of a long guidance paper, in the form of questions and answers, which the Taoiseach had drafted for use by Fine Gael TDs – a document which showed a remarkably detailed and accurate understanding of the negotiating background and the various compromises which had been struck along the way. While I read it, Michael paced restlessly up and down the room until I suggested that he should say the Rosary.

When the Prime Minister and the Taoiseach emerged from their tête-à-tête they had decided that there was no need for a plenary meeting, so we all straggled into the large room where the signing and the press conference were to take place. Mrs Thatcher immediately began to move the flowers about, checked that the picture on the wall behind the table at which she and the Taoiseach would sit had no overtly green or orange connotations (it was an 18th century view of Windsor – 'from the playing fields of Eton', Robert Armstrong whispered to me) and then, summoning Garret and Geoffrey Howe to her aid, began moving the table and chairs. The rest of us watched uneasily. 'You have to have Prime Ministers to move the furniture around here,' observed Peter Barry dryly. Mrs Thatcher complained about the absence of any Belleek porcelain and continued to fuss about in her half bossy, half humorous way until it was time for lunch.

We sat down sixteen at the lunch table. My immediate neighbours were Alan Goodison and Seán Barrett, the Irish Minister of State and Fine Gael Chief Whip, a pleasant, unremarkable man who told me that he was an insurance salesman who had come into politics through an argument at the local golf club after a fourball match. Mrs Thatcher, who looked drawn and older, with her teeth more prominent, sat between Garret and Dick Spring. I noticed increasing periods of silence between them as the meal progressed, with Spring having to make a visible effort to nerve himself to say something to the Prime Minister. It was not until later that I learned that she had just received Ian Gow's letter of resignation as a Treasury Minister and was badly rattled by it.

From lunch we went straight to the signature ceremony. The room was crammed to bursting point with journalists and cameramen, who had seized all the seats reserved for officials. The signing was quickly over, and we then adjourned to give the journalists twenty minutes reading time before the press conference. I accompanied the Prime Minister upstairs, where she promptly went into an agitated drafting session on her opening statement for the press conference, writing on scraps of paper and reading out phrases as she wrote them in or crossed them out. Tom King stood in front of the fireplace booming out suggestions. My only contribution was to stop her using the word 'Treaty' to describe the Agreement, the name

'Anglo-Irish Treaty' having unwelcome historical connotations for the Irish.

We then went down to the press conference. The room was now more crowded and hotter than ever, and protesting bellows from the Paisley-led crowd outside were faintly audible in the distance. Both the Prime Minister and the Taoiseach performed well, both being visibly nervous until the questions began. Garret FitzGerald was careful and measured in his replies, sticking faithfully to the pre-agreed lines. Mrs Thatcher was much more emotional, her eyes widening, her adverbs emphatic, declaring herself 'a unionist and a loyalist' who was sitting beside 'a nationalist and a republican'. However, she avoided anything likely to jar Irish sensitivities too sharply, and used a reasonably positive formula on mixed courts.

Bernard Ingham was a ruthlessly tough compere, allowing each journalist only one question and cutting the proceedings off sharply at 3.30 pm. Through the subsequent melee I returned to the Prime Minister's room upstairs to find her with Geoffrey Howe agonising over her reply to Ian Gow's resignation letter. Written in a dignified tone of sorrow rather than anger, this roundly rejected the charge of 'treachery' which Enoch Powell had brought against the Prime Minister in the House of Commons the previous day; but it recorded Gow's belief that 'the change of policy in Northern Ireland, including the involvement of a foreign power in a consultative role in the administration of the province, will prolong, and will not diminish, Ulster's agony'. It appeared from her dismay that this defection of someone on whose friendship and loyalty she had relied so closely had not only come as a personal blow, but had revived her visceral misgivings about what had just been accomplished.

The Irish now took their leave, the Taoiseach shaking me warmly by the hand and thanking me 'for everything', and we followed them without further delay. In the returning helicopter, Geoffrey Howe and I were seated side by side under a bulkhead, the view immediately above us being of the pilot's buttocks on his canvas seat and the lower part of his legs. The din of the engines made conversation impossible, but Geoffrey Howe gave one of his Welsh giggles and wrote jerkily on the back of an envelope: 'Rather an unusual view'. As we parted at Heathrow, he renewed his thanks. The Prime Minister never spoke to me.

Over the next few days reactions to the Agreement, both nationally and internationally, were overwhelmingly favourable. Sinn Féin was hostile, but unionists were otherwise virtually isolated in their fierce opposition to it. In the Republic, Garret FitzGerald's standing in the opinion polls rose sharply and Charles Haughey felt obliged to modify his initial dismissal of what the Taoiseach had achieved.

I was in the Officials' Box for the Prime Minister's Statement on the Agreement in the House of Commons on 18 November, and found it a mildly disappointing occasion. She read her script rather unimpressively, but got immediate warm support from both sides of the House. The first question came from Roy Hattersley, who commended the Agreement, as did David Steel and most Tory backbenchers with one or two exceptions. Then came bursts of outrage from the unionist benches, and notably from the DUP, all of whom were called. 'Treachery', 'deceit', 'desolation', 'fury' were hurled about at the top of angry Ulster voices. Enoch Powell asked only a cold question about mixed courts, which Mrs Thatcher answered fairly. She stressed over and over and over again that the purpose of the Agreement was 'to defeat the men of violence'; that there could be 'no change in the status of Northern Ireland without the consent of the majority'; and that there was no derogation from British sovereignty.

She was at her most effective in meeting anger with restraint; and there was genuine warmth in her response to a helpful question from John Hume. But there was little sense of style in her replies. Despite the fact that she, as Prime Minister, had been directly involved in the most extended and potentially far-reaching negotiations between Britain and Ireland since the Anglo-Irish Treaty of 1921, she made no attempt to set the Agreement in any sort of historic context or offer any broader vision of its purpose or implications beyond defeating terrorism and keeping British sovereignty intact. Many of the questions too were lamely phrased. Only Ian Gow (whom I had mistrusted from afar, without ever knowing him) rose to the occasion with a short and dignified intervention appealing for restraint and saying that the application of the word 'treachery' to the Prime Minister was deeply resented by him. All in all, despite the tension and the underlying emotions, it could hardly be ranked as a great parliamentary event.

The Agreement, however, was now in place. Its implementation and subsequent history are outside the scope of this narrative, nor, writing thirteen years after the event, do I want here to assess its significance with the benefit of hindsight. What I thought at the time is contained in a minute which I wrote to Antony Acland, the Permanent Under-Secretary at the FCO, on 9 December 1985: 'As both governments have emphasised, the Agreement is not a solution to the Irish problem: it is intended to create a framework within which, once the dust has settled, both communities in Northern Ireland can feel secure and reconciliation between them may become possible. Judged objectively, it neither blocks Irish unification nor represents a step down the "slippery slope" towards it: but it adjusts the Anglo-Irish geometry so as to take some account of the uniqueness of the relationship between the two parts of the island of Ireland and between both parts of Ireland and Britain. In the Secretary of State's (Geoffrey Howe's) phrase, that is probably as much as can be done "for this generation"'.

DAVID GOODALL
Ampleforth, 1992-1998

*Edging Towards Peace**

MICHAEL LILLIS AND DAVID GOODALL

I

Emerging from Despair in Anglo-Irish Relations

MICHAEL LILLIS

HOW OFTEN I HAVE been asked by thoughtful foreign friends if I, a non-specialist, could recommend a single serious and modern history of our country from early to modern times suitable for the general reader – and have had to say that I don't know of any in English! A modest proposal: Pierre Joannon's *Histoire de l'Irlande et des Irlandais* (Paris, 2006) should be translated into English (and other major languages) and made available in Ireland and throughout the world as a reliable and highly readable chronicle. Up-to-date and sedulous in research and sober in judgment, the narrative is connected and enlivened by the author's unflagging enthusiasm for his subject in every epoch and by a continental European perspective which persistently broadens the context of Irish history beyond the cauldron of Anglo-Irish claustrophobia. He was perhaps more clairvoyant than even he himself intended in 2006 in cagily entitling his upbeat concluding section *Épilogue Provisoire* (especially given the later Lisbon Treaty referendum result and today's financial crisis), but he was insightful when he quoted James Joyce: 'ce que je veux faire par mes écrits, c'est européaniser l'Irlande et irlandiser l'Europe'. His history of Ireland and of the Irish people and the entire body of his distinguished work on Irish history, biography and culture achieve precisely Joyce's goals and we are profoundly in his debt.

The negotiation by Dr Garret FitzGerald and Mrs Margaret Thatcher of the Anglo-Irish Agreement of 1985 provided an important example,

* This article was first published in the *Dublin Review of Books* in 2010 and is reprinted here with the kind permission of Maurice Earls, Editor of the DRB

even if fundamentally circumstantial, of the importance of Europe at a moment of despair in Anglo-Irish relations. Dr FitzGerald in his autobiography *All in a Life* gives a definitive, masterly and entertaining account of the negotiations in all their complexity (to be compared only perhaps with Jonathan Powell's account of the labyrinthine negotiations leading to the Good Friday Agreement in *Great Hatred, Little Room*). The following 'footnotes' disclose nothing as to the facts beyond. Dr FitzGerald's account and other published reports, except to suggest an interpretation of the Agreement itself, its significance and one aspect of its origins, as seen in the perspective of elapsed time.

Dr FitzGerald justly says that when he came into office as Taoiseach at the end of 1982 'the state of Anglo-Irish relations was little short of disastrous'. In Northern Ireland the residue of the hunger strikes, which had themselves provoked the most intransigent – visceral may not be too strong a word – reaction from Mrs Thatcher, continued to churn dangerously, despite the heroic efforts of John Hume and the SDLP to hold the ring for a political way forward. The minority nationalist community was increasingly alienated from the British government, from the security forces on the ground and from the system of justice. The 'long war', the brutal and sometimes nakedly sectarian violence of the Provisional IRA, continued seemingly endlessly, while political support for Provisional Sinn Féin was filling a nihilistic vacuum among many young Catholics; the aims of the Provisionals were summarised at the Sinn Féin *Ard-Fheis* of 1981 by Danny Morrison: 'with a ballot paper in this hand and an Armalite in the other, we take power in Ireland'. The unionist majority, understandably outraged at the violence of the Provisional IRA, was nevertheless encouraged in its own entrenched resistance to any political compromise by the capitulation of the Wilson government eight years previously in 1974 to the British Army's reluctance to confront the resistance of loyalist mobs to the Sunningdale Agreement, a betrayal of democracy which dwarfed the Curragh Mutiny of 1914. Unionists were as convinced in 1982 as they had been for the previous eight years that they held a veto over any proposal whatsoever from London. Butchery of innocent Catholics by Loyalist extremists continued, with plausible (and subsequently proven) suspicion of degrees of collaboration by elements in the RUC Special Branch and the UDR [Ulster Defence Regiment].

In the perspective of today's peace in Northern Ireland and the warm relations between Dublin and London it is difficult to conjure up the condition of Anglo-Irish relations in late 1982. A low intensity civil war that could explode at any moment – provoked perhaps by an IRA, a British security force or a Loyalist outrage – was simmering in Northern Ireland. The British Prime Minister, a fearless 'conviction politician' with the rawest commitment to confronting and defeating terrorism at whatever political cost, was proud to proclaim herself a unionist. She had (to state the matter politely) little interest in and less sympathy with Irish nationalist aspirations. She made no secret of the fact that she had been stung by Dr FitzGerald's predecessor, Mr Haughey, when he had unsuccessfully sought to defeat British policy on sanctions against Argentina at the UN Security Council during the Falklands crisis. She was particularly enraged by Dublin's public suggestion that the term 'the totality of relations' in an Anglo-Irish communiqué somehow implied a British commitment to withdraw from Northern Ireland or to support Irish unity when its purpose had been to foster a series of studies within an institutionalised Anglo-Irish framework on the common ground shared across a set of routine policy issues in the two countries. There was literally no Anglo-Irish political dialogue on Northern Ireland and little prospect of it when Dr FitzGerald became Taoiseach. Mrs Thatcher had none of the goodwill towards Anglo-Irish relations, much less the determination to work with Dublin to solve the problem of Northern Ireland, of Edward Heath at Sunningdale, of John Major of the Downing Street Declaration, or of the visionary Tony Blair. On the contrary.

How then did the Anglo-Irish Agreement, facilitating the most intrusive role for Dublin in the affairs of Northern Ireland of any Anglo-Irish arrangement before or since, come about?

There can be little doubt that, but for the regular cycle of European Community summit meetings, on the margins of which the Taoiseach and the British Prime Minister invariably met – usually on Dr FitzGerald's initiative – without fanfare of any kind, the negotiation of any type of agreement between Dublin and London on Northern Ireland would have been next to impossible. Mrs Thatcher was, particularly during the first year of Anglo-Irish exchanges, nervous – almost paranoid – about any publicity which might be interpreted as suggesting that she was selling out the unionists behind their backs to their enemies in Dublin. As time went on and as the momentum of negotiation gathered pace, there were occasional meetings between the two heads of government in London or Chequers, where discussion was somewhat inhibited by crowds of ministers and officials. The settlement of most of the more 'neuralgic' points (a term of London-Dublin diplomacy made current between the teams of officials on both sides by a senior Cabinet Office official, David Goodall) took place discreetly between the two heads of government in the presence of at most one or two senior officials from either side on the margins of these Community occasions. As Dr FitzGerald implies, but does not perhaps adequately emphasise in his memoirs, sometimes the tone of the exchanges was quite lively, not to say dramatic. Contrary to his genial public persona, in several of these critical encounters, Dr FitzGerald proved himself to be an extraordinarily dogged, if always courteous, advocate. Mrs Thatcher, formidable as always, was, even in her most tense moods – and certainly the topic of Northern Ireland often seemed to make her somewhat uptight – well-matched.

Other ministers on both sides, notably the Tánaiste, Dick Spring, and the Minister for Foreign Affairs, Peter Barry, and the British Foreign Minister, Sir Geoffrey Howe, and Secretary of State for Northern Ireland, Douglas Hurd, played important roles, but Mrs Thatcher insisted on keeping the decisive discussions for herself and the Taoiseach. In the case of our government, Mr Spring and Mr Barry both made crucial contributions in numerous meetings with their British opposite numbers and in internal discussion and planning (which Dr Henry Kissinger has correctly described as comprising more than 80 per cent of the diplomatic process). Mr Barry brought to the Dublin approach his unique 'feel' for the 'nightmare of the Northern nationalists' (his description). Mr Spring's stern insistence on stark realism – and his occasionally mordant humour – kept the Taoiseach's approach tenaciously focused. Dublin's planning was at all stages critically enhanced by the deep strategic thinking of John Hume. We learned that Sir Geoffrey played a key role in keeping Mrs Thatcher 'positive' when, as regularly occurred, the negotiations seemed to run into the ground. Mr Hurd on the other hand worked hard, as we would have expected from the political head of the extremely sceptical and, in our view at that time, for the most part pro-unionist, Northern Ireland Office, to narrow the scope of the eventual agreement. He argued, for example, to the intense irritation of Irish ministers, that Dublin should not risk politically an associated referendum on Articles 2 and 3 of our Constitution and that, therefore, the overall package need not be particularly significant. His success in this endeavour was in the end limited.

The Agreement that eventually emerged was essentially of Mrs Thatcher's and Dr FitzGerald's creation. This circumstance was significant for later British negotiators, who thus won unassailable domestic political cover, especially from what might be called the Enoch Powell wing of the Conservative Party, from the concessions this ardent British unionist had made to the Irish side in 1985. Paradoxically, they themselves in the Good Friday Agreement had to concede less ground to Dublin 'intrusiveness' than she did, and this in return for the far more significant concession from Dublin of a radical dilution of the territorial claim on Northern Ireland in the Irish Constitution than anything conceded by Dublin to London in the '85 Agreement.

All of the detailed negotiation was conducted by two small teams of officials, led by the respective cabinet secretaries, Dermot Nally and Sir Robert Armstrong, both men of long experience of Anglo-Irish negotiations (both were in Sunningdale in 1973) and both happily imbued with high intellectual acumen, charm and – perhaps even more important – the patience of Job. Their mutual trust was the cement of the process. David Goodall, seconded to the Cabinet Office, was the senior Foreign Office representative: a creative but tenacious negotiator of immense intellectual energy and commitment, a gifted watercolourist, with perhaps a deeper knowledge of certain aspects of Irish history – notably Wexford in 1798 whence some of his ancestors had come – than any of us on the Irish side of the table. The British ambassador in Dublin, Sir Alan Goodison, was a skilled diplomat of quite unique sensitivity and good will. His sincerity endeared him to everyone and his passionate interest in Christian theology created a bond with the Taoiseach and Mrs FitzGerald. The Secretary of the Department of Foreign Affairs, Seán Donlon, brought many years of experience (also including Sunningdale) and a clear-sighted realism to our efforts, along with his unique access to President Reagan and the White House, a set of contacts that were to provide indispensable leverage in moving Mrs Thatcher from positions of inflexibility as the process unfolded. Noel Dorr (later Secretary of Foreign Affairs) was Ambassador in London: also immensely experienced (again including Sunningdale), his philosophic cast of mind (as I encountered it) and his gift for elegant drafting solutions to negotiating conundrums were a valuable resource for both sides. There was also myself, in my capacity as head of the Anglo-Irish Relations division of Foreign Affairs. The two teams met usually for two-day sessions successively in Ireland and Britain, sometimes in the respective capitals, sometimes in remoter country houses, approximately every six weeks during 1984 and 1985.

Later the teams of officials were supplemented by officials from other government departments on both sides. Two stand out in my memory: Andy Ward was Secretary of our Department of Justice and his was intellectually the most brilliant and creative mind I have encountered in a lifetime of diplomacy and international business. And Tony Brennan, a senior official at the Northern Ireland Office, was endlessly ingenious in drafting workable structures for devolution in Northern Ireland within the challenging intricacies of British constitutional and secondary law: a gifted problem-solver.

The diplomatic fieldwork of Dublin with the spectrum of Northern nationalists (but never including hard-line supporters of violence) was led with devotion and outstanding success by Dáithí Ó Ceallaigh (later Ambassador in London). Richard Ryan (later Ambassador at the UN) ran a campaign in the clubs of St James's (and the grouse moors of the north), using charm and cogent advocacy to win support for the concept of Dublin-London cooperation to address the political crisis in Northern Ireland among the often sceptical grandees of the Conservative Party and their backroom henchmen, now crucial constituencies for our purpose, but which hitherto had been relatively unexplored by Dublin: this has rightly become the stuff of legend.

The New Ireland Forum, in practice a constitutional nationalist assembly, was established by the main parties in the Dáil and the SDLP in May 1983 with a view to hearing opinions from all sides, except from those who supported the use of violence, and to analysing the crisis and its causes and to proposing possible solutions. Usefully it agreed, at Dr FitzGerald's initiative and under John Hume's untiring shuttle diplomacy between the main Dublin parties, a set of accurately and cogently expressed 'Present Realities and Future Requirements', including acknowledging not alone the problems, aspirations and rights of the nationalist minority but the British identity of the unionist community and its right, equal to that of the nationalists, to have that identity fully accommodated in the institutions of government. The Forum concluded with a description of the advantages and disadvantages of three possible models for a solution: a unitary state, a confederal Ireland and a structure of joint authority (to be distinguished from joint sovereignty) between Dublin and London for the government of Northern Ireland. This 'menu', and most centrally the 'Realities and Requirements' section, were intended by the government to provide room for a flexible negotiation with London. As is notorious, Mrs Thatcher later peremptorily dismissed all three models: they were 'Out, Out, Out', she declared after the Anglo-Irish Summit at Chequers on 18 November, 1984, creating a brief crisis in Anglo-Irish relations and much political difficulty for Dr FitzGerald's government at home.

But the fundamental challenge from the beginning was somehow to overcome Mrs Thatcher's strong reluctance to engage with the Irish government in any way in working for a solution to the impasse in Anglo-Irish dialogue and in Northern Ireland.

Dr FitzGerald has recounted in his memoirs that in early September 1983, I was authorised by him to advance a particular line of argument to the British side based on an analysis which he and I discussed (FitzGerald, *All in a Life*, p. 473 and passim). This was to be presented as strictly a personal view of mine, in the first instance to David Goodall. He was joint chairman with myself of the rather grandiosely named Co-ordinating Committee of the Anglo-Irish Intergovernmental Council, where we led inter-departmental teams from our respective administrations to review complementary possibilities in non-political areas, such as mutual recognition of professional qualifications and the like (in the context of the somewhat glorified Anglo-Irish Studies). The first opportunity to do so arose during an afternoon walk back and forth along the delightful and tranquil stretch of the Grand Canal between Leeson Street and Baggot Street bridges, so beloved of Dubliners and immortalised in Patrick Kavanagh's lines inscribed at that time on the side of his commemorative bench which we quietly pondered and which are reproduced at the end of this essay (they were not replicated on the more recent second Kavanagh bench on which a fine sculpture of the poet is seated).

The argument could hardly have been simpler. It was moreover marshalled with full sincerity on my part in terms of the frightening true facts on the ground in Northern Ireland, while also intended to engage the attention of a British Prime Minister whose entire focus on Northern Ireland was exclusively on security concerns and specifically the defeat of terrorism.

1. Trust on the part of the nationalist community in the British security forces, including the RUC and the UDR as well as the local judicial system, had completely broken down. The situation was simply beyond repair and was now feeding the alienation of young Catholics in particular and creating a major political opportunity for the IRA's terrorism. By now even the least dramatic quotidian encounter between most Catholics and the British system of authority, such as being stopped at a routine road block, was entrenching and spreading the poison of alienation and in many cases hatred. The situation was now so far out of control that the Irish government were seriously concerned at destabilisation spilling over into the South. There was nothing in the present security or political arsenal of the British as it existed that could begin to address this disaster or to arrest its further deterioration.
2. A profound and imaginative transformation was urgently needed 'on the ground' so that the majority of Catholics could start to identify positively with the agents of authority, be they soldiers, police or judges. This could only be achieved by the direct involvement of the Irish government's security forces and courts 'on the ground' especially in nationalist areas where people would see them as 'their own', just as unionists saw the RUC, UDR, British Army and the existing courts as constituting their own tribal security system. This should be done only because it was vital to arrest the spreading pathology of alienation and in order to establish a solid basis for security and stability – and not for merely 'political' reasons.
3. It was understood on our side that there would be a need to address the fundamental insecurities this project would inevitably create among unionists and that we should be ready in the interest of stability to do what was necessary to allay those insecurities, including reviewing the articles of our Constitution which they read as constituting a territorial claim on Northern Ireland.
4. This argument had, of course, an unspoken but inescapable subtext. For such an initiative to be attempted and to succeed, a political and institutional

scaffolding would have to be constructed which would facilitate a command and control system for our forces and an authority system for our courts such as would have the support of an extremely sceptical and reluctant public opinion in the South and be consistent with our Constitution and laws. This in practice would have to be in the form of some version of joint authority for Dublin and London in Northern Ireland, or indeed joint sovereignty. None of this was stated in terms because to have done so at that stage would have vitiated any possibility of the 'alienation' argument and the associated proposal for an Irish dimension on security and the courts being considered in London. Yet it was beyond doubt that experienced British officials would fully appreciate this underlying dimension to our argument and anticipate these major issues involved for Dublin.

Several conversations about the same ideas that ensued in the following weeks confirmed that this was the case. An authorised reaction from the British side inquired, for example, whether the Irish government might be prepared to act to 'remove' the constitutional claim on the territory of Northern Ireland in the event that our ideas were in some fashion adopted. On the same personal basis as previously, I said that I believed the answer would be yes, if the arrangements envisaged on the ground were politically defensible. To be fair, it was clear to me that my interlocutor was very reasonably assuming that I was speaking with guidance from the Taoiseach, even if my remarks were without formal attribution to our government. We were also learning, as Dr FitzGerald narrates, that Mrs Thatcher was beginning to consider whether it might be more dangerous to do nothing than to attempt an initiative with himself.

When the Taoiseach and the Prime Minister met at Chequers on 7 November 1983, it was clear that Mrs Thatcher had begun to consider ways to cooperate with Dublin to launch a serious project on Northern Ireland. The Taoiseach confirmed to her that the ideas I had informally conveyed had his personal approval. She said she wished the informal discussions between officials to be discontinued so as to be able to defend herself against the accusation that secret negotiations were going forward. Having said this, she also implied some approval of the initiative we had taken.

The account in Dr FitzGerald's memoirs of the Forum and the negotiations that continued intensively for two years after this meeting until the signing of the Anglo-Irish Agreement on 15 November 1985 is essential reading – absorbing, at times heart-stopping, intermittently hilarious – for anyone interested in Anglo-Irish history or negotiation or the personalities involved, most notably Mrs Thatcher. His account is structured in a separate section of *All in a Life*, in Chapters 14 to 17 inclusive, so that it can be read – and could have been published separately – as an autonomous narrative. Similarly, his Chapters 8, 9 and 10 on the establishment and betrayal (he, as ever, more politely, calls it 'collapse') of the Sunningdale power-sharing government of Northern Ireland stand as a unique and complete account by its most articulate protagonist.

Before coming to the Agreement itself, there is one episode which flowed directly from these earlier informal conversations which merits a brief 'footnote' from me, as conscience suggests that I may have provoked it as well as some attendant misunderstandings.

On 1 March 1984 the British negotiators, led by Sir Robert Armstrong, presented to the Irish side a remarkable proposal – remarkable coming from the emissaries of Prime Minister Thatcher – on behalf of their government. They proposed that a 'security band' be established along the border to be overseen and jointly policed under a joint security commission. Ideas like this, they said, could be viewed as building blocks for future political arrangements and that the 'security band' might also apply in West Belfast for example. A law commission, with the possibility of an all-Ireland court, was envisaged. Reform of the voting laws of Northern Ireland and repeal of the Flags and Emblems Act would be on the agenda. As counterpart, a guarantee by Dublin of the status of Northern Ireland, including possible action on Articles 2 and 3 of our Constitution, would be needed.

Some weeks later our team, on the instructions of the Taoiseach, Mr Spring and Mr Barry, provided a somewhat dismissive reaction in London, arguing that a security band straddling the border would be counter-productive, inciting further terrorism, and that both sides should begin a negotiation based on an agreed set of principles. Behind this approach were the 'Principles' in the excellent 'Present Realities and Future Requirements' section of the Forum Report which was emerging at this time and was very much in the minds of our ministers. With the convenient perspective of hindsight and spurred by keen shafts of embarrassment

1. Chequers Summit, November 1983. *Left to right* Geoffrey Howe, British Foreign Secretary; Peter Barry, Irish Foreign Minister; Prime Minister Margaret Thatcher; Taoiseach Garret FitzGerald; Tánaiste (Irish Deputy PM), Dick Spring; Northern Ireland Secretary, James Prior.

2. The signing of The Anglo-Irish Agreement, 15 November 1985. Taoiseach Dr Garret FitzGerald and Prime Minister Margaret Thatcher at Hillsborough Castle, Northern Ireland. © *Alamy Limited*

incited again recently by an encounter with two of the former British negotiators, I today believe that we may have missed an opportunity at that time. Instead of trying to engage the British side in a consideration of first principles – never (as events confirmed) the vernacular in which 'pragmatic' British ministers and officials are most at home (and apparently an entirely foreign language to Mrs Thatcher) – we should perhaps have boldly and firmly fought for our needs based on the ground of their proposal. We should perhaps have insisted that the approach should be that we should do only what was strictly necessary to make the authority system – police, army, courts – acceptable to those who were alienated from it, but that we should not do anything that would exacerbate alienation or further destabilise the situation in the North or in the South. So, the 'security band' should be where it was required, that is, in nationalist centres in Northern Ireland, and not where it would create chaos and new alienation, such as in perfectly stable communities in the South. And in the next round we would insist that the structure of the role of Dublin's presence be such that it would promote a sense of confidence in the system on the part of the minority community, that is that Dublin's agents be seen to be institutionally and constitutionally subject to Irish political control. 'You need our help. Our help will be effective only if our presence is unequivocally an Irish governmental presence.' We should on the other hand fully accept the need to avoid the mistakes of the British: our presence, unlike that of the British Army (as seen by nationalists), should not be seen by unionists as that of an army of occupation and thus we on our side should be open to finding solutions, including if necessary constitutional solutions, which would avoid such extreme provocation.

This approach would have produced a quite different type of negotiation and probably a different type of Agreement from the tortuous but eventually successful process that took another two years to complete. Or not, as the case might be: this is mere speculation. I mention these considerations here partly because the British proposals of 1 March 1984 were clearly at least to some extent inspired by the earlier informal exchanges between officials of which I had been a protagonist. And I can only begin to imagine the toilsome process involved internally in London in formulating a first step proposal for a negotiation on behalf of Mrs Thatcher (of all British leaders) to Dublin which could be read (as I interpreted it – or perhaps overinterpreted it – privately) as a British government inviting Irish security forces into nationalist areas in Northern Ireland!

So much for water under troubled bridges, as I have decided to call this episode. The negotiations that ensued produced, after many vicissitudes, a very remarkable Anglo-Irish Agreement, in many ways even more surprising than the British proposal of 1 March 1984.

It is worth recalling that the Agreement set up a mechanism for the central involvement of Dublin in the processes of government of Northern Ireland. Article 2 (a) set up an Intergovernmental Conference at ministerial level 'concerned with Northern Ireland and with relations between the two parts of Ireland, to deal on a regular basis with: (i) political matters; (ii) security and related matters; (iii) legal matters including the administration of justice; (iv) the promotion of cross border co-operation'. Article 2 (b) laid down how the process would work: 'The United Kingdom government accept that the Irish government will put forward views and proposals on matters relating to Northern Ireland within the field of activity of the Conference insofar as these matters are not the responsibility of a devolved administration in Northern Ireland. In the interest of peace and stability determined efforts shall be made through the Conference to resolve any differences ...'

Article 2 (c) also made it clear – on British insistence – that this was not joint sovereignty: 'There is no derogation from the sovereignty of either the Irish government or the United Kingdom government, and each retains responsibility for the decisions and administration of government within its own jurisdiction'. In fact, this qualification effectively anticipated and rebutted a charge later used as the grounds for the Opposition in the Dáil to oppose the Agreement as purportedly involving a helpless Dublin government in assuming responsibility for British decision-making. A working crib agreed by the two sides for use with the press by the two heads of government established that the process involved 'consultation but more than consultation'.

On the achievement of agreed devolution in Northern Ireland (a policy now formally shared under the Agreement between Dublin and London), the Irish government was acknowledged under Article 2 (c) as the advocate of the Northern minority's interest under the regime of 'determined efforts to resolve differences': 'Both governments recognise that devolution can be achieved only with the co-operation of constitutional representatives within Northern Ireland of both traditions there. The Conference shall be a framework within which the Irish government may put forward views and proposals on the modalities of bringing about devolution in Northern Ireland, in so far as they relate to the interests of the minority community.' The other side of this coin was the implication that the British would represent the unionist community's interests in this process as they were perceived in London.

The exchanges between British and Irish officials on controversial events and sensitive policy issues which subsequently took place both in the ministerial conference, and on a daily (and often a nightly) basis at the Agreement's secretariat's embattled and somewhat primitive premises in Maryfield, Belfast (known to its denizens on both sides as the 'Bunker'),[1] where a small team of Dublin officials (Dáithí Ó Ceallaigh and myself included) lived in the first years following the Agreement, were betimes tense. It sometimes became necessary to call in formal terms for 'determined efforts to resolve differences' from our British colleagues and sometimes it was useful to be able to remind them that their obligation – as well as ours – to join in these efforts was, in the terms of an international treaty registered at the United Nations, 'in the interest of peace and stability', the two ingredients starkly most lacking in the life of Northern Ireland. This arrangement was and remains without parallel in conflict resolution structures between states for the government of territory which is 'disputed' between them.

Dr FitzGerald and John Hume had successfully pressed for the inclusion of a 'joint authority' model in the conclusions of the report of the New Ireland Forum, knowing that their preferred model of 'joint sovereignty' would not be considered by the British side: basically an Anglo-Irish ministerial Joint Authority would concern itself with the issues (i) to (iv) as listed in Article 2 (a) of the Anglo-Irish Agreement (see above), but would have no role in the areas which were core prerogatives of the sovereign government, most notably external defence, finance and foreign

1. This was the nickname for the rather primitive building – formerly an out-office of the Motor Registration Authority – located at Maryfield in Belfast where the Joint Secretariat had its offices and where the Irish team lived and slept. For the first six months it was the object of round the clock Loyalist demonstrations.

policy. It became clear that the Irish government could not, as a fundamental political matter, assume responsibility for any decisions, particularly internal security matters in Northern Ireland, for which it could not have eventual sovereign responsibility, even though it might have the maximum influence otherwise possible in the formation of those decisions under the intrusive mechanisms of the Agreement. In fact, the Agreement in its mechanisms and formulations came as close as one could imagine in practical political terms to achieving a form of Joint Authority, between the sovereign British government and the 'intrusive' role of the Irish government, in the particular circumstances of Northern Ireland. Given the British Prime Minister's trenchant dismissal of joint authority ('that's out!'), as well as a shared desire to avoid provoking unionist hysteria, it went almost without saying that Dublin ministers did not make such a large claim for the institutional machinery of the Agreement at that time.

As will be recalled, unionist reaction to the Agreement was convulsively negative: unionist legal opinion held that the process was indeed one of only thinly disguised joint sovereignty or, as described by some of their scholars, a 'condominium' or 'Anglo-Irish Joint Protectorate' (for example Hugh Roberts's Northern Ireland and the Algerian Analogy). So extreme and violent was their reaction that the Irish government, at the urgent request of British ministers, forbore from stressing publicly the substantial political gains in the Agreement from a long-term nationalist point of view, a mistake in the opinion of Seamus Mallon, deputy leader of the SDLP. In retrospect, it has sometimes seemed to me that he was right. On the other hand, some even in the South felt that the Agreement had gone too far in undermining the interests and rights of the unionist community: Senator (later President of Ireland, later head of the UN's Commission on Human Rights) Mary Robinson resigned on these grounds from the Labour Party, the second party in Dr FitzGerald's coalition government.

The mechanisms of the Agreement were instrumental in improving the circumstances of life of the minority community in a multiplicity of ways during its first fifteen months of operation. Examples were: repeal of the Flags and Emblems Act, improved rules for fair employment, vastly improved representation of the minority on public bodies, demolition and replacement of three notorious ghetto 'developments': Divis, Unity and Rossville Flats, better rules for the routing of controversial parades, establishment of a Police Complaints Commission, full investigation and reporting and discussion of sensitive incidents, improvements in habeas corpus rules and procedures, some (not enough) improvement in the rate of RUC accompaniment of the UDR, a new code of conduct for the RUC, substantial improvements in prisons policy and on issues such as compassionate leave, shifting of the onus of proof to the prosecution in bail applications, tighter rules on admissibility of evidence (particularly 'coerced evidence'), measures to reduce delays and expedite trials; strengthening of the law on incitement to hatred and improved rules for fair employment.

Within a decade the changes in legislation, regulation and in practice that resulted from Irish advocacy in these areas through the mechanisms of the Anglo-Irish Agreement (as well as from the excellent work of professional and voluntary agencies), helped to transform Northern Ireland by eliminating many of the deep-seated grievances of the nationalist population which had been key factors in the alienation of the minority.

Perhaps nothing more dramatically illustrated the importance of the Agreement for the mass of nationalists than the fury of the unionist reaction on the one hand (which after so many years of Orange triumphalism they naturally found to be gratifying), and on the other, the discipline and determination shown by the RUC, the British Army and, at a remove, Mrs Thatcher's government in not being intimidated by that fury. Nothing in their experience as a disadvantaged community could match these two phenomena.

Paradoxically it was precisely the intensity of the hysterical unionist fury that obscured for many the 'real' achievements of the processes of the Agreement such as the illustrative list above. The British authorities were understandably opposed to publicising these measures as outcomes of the Irish government's advocacy under the Agreement for fear of further provoking the unionists and, as Dr FitzGerald later acknowledged (FitzGerald, *All in a Life*, p. 575), Dublin went along with this approach perhaps excessively. I believe he was correct in this assessment.

The two sets of negotiators had with great care agreed that following the signature of the Agreement, the British authorities would announce in the debate in the Commons that a period of reduction of the level of violence would have significant influence in the regular process of review of prison sentences in the case of those sentenced on terrorist crimes. This device was inspired by Fr Denis Faul's passionate conviction that, even in extreme circumstances such as the most dramatic hunger strikes, the influence of families was critical with the leadership of the Provisional IRA. In the event, and reflecting the degree of British government distress at the enormity of the unionist public reaction to the Agreement, nothing was said in the debate and only a virtually unnoticed and ambiguous brief statement was made by minister Nick Scott in the graveyard hour of a later overnight debate. This was most regrettable.

The daily pageant of unionist resistance to the 'diktat', as they called the Agreement, also constrained our ability on the Irish side to press for immediate implementation of a sensitive but central part of the agenda laid down in it, namely a profound review and reform of policing. There was some progress made in areas of police reform in the early days of the Agreement, but events on the ground made it difficult to demand more at that point. The RUC, courageously led through this episode by Sir John Hermon, was itself being seen nightly on television being vilified and physically attacked 'by their own people' as it carried out the undoubtedly unwelcome role which fate – and Mrs Thatcher – had imposed on it of defending the Anglo-Irish Agreement on the streets.

The change of government in Dublin in March 1987 was at this stage something of a relief to the British, who, still unhappy at the depth of unionist revulsion, expected that Fianna Fáil, having opposed the approval of the Agreement in Dáil Éireann and repeatedly derided its aspirations, would not work its mechanisms in government as central instruments of its policy on Northern Ireland. This was certainly the hope of Tom King, Secretary of State since the Agreement was inaugurated: a man of considerable charm who showed much kindness to the Irish officials resident in the 'Bunker' and much courage in the face of several physical attacks on him by loyalists as well as assassination attempts by the Provisional IRA, he clearly thoroughly disliked the hurt and dismay the Agreement caused the unionist people and felt it was unfair on them. In fact, Mr Haughey's administration operated the Agreement in a workmanlike way and did not, as he had earlier threatened, attempt to renegotiate it. But the combination of British horror, notably that of the Prime Minister herself, at being seen as the betrayers of 'decent unionists' and a lack of enthusiasm in Dublin did not augur well for the achievement of the rich promise foreseen by its negotiators.

Nevertheless, the Agreement was a significant historic event in itself, changing irreversibly the relationships between the two communities in Northern Ireland with the two governments and also the relationship between the two governments. The unique mechanisms of the Agreement had begun to function and to rebalance the internal inequities of Northern Ireland and it was, in my view, profoundly regrettable that this initial momentum was lost. The Anglo-Irish Agreement was an extraordinary feat of diplomacy by Dr FitzGerald in circumstances which could hardly have been more challenging. It created profound and enduring effects which were useful, in fact indispensable, to subsequent negotiators.

For constitutional nationalists North and South, the perception that unionists had a veto over any substantial British government proposal for political matters even within Northern Ireland had been, since the Wilson government capitulated to the loyalist workers' strike against the Sunningdale Agreement eight years previously, an enormous and depressing stumbling block to any kind of political progress. The existence of the 'veto' had been for years exploited politically by the Provisional IRA as proof that only their violence and not the political efforts of the SDLP and Dublin could wring concessions from Britain: this proposition was widely believed in even by thousands of Northern nationalists who themselves passionately opposed the use of violence. The power of this 'veto' was also profoundly relied upon by both moderate and hard-line unionists as it reinforced their conviction that no significant concessions need ever be made to the other tribe. Belief in the reality of the 'veto' permeated policy in the Northern Ireland Office and was reflected in the wholly inadequate 'initiatives' of every secretary of state from Merlyn Rees and Roy Mason to Jim Prior's 'rolling devolution' local government project.

The Anglo-Irish Agreement demolished this unionist 'veto' once and for all and created a different landscape. Unionist trust in the most palpably 'loyal' of British prime ministers, and thus in any possible Conservative or Labour alternative, was at an end.

In the perspective of twenty-five years, it is beyond question that this perceived 'betrayal' of the unionists by Mrs Thatcher – their very talisman – created over time a gradual but profound reappraisal in the first place by the UUP and finally by Dr Paisley's DUP. Without it, and, of course, without the decision of the IRA to cease violence in response to the indefatigable campaign of John Hume, in combination with the efforts of Taoiseach Albert Reynolds working with John Major, the remarkable and historic achievement of Messrs Ahern and Blair on Good Friday, 10 April 1998 would have been unthinkable.

(A separate but unavoidable footnote: Mr Mallon's lapidary characterisation of the Good Friday Agreement as 'Sunningdale for slow learners' takes nothing from the importance and enormity of that achievement by the two governments, but, with each passing day, it gathers ever more depth of implacable anguish: why did so many have to die, why did such utter misery have to be endured by so many thousands of individuals and families during thirty years of horror, when finally not a single one of the 'war aims' of the Provisional IRA was achieved and when in 1998 they were to settle for the 1973 Sunningdale terms plus the entrenchment of partition in the changes in Articles 2 and 3 of the Irish Constitution?)

Mrs Thatcher in later times may have decided that she disliked the Anglo-Irish Agreement, but she deserves much credit for the benefits her decisions created for the next cycle of negotiation. The Agreement was carried in the House of Commons by the largest margin of any vote in the twentieth century, but Mrs Thatcher was attacked in the debate by two allies she revered, Ian Gow, who resigned from the government (he was murdered on July 30th, 1990 by the Provisional IRA because he was 'a close personal associate' of Mrs Thatcher's on her Northern Ireland policy!), and Enoch Powell, who accused her of 'treason' and promised her 'public contempt'. This dramatic paradox of history can only be compared with President Nixon's betrayal of his own party's heartfelt opposition to any recognition of communist China, which led on to one of the greatest successes of modern diplomacy.

Dr FitzGerald too had to overcome his profound unhappiness at having to leave the unionists (including members of his extended family) out of the consultation process that led to the Agreement. All I can say today is that most unionists were at that time so immured in their veto-proofed immunity from any other reality that they would have wrecked the negotiation process had they been included in it.

Constitutional nationalists were, largely because of the hysterical reaction of unionists, heartened and reengaged. What was most enduringly significant and impressive, but has been insufficiently acknowledged, was that Mrs Thatcher, a unionist by passionate conviction and no friend to Irish nationalism, unlike her Labour Party predecessor, the self-proclaimed supporter of Irish unity, Harold Wilson, did not flinch in the face of fiery loyalist intransigence. As she had not flinched from continuing the, by then, intensive Anglo-Irish negotiations with Dr FitzGerald in the aftermath of IRA bombs in her Brighton hotel on 12 October 1984 which killed several of her closest supporters and friends and would almost certainly have killed her but for an uncovenanted stroke of good luck.

The Provisional IRA were taken aback. In public they were dismissive, but a 'Kremlinologist' re-reading of *An Phoblacht* editorials from early 1986 discloses intermittent subtle acknowledgements that politics had changed. Some of us had the opportunity to gauge this process of decongealing among their leaders, none more than the extraordinarily determined John Hume.

In a truly tragic development the opposition in Dublin, to the delight of the Provisionals, sought to damage the success of the Agreement from the constitutionalist nationalist perspective by opposing it in the Dáil, but this in turn was somewhat reversed by the unprecedented public outrage against them of the SDLP. Hitherto that party had always striven, as a strategic matter, to exclude from the normal parliamentary wars of Dublin the issues of Northern Ireland. Their reaction was trenchantly reinforced by the acid reception given in Washington to Mr Haughey's emissary on this subject by US House Speaker Tip O'Neill, Senator Edward Kennedy and their powerful lobby of President Reagan's White House. When Mr Haughey returned to power in 1987 he did not, as he had promised, attempt to renegotiate the Anglo-Irish Agreement but rather worked its processes with at least a minimum of application.

Mrs Thatcher demonstrated effectively at the joint press conference at Hillsborough on 15 November 1985 and in the subsequent debate on the Agreement in the House of Commons that she fully understood the mechanisms of the Agreement whereby the 'carrot' of removing the Irish governments role (the 'stick') in respect of certain issues should logically be attractive to unionists, if those issues were devolved to a cross-community assembly and a power-sharing executive. In those circumstances the role of the Irish government would be 'out', as she so characteristically put it. The achievement of power-sharing devolution was also a strategic priority for Dr FitzGerald. He would have been happy to sacrifice the Irish government's new role in making 'determined efforts to resolve differences' with the British government on those issues had this produced a power-sharing government in Northern Ireland.

It is regrettable that almost two decades had to pass before this message was digested fully by unionist leaders. It was remarkable that Dr Paisley cited precisely Mrs Thatcher's argument of November 1985 to his own followers as the grounds for his 'reluctantly' acceding to the St Andrews Agreement, the basis of the present political structure of power-sharing government in Belfast between the DUP and Sinn Féin. Peter Hain, the Secretary of State for Northern Ireland at that time, for his part employed the same logic with bludgeon force in the run up to the St Andrews Agreement, overtly threatening that the alternative to power-sharing would be a system of joint authority with Dublin. His threat was articulated in the words and (by then) diluted mechanisms of the '85 Anglo-Irish Agreement, insofar as they were preserved in the Good Friday texts. The secretary of state for Northern Ireland thus gave an interpretation to those mechanisms which Dublin would dearly have liked, but could scarcely have dared, to attach publicly to the original substantially stronger terms back in '85, because of alarm in London (and indeed in Dublin too) at the violent reaction at that time on the unionist side.

In short, this particular device survived and eventually proved as effective as it was originally intended to be by Dr FitzGerald and Mrs Thatcher in securing cross-community government in 2007 – and by two parties, Sinn Féin and the Democratic Unionist Party, which back in '85 could not by anyone's wildest imaginings have been thought susceptible to its 'sticks and carrots'. A further paradox is that, in a yet wider sense, the 'carrots and sticks' provided by the very existence of the Anglo-Irish Agreement proved effective in securing the Good Friday Agreement. Thus, the Anglo-Irish Agreement itself, the hated 'diktat', was formally abrogated by the Good Friday Agreement as a key concession to Mr Trimble. Had the Agreement not existed it would have been difficult to invent as effective a 'carrot' to secure unionist acceptance. Despite this, the words and mechanisms of the Anglo-Irish Agreement of 1985 were enshrined (with diluted powers for the role of the Irish government in Northern Ireland), but with the minimum of textual amendment, in the Good Friday Agreement of 1998.

Lines Written on a Seat on the Grand Canal, Dublin
'Erected to the Memory of Mrs Dermot O'Brien' *

O commemorate me where there is water,
Canal water, preferably, so stilly
Greeny at the heart of Summer, Brother
Commemorate me thus beautifully
Where by a lock niagorously roars
The falls for those who sit in the tremendous silence
Of mid-July. No one will speak in prose
Who finds his way to these Parnassian islands.
A swan goes by head low with many apologies,
Fantastic light looks through the eyes of bridges -
And look! a barge comes bringing from Athy
And other far flung towns mythologies.
O commemorate me with no hero-courageous
Tomb - just a canal-bank seat for the passer-by.

Patrick Kavanagh

* Reprinted from *Collected Poems* edited by Antoinette Quinn (Allen Lane, 2004), by kind permission of the Trustees of the Estate of Katherine Kavanagh, through the Jonathan Williams Literary Agency.

11

An Agreement Worth Remembering

DAVID GOODALL

A QUARTER OF A CENTURY after it was signed at Hillsborough Castle, the Anglo-Irish Agreement of 1985 is almost forgotten, overshadowed by the landmark developments in the handling of the Northern Ireland question which have happened since: the Downing Street Declaration of 1993, the Good Friday Agreement of 1998; the piecemeal ceasefires by the Provisional IRA and loyalist paramilitaries; and lastly the St Andrews Agreement of 2006, which seemed to signal an end to terrorist violence and at least a provisional willingness on the part of republicans and unionists to cooperate in running a territory which remains a part of the United Kingdom.

The 1985 Agreement, although it was acclaimed at the time by all political parties in Britain, except the Ulster Unionists, today tends to be seen as at best a small step forward, significant in improving relations between the British and Irish governments, but failing in other respects to bring a peaceful settlement in Northern Ireland much closer. Arguably, however, none of the developments which eventually followed it would have taken place without it. So, what were the participants in the negotiations hoping to achieve and how far were they successful? And why did Margaret Thatcher, as is evident from her account in *The Downing Street Years*, take a negative view of what was regarded at the time as one of the important achievements of her premiership?

Both the principal authors of the Agreement – one may properly call them the protagonists – have published their accounts of the negotiations, Dr Garret FitzGerald in *All in a Life* and Lady Thatcher in *The Downing Street Years*. Geoffrey Howe, another important participant, has devoted a chapter to them in *Conflict of Loyalty*, and they are covered also, although only briefly, in Douglas Hurd's memoirs. The face-to-face meetings between the Taoiseach and the Prime Minister in the margins of EC summits and at Anglo-Irish summits at Chequers were key moments in the process, and in its later stages Geoffrey Howe played a crucially constructive role on the British side. But although the decisive bargains were struck, and the outcome shaped, by the political leaders, the detailed negotiations were carried on by a very small group of Irish and British civil servants, meeting frequently and intensively over a period of more than two years.

Of these, the outstanding figures, without whom the Agreement would never have been reached, were Sir Robert Armstrong and Dermot Nally. Both were highly skilled negotiators and draftsmen with first-hand experience of Sunningdale behind them; both had inexhaustible patience and a sense of humour; both liked and trusted one another; and both had the confidence of their principals. If Robert Armstrong had not had Mrs Thatcher's confidence the negotiations would never have got off the ground and would certainly have been broken off before the finish.[2]

Of the published ministerial accounts, Garret Fitzgerald's is by far the fullest and most detailed, describing with notable frankness each twist and turn in the negotiations and the calculations made by the Irish side as they proceeded. It is also commendably fair and, as far as my own knowledge goes (I was not present at the various tête-à-tête meetings between the two prime ministers), broadly accurate, although a British participant will detect here and there a judicious understatement. No one on the British side has produced – or could produce – anything comparable. Margaret Thatcher's account is a good deal less detailed, as well as reflecting the distaste she apparently came to feel for the whole business. The best account from the British side is Geoffrey Howe's. Although relatively

2. Michael Lillis has described most of the other participants. But from the British side there are two to be added: Robert Andrew, then Permanent Secretary of the Northern Ireland Office in London, who joined the British team half-way through. As the head of the department responsible for maintaining law and order in the North, he had the necessary but not always grateful task of ensuring that the realities of the situation on the ground were not overlooked in moments of negotiating euphoria – a task he discharged with determination and good humour. Then for the final stage of the negotiations the British team was joined by my successor but one at the Cabinet Office, Christopher Mallaby (afterwards ambassador at Bonn and Paris).

compressed, it provides a corrective to the grudging tone of the Irish chapter in *The Downing Street Years*, fairly reflecting the positive element in the British approach as well as the critical importance of his own contribution.

Mrs Thatcher's views on the Northern Ireland problem and on the negotiations are given with characteristically forthright clarity in *The Downing Street Years*. But the tone of voice and the vehemence tend to overlay the basic rationale for her attitude. So, it may be worth trying to describe it, shorn of the vehemence, from the vantage point of someone who worked for her throughout the two-year period of the negotiations.

On Northern Ireland itself, she was, of course, a self-proclaimed unionist, and for much the same reasons as had led her to take Britain to war to recover the Falkland Islands: because she believed that the North was British territory, a clear majority of whose population had through many generations regarded themselves as British and demonstrably wished to remain so. She was allergic to the concept of 'alienation', which I think she regarded as Marxist, but she recognised that the nationalist minority had had legitimate grievances and had suffered serious discrimination. By 1982, however, she thought that the most serious grievances had been attended to and (like the Irish Catholic bishops at the time of the Fenians) that such grievances as remained could not justify armed rebellion, let alone a campaign of systematic murder. The same system of democratic, parliamentary government was in operation in the North as in the rest of the United Kingdom, giving equal rights to members of both communities. As for the consideration that the minority was relatively too small ever to bring about a change of jurisdiction by the normal democratic process of one man one vote, she saw this as a situation which minorities everywhere had to accept. To argue otherwise was to defend Sikh terrorist-backed separatism in India or Hitler's intervention in Czechoslovakia on the ostensible behalf of the large German community in the Sudetenland (which had been incorporated into the new state of Czechoslovakia against the wishes of the Sudeten Germans). Both these analogies surfaced from time to time in her conversations with Dr FitzGerald as well as with her own collaborators.

At the same time, Mrs Thatcher hated loss of life. The losses incurred in the Falklands campaign had caused her personal anguish. Consistent with this, she had a hatred of terrorism and a conviction that terrorists were murderers who should never be rewarded for their terrorism: hence her intransigence over the hunger strikes. (The canard that she authorised the sinking of the Belgrano in order to make armed conflict inevitable would have been totally out of character.) The aspect of the Northern Ireland troubles which most concerned her was the drain they caused on lives – lives for which the British government was responsible. Given that the declared aim of all parties in the South, as reflected in Articles 2 and 3 of the Irish Constitution,[3] was the same as that of the IRA, namely the incorporation of the North into the 'national territory' of a united Ireland, she believed that successive Irish governments were less than wholehearted in combating IRA terrorism, insufficiently vigorous in preventing terrorists from using Southern territory as a safe haven, and disposed to put obstacles in the way of cross-border cooperation between British and Irish security forces. (High-level liaison between the RUC and the Garda Síochána was limited and the Irish government did not permit operational contact between the Irish and British military authorities.)

Her lack of sympathy for Irish nationalism had been fuelled by the long IRA terrorist campaign, still at its height in 1983; by the assassination of Airey Neave, a personal friend and mentor; and by the mutually embittering tensions of the hunger strikes. Then the anti-British stance adopted by the Haughey government during the Falklands crisis had come not just as an affront, but as a stab in the back at a time when she was under great personal strain and needing the support of all her European allies – support which had been forthcoming even from President Mitterrand, who had telephoned her himself to assure her of his understanding of what the British were having to do. Instead (as it seemed in London), Mr Haughey had chosen to act once again on the principle that England's difficulty was Ireland's opportunity.

3. These Articles read: '2. The national territory consists of the whole island of Ireland, its islands and territorial seas. 3. Pending the re-integration of the national territory, and without prejudice to the right of the Parliament and Government established by this constitution to exercise jurisdiction over the whole of that territory, the laws enacted by that Parliament shall have the like area and extent of application as the laws of Saorstát É ireann and the like extraterritorial effect.' They have since been amended, following the Good Friday Agreement.

To spell out Mrs Thatcher's attitude in this way is not to ignore all the countervailing considerations, historical and contemporary, which led others of us on the British side, including Geoffrey Howe, to recognise that peace would only be restored in the North through some degree of compromise with Irish and nationalist demands. But it is necessary in order to understand why Mrs Thatcher herself found this recognition hard to accept; why her attitude to the negotiations and the eventual Agreement fluctuated in the way it did; and also, I suspect, why Enoch Powell's accusation of 'treachery' after the Agreement was signed touched a raw nerve.

The adamant refusal of Northern unionists to contemplate any settlement which included an 'Irish dimension' (believing that this was bound to be a step down the slippery slope to a united Ireland), matched by the SDLP's refusal to operate any settlement which did not include an Irish dimension, had, by the end of 1982, left the British government temporarily bereft of new ideas for tackling the Northern Ireland problem. The alternatives before it seemed to be: integrating Northern Ireland fully into the United Kingdom's administrative structure – to treat it as being (as Mrs Thatcher had once said) as British as Finchley; finding some way of meeting the main concerns of the constitutional nationalists (the SDLP) while at the same time confirming the union; or simply carrying on with direct rule with a view to defeating the terrorists militarily and in the hope of being able eventually to restore some form of devolved government. All three courses had their advocates, but politically only the third appeared for the moment to be feasible.

Since I became heavily involved, in a subordinate capacity in the subsequent negotiations with the Irish government, I should perhaps say something here about my personal position and view of the Irish question. Early in May 1982, I was transferred from the British embassy in Bonn to the Cabinet Office, on temporary secondment from the diplomatic service, as deputy secretary to Robert Armstrong for foreign and defence matters. I had until then had no professional involvement with Ireland or Anglo-Irish inter-governmental relations. My interest in Ireland derived from my exploration of the history of the Goodall family. Originally from Yorkshire, this family had been in Co Wexford since at least the end of the sixteenth century; but my grandfather had moved to England in the 1880s and married an Englishwoman and my own branch of the family thought of itself as wholly English.[4] I had taken little interest in twentieth century Irish politics and virtually none in dealings between the British and Irish governments since partition. But my researches into family history and the contacts I had made in the process had given me some feeling for what it was like to be an Anglo-Irish Protestant and what it was like to be a Catholic nationalist.

So, I did not think of Ireland as a 'foreign' country. Rather it seemed to me that the relationship between our two islands was a historic mess, and one for which the British bore much (but not all) of the responsibility. The result was a legacy of alienation, mistrust and even hatred in a country whose natural relationship to Britain in terms of culture, propinquity and interbreeding was one of close cousinship. I had no sympathy with the idea that the unionists of the North should be pushed or eased into a united Ireland against their will; in so far as I had a coherent opinion on the matter, I thought that the long term aim should be to bring the island of Ireland as a whole, within the framework of the European Community, freely back into some closer relationship with England, Scotland and Wales – a relationship which could not be defined in advance and which would have to evolve over time as animosities cooled and the border between North and South became gradually less significant.

For the first few months of my time at the Cabinet Office, I was mainly concerned with the Falklands conflict and its aftermath. At the end of 1982, however, I found myself talking to Mrs Thatcher after a dinner at

4. Garret FitzGerald (*All in a Life*, p. 474) kindly says that a forebear of mine 'had been a member of the Irish Parliament who in the middle of the eighteenth century had been actively involved in one of the earliest challenges ... to the Dublin Castle establishment'. The truth is rather less flattering. The Wexford Goodalls at their most prosperous were never more than what Sir Jonah Barrington called 'half-mounted gentry', and none of them sat in the Irish Parliament. But in 1754 one John Goodall voted for the anti-Castle candidate in a parliamentary by-election for the county of Wexford and his vote was disqualified on the ground that he was married to a 'popish wife'. He protested that his wife had formally recanted before their marriage and had a certificate of conformity to prove it. When accused of having been married to her before that, he made the memorable reply that 'there was a ceremony or a sort of a ceremony, but he did not look upon it as a marriage as there was no consummation in consequence of it, nor even a ceremony of marriage, as he was drinking all the time. (*Journal of the House of Commons (Ireland)*, Vol IX, p. 407 and David Goodall, 'All The Cooking That Could Be Used', *The Past*, No 12, 1978).

No 10, and the conversation turned to Ireland. This led me to draw attention to what I suggested was the often overlooked and scandalous fact that the only place in the world where British soldiers' lives were then being lost in anger was in the United Kingdom itself, that is, in Northern Ireland. Mrs Thatcher readily took this point; and although there was no mistaking her lack of sympathy for Irish nationalism, I was struck by the seriousness of her interest in Northern Ireland and the extent of her background reading on the subject. I reminded her of General de Gaulle's handling of the Algerian problem, and she turned the analogy over in her mind. Our conversation ended with her saying reflectively 'If we get back next time' (looking ahead to the forthcoming general election in 1983) 'I think I would like to do something about Ireland'. In the event, before she had had time to formulate what that 'something' might be, the Irish took the initiative.

In early 1983, Dr Garret FitzGerald replaced Mr Haughey as Taoiseach, and in June Mrs Thatcher won her comfortable election victory in Britain. Although in *The Downing Street Years* she professes to have found Mr Haughey easier to deal with than Dr FitzGerald, at the time (as Geoffrey Howe makes clear) [5] she had a high regard for Garret FitzGerald's honesty of purpose and indeed (so it seemed to me) even a degree of personal affection for him. Although she found him unduly loquacious and tended to call him 'Gareth' ('She seems to think I'm Welsh,' he observed ruefully), he was a man (like Gorbachev) she 'could do business with'; had this not been the case, the negotiations would almost certainly have been broken off before they had got properly under way.

As he has told us, Garret FitzGerald had entered politics fired with a determination to bring about a reconciliation between the two parts of Ireland; and with governments in place in Dublin and London looking likely to be secure in office for the next two or three years, he saw an opportunity of achieving his ambition. For good or ill, this chimed in with Mrs Thatcher's somewhat differently motivated feeling that it was time 'to do something about Ireland'. It also meant that, as is apparent from a comparison of the four ministerial accounts I have mentioned, Garret FitzGerald and his negotiating team had a clearer view at the start of what they were aiming for than did the British participants, whose negotiating position was developed in response to Irish proposals. All

5. Howe, *Conflict of Loyalty*, p. 427.

that was common to both sides was the desire for an agreement of some kind which would hopefully make the situation in the North better and at least not make it worse.

So, as soon as the British election was over, Dermot Nally was despatched to London to propose to Robert Armstrong the reactivation of the 'Anglo-Irish Intergovernmental Council' – a grandiose name for regular meetings between the two heads of government, to be serviced by a joint 'Steering Committee' of officials from both sides. This entity had been agreed upon between Mrs Thatcher and Mr Haughey in 1981 during their brief political honeymoon, but aborted by their subsequent falling out over the Falklands. As we sat round the table with Dermot Nally and his colleagues in the Cabinet Secretary's large and elegant office discussing the Irish proposal, the sound of martial music and military commands were wafted into the room from Horse Guards Parade, where guardsmen in scarlet could be seen rehearsing for a Beating of Retreat. It was almost exactly a year since a detachment of the Household Cavalry, assembling for a similar event on the Horse Guards, had been blown up in an IRA bomb attack. This latest attempt at Anglo-Irish reconciliation thus opened, not altogether inappropriately, against a background of 'England's cruel red' in its peaceful mode.

It was agreed that the Steering Committee – in effect the two Cabinet Secretaries, Dermot Nally and Robert Armstrong – should be mandated simply to identify practical areas for closer Anglo-Irish cooperation and report to a summit meeting of the two heads of government in the autumn. The detailed work was to be done by a coordinating committee of officials from the interested departments within the two governments. The Irish team was to be headed by Michael Lillis, responsible for Anglo-Irish affairs at the Irish Department of Foreign Affairs; and I was to lead the British team by virtue of the Cabinet Office's co-ordinating role within Whitehall. At that time, however, we were not aware that the Irish were contemplating any new initiative beyond an intensification of high-level political and official contacts.

So, it was a complete surprise when, at the first meeting of our co-ordinating committee in September 1983 in Dublin, Michael Lillis invited me to take a quiet walk with him along the Grand Canal and proceeded to sketch out the possibility of radically new arrangements for Northern Ireland. He made it clear that these were not yet the ideas of the Irish government, but indicated that they were the lines on which the Taoiseach was thinking.

No two interlocutors approaching a subject from differing points of view ever carry away exactly the same understanding of what was said. With that qualification, my understanding from Michael of what the Taoiseach was tentatively envisaging was unequivocal Irish acceptance of the Union, if necessary, including amendment of Articles 2 and 3 of the constitution, and a revived Northern Ireland parliament, in return for an Irish political presence in the North together with the participation of Irish police and security forces in operations there and of Irish judges in terrorist trials. This stemmed from a recognition that unification was not a realistic goal for the foreseeable future; and that unless the Catholic minority in the North could be brought to identify themselves with the institutions of law and order there (from which they were profoundly and increasingly alienated), Sinn Féin would replace the SDLP as the legitimate representative of the nationalist community, with disastrous consequences for the island of Ireland as a whole. The Taoiseach accordingly believed that outright acceptance of the Union would be a price worth paying for measures which, by addressing Northern nationalists' concerns, would end their alienation from the institutions of the state in the North and demonstrate that constitutional – that is non-violent – nationalism could achieve more for nationalists than Sinn Féin and the IRA.

Having had no previous dealings with Michael Lillis, and being a newcomer to the Anglo-Irish political scene, I was uncertain what to make of these (to me) astonishingly far-reaching ideas and not sure how far they were to be taken seriously. I also had some difficulty in believing that I had been chosen as the channel for conveying to London a major new initiative by the Taoiseach. But Michael Lillis, while leaving me in no doubt that he was by background and conviction a strong and emotional Irish nationalist with his fair share of historic resentments about the British role in Ireland, impressed me as being honest, intelligent and capable of being both imaginative and objective. While I thought that any idea of Irish troops or police operating in the North would be a non-starter in London, it seemed to me that unequivocal Irish acceptance of the Union, confirmed by the amendment of Articles 2 and 3, might be a step of sufficient symbolic and political importance to justify the introduction of an 'Irish dimension' of some kind into the Northern Ireland administration. So, I duly reported my understanding of what Michael Lillis had said.

This report engaged Mrs Thatcher's interest. But it was received in Whitehall with scepticism, and subsequent exploratory encounters at various levels were needed to establish that these were in fact the Taoiseach's ideas. When it seemed that they really were, it was thought that on the one hand they went well beyond what the Taoiseach would ever be able to deliver, and on the other that they were incompatible with the maintenance of British sovereignty over the North. Eventually however a consensus was reached that, at the forthcoming November summit, the Prime Minister should be recommended simply to explore the Taoiseach's thinking further, while making it crystal clear that British sovereignty over the North was non-negotiable; and this is essentially what she did.

It was at this meeting at Chequers on 7 November, 1983 that the Taoiseach made his case to the Prime Minister for what became known among the negotiators as 'the basic equation': outright Irish endorsement of the Union and closer security cooperation in return for an Irish role in the government and administration of justice in the North. Since joint sovereignty was firmly ruled out, Garret FitzGerald made his pitch for 'joint authority'. Mrs Thatcher thought this was equally unacceptable, a distinction without a difference. But the Taoiseach had persuaded her that there was at least enough common ground between them to justify taking matters further; and immediately after the Irish left, she convened a meeting of the British participants round the fire, at the end of which officials were commissioned to produce counterproposals for presentation to the Irish in the new year (1984).

The main stages in the negotiations which followed are succinctly summarised by Garret FitzGerald in *All in a Life*.[6] Essentially, they comprised a long series of probing operations in which the two sides jointly tested the relative weight which each of the two elements in 'the basic equation' could be made to bear and discussed ways of putting the results into mutually acceptable language. In return for endorsing the Union, the Irish wanted to maximise the political role to be accorded to the Irish government in the North and limit the emphasis on security. The British wanted to restrict the Irish role as far as possible to the security field, while wanting Irish endorsement of the Union to be as formal and explicit as possible. The Irish (encouraged by the SDLP) wanted measures which would demonstrate to the minority community that, although the Union had to be accepted, the institutions of the state were becoming Irish as well as British; the British wanted

6. FitzGerald, *All in a Life*, pp. 460–462.

a visible and effective Irish commitment to joint anti-terrorist operations.

The official negotiators fairly quickly came to understand the political constraints on what each other's government would find tolerable. Ministers on either side were – understandably – slower to do so or, having done so, to adjust their expectations accordingly. The British were reluctant to accept that an Irish government could not commit itself to joint counterterrorist operations without being given some share of real political responsibility for what was being done. (Mrs Thatcher regarded this 'bargaining about security' almost as a form of blackmail.) Dr FitzGerald was equally reluctant to see that British acceptance of 'joint authority' with the Irish over the North would *ipso facto* amount to a dilution of British sovereignty and be seen by the majority community as a large a step down the road to a united Ireland. The Irish could not see why, if Irish police or security forces were to operate along the northern side of the border, this could only be on a reciprocal basis, with British forces being allowed to operate along the southern side. The British found it difficult to acknowledge that, to be politically saleable in the South – or to achieve its agreed aim of ending the alienation of the minority community from the institutions of the state – any agreement involving endorsement of the Union had to address continuing nationalist concerns about the conduct of the security forces, the impartiality of the courts and the need for some identifiable Irish presence and influence in the North.

The hint of a repeal of Articles 2 and 3 of the Irish Constitution was very important at the start in catching Mrs Thatcher's interest in a possible agreement (although the Irish did not put it fully on the table until a later stage in the negotiations) but its attractiveness from the British point of view declined as it became apparent that the political price expected for it in terms of Irish involvement in the North – 'joint authority' – was too high.

One other important component of the negotiating package (and of the eventual Agreement) was the proviso that the Irish government's role in the administration of the North would lapse to the extent that it could be assumed by 'a devolved administration' – in other words an administration in which unionists and nationalists were sharing power.[7] This important and welcome proviso was offered by the Irish early on, and one

7. Articles 2(b), 4(b) and (c), 5(c).

of the hiccups which punctuated the negotiations occurred when they were mistakenly given the impression that the British were making any Irish involvement in the North conditional on the prior establishment of a power-sharing administration – something which, given the attitude of the main political parties in the North at that time, looked unachievable in the foreseeable future.

The negotiations had other ups and downs but attracted relatively little public attention in Britain until the 'Brighton Bomb' on 12 October 1984, when the Provisional IRA narrowly failed to assassinate Mrs Thatcher, together with most of the British Cabinet and their wives, at the annual Conservative Party Conference. Nothing could have illustrated more vividly the reality of the antagonism we hoped an agreement would help to defuse than the singular brutality of the language with which the IRA claimed responsibility: 'Today we were unlucky but remember we only have to be lucky once.' In the light of her ingrained suspicions about Irish sympathy for the terrorists and her doubts about the direction the negotiations were taking, Mrs Thatcher would have been only human if she had responded by withdrawing from the negotiating process; and I half expected her to do so. But I had underestimated both her courage and her determination. In the event, she appeared outwardly unruffled, and the negotiations were allowed to continue.

The next Anglo-Irish summit meeting, however, which followed only five weeks later on 18 November, 1984 (at Chequers instead of in Dublin), culminated in the celebrated 'Out, Out, Out' episode, when Mrs Thatcher, in answer to a question at her press conference, forcefully dismissed all three 'models' for the future of Northern Ireland put forward in the Forum Report,[8] thereby gravely – but quite unintentionally – creating serious difficulties for Garret FitzGerald at home and precipitating a crisis in the negotiations.

At the time, this looked like a disaster which threatened to derail the

8. A unitary state for the whole of Ireland, a federal state embracing North and South or 'joint authority' over the North. The Forum Report had never loomed as large in the British government's thinking as it did, for obvious reasons, in that of Dr FitzGerald's government, and it was regarded in London as of only peripheral importance. Mrs Thatcher had already made it clear to Dr FitzGerald privately that the models it proposed were unacceptable to the British. But, as on other occasions, it was the vehemence with which she gave her views, as much as their substance, that caused offence.

negotiations altogether. In the light of hindsight, however, it probably saved them, by forcing each side to realise the limits of what was politically feasible for the other. When the official negotiators re-convened, somewhat chastened, early in January 1985, the 'basic equation' had been effectively clarified: no amendment of Articles 2 and 3, but a formal acceptance by the Irish government of Northern Ireland's status as part of the United Kingdom (unless and until its people should freely choose otherwise), as a basis from which the Irish government could have an institutionalised influence on British decision-making there without any diminution of British sovereignty.

Once this lowering of expectations had been mutually digested, there still remained important issues to be resolved, including the range of subjects on which the Irish were to have the right to bring their influence to bear, the nature of the Irish presence in the North, the way in which Northern Ireland's status as a part of the United Kingdom was to be recognised and, of course, the wording in which all this was to be expressed. How to reconcile the Irish requirement for something more than a right to be 'consulted' (and therefore, by implication, to be disregarded) with the British requirement to leave no doubt that this was all that was on offer taxed all Robert Armstrong's and Dermot Nally's drafting and bargaining skills, not only with one another but also with their respective principals, and was problematic almost up to the last moment.[9] So, the negotiations went on at an intensifying pace – and with more than one cliff-hanging moment – until the beginning of November 1985. But by the middle of the year the essence of what was to be agreed had been tacitly accepted by both sides and the prospect of possible failure to reach agreement effectively discounted.

The Agreement which finally emerged represented 'the most significant and carefully prepared development in the relationship between Britain and Ireland since the partition settlement of the 1920s'. But like all freely negotiated agreements between parties with conflicting objectives, it was a compromise in which neither side achieved all it had tried for. The Irish

9. See Article 2(b) of the Agreement. The word 'determined' here, in the phrase 'that in the interests of peace and security determined efforts shall be made ... to resolve any differences' was eventually chosen after 'every effort' was thought too strong by one side and not strong enough by the other.

did not get joint authority, but the 'consultative' structures established under the Agreement, and the range of subjects covered constituted in practice a significant degree of joint responsibility. From that joint responsibility developed the mutual confidence between the two governments and successive prime ministers of both countries without which it is doubtful whether the subsequent agreements, leading to the Good Friday Agreement, could ever have come about.

The British got only a conditional Irish endorsement of the Union, but in the context of the Agreement as a whole and of the institutionalised consultation between the two governments which it initiated, it was clear that the Irish government no longer contested the legitimacy of British sovereignty over the North, and any idea that an Irish government might seek to coerce the North into a united Ireland against the wishes of the unionist community was laid to rest. Cooperation between the RUC and the Garda Síochána at senior levels became closer.

In the short term, the measures taken to reconcile the nationalist community to the institutions of the state in the North had only limited impact. The leaders of the SDLP warmly welcomed the Agreement, but made no move to try to open a dialogue with the unionists. For a time, the level of violence actually increased. But in the elections which followed the Sinn Féin vote dropped significantly and the SDLP vote increased. None of this was lost on the Sinn Féin leadership.

An undoubted flaw in the whole process was the exclusion of the unionists, who were party neither to the Agreement itself nor to the negotiations leading up to it (unlike the SDLP, who were in the Irish government's confidence throughout and whose leaders were regularly consulted by Dublin.) The inescapable reason for this was the sustained and implacable opposition of both unionist parties to any form of 'Irish dimension' in the North or to any discussion with Dublin about such a possibility. The state of feeling in Northern Ireland, and the attitude of the unionist leaders, meant that there was simply no prospect at that time of a constructive negotiation between the two governments involving all the main political parties there; and if the unionists had been brought in from the start there would have been no negotiation and no Agreement.

As it was, the unionists reacted to the Agreement with outrage and refused either to be comforted by the provision that there was 'no derogation from sovereignty of . . . the United Kingdom government' or to take advantage of the opening created for the establishment of a devolved, power-sharing administration in which the Irish government would then have no say.[10]

The anger and resentment of the unionist community was understandable, if mistaken; and the fierceness of their reaction blunted any positive impact the Agreement might have had in the short term on inter-community relations. But the fact that it was concluded solely between the two governments, and that none of the political parties was a party to it, turned out to be its strength. The Sunningdale Agreement had collapsed mainly because it had depended on the unionists' willingness to operate it, and the unionist leaders had walked away from it under pressure from their own people. The 1985 Agreement could only have collapsed if one or other government had walked away from it, and neither of them did. As a result, it remained in force long enough to change the political chemistry in the North and oblige all the political parties – even in the end Sinn Féin – reluctantly and privately to realise that it would not go away unless and until they could jointly agree on a mutually acceptable alternative.

Looking back on the negotiations at a distance of nearly twenty-five years, I am struck by how important a part was played in producing a positive result, first by mutual trust between the negotiators and then by the two governments sticking to what had been agreed, even though neither was satisfied with it. As it happened, shortly after the Agreement was signed, I was posted to India, where I found that the long running dispute with Pakistan over Kashmir had striking similarities with the Northern Ireland problem. Both disputes had deep historical roots and arose from the partition of a territory (the island of Ireland and the Indian sub-continent) which was previously under a single jurisdiction. Both sets of troubles arose from antipathy between two communities who defined themselves by their religious allegiance (in Kashmir, Hindu and Muslim). Both involved one of those communities (the Muslims in Kashmir) being left on the side of the border with which they did not identify in religious and cultural

10. Tom Hadden and Kevin Boyle, *The Anglo-Irish Agreement: Commentary, Text and Official Review* (Sweet and Maxwell Ltd,: London, 1989), p. 110. Article 2(b).

terms, separated from those with whom they did; and in both cases the country across the border effectively laid claim to the territory concerned.

Given these similarities, the Kashmir dispute seemed to cry out for a peaceful settlement on lines similar to those adumbrated in the 1985 Hillsborough Agreement and filled out in the Good Friday Agreement of 1998. I found many people in both India and Pakistan interested in such a possibility and keen to understand how it was being realised in negotiations between Dublin and London. But what was missing, and is sadly still missing in the sub-continent, were the key ingredients of mutual trust, together with stable governments on either side willing – and able – to ride out the ensuing turbulence. The 1985 Agreement and its successors exemplify the fact that Britain and Ireland in recent years have been fortunate in both respects.

A British View

I

What British Politician Will Ever Really Inderstand Northern Ireland?

ROBIN RENWICK *

NO PRIME MINISTER could have had a closer or more personal experience of Irish terrorism than Margaret Thatcher. Airey Neave, hero of the attempts to escape from Colditz prison camp during the war, had played a crucial role in her campaign for the party leadership against Ted Heath. Appointed by her as shadow Northern Ireland Secretary, he was killed by a car bomb planted by an extremist Irish terrorist group, the Irish National Liberation Army (INLA) within the precincts of Parliament on the eve of the election in 1979.

This was followed by the murder of Lord Mountbatten and members of his family in Ireland in August 1979 and the ambush and killing by the Irish Republican Army (IRA) of eighteen British soldiers near the border with the Irish Republic. Mrs Thatcher went post haste to Northern Ireland, receiving an enthusiastic reception in Belfast's main shopping centre before spending time with the army and police. Her attempts shortly afterwards to agree on increased security cooperation with the Irish authorities met with no response whatever from the Irish Prime Minister, Jack Lynch.

Her own instincts were, as she said herself, 'profoundly unionist', despite her sometimes troubled relationship with them. She was firmly committed

* This chapter is taken from chapter VIII of Robin Renwick's book, *A Journey with Margaret Thatcher: Foreign Policy under the Iron Lady* (Biteback Publishing Ltd.: London, 2013) and is reproduced here with his kind permission.

to the defence of the union. She considered that the North was British territory, a clear majority of whose population had through many generations regarded themselves as British and demonstrably wished to remain so. She had the highest admiration for the people of Northern Ireland, who greeted her warmly on the visits she made there after nearly every major terrorist attack, and she felt responsibility for them acutely.

'But what British politician', she added, 'will ever really understand Northern Ireland?' It was her realization that this was indeed the case that led her to move from a very conservative position to a more adventurous one. Her starting point was that the nationalist minority had legitimate grievances and had suffered serious discrimination. This could not justify armed insurrection, let alone a campaign of systematic murder, but the political realities prevented a return to self-government based on majority rule. Enoch Powell had been campaigning for full integration and an end to any special status for Northern Ireland, an idea she rejected. There was going to have to be some form of power-sharing.

As the declared aim of all parties in the South, as reflected in Articles 2 and 3 of the Irish Constitution, was the same as that of the IRA, namely the incorporation of the North into the 'national territory' of a united Ireland, she believed that successive Irish governments were less than wholehearted in combatting IRA terrorism, lax in preventing terrorists from using Southern territory as a safe haven and prone to placing obstacles in the way of effective cross-border security cooperation.

In December 1979, Charles Haughey became the Irish Prime Minister. In 1970 he had been accused but acquitted in a case of gun-running for the IRA. Despite the unpromising background and allegations of corruption which followed him throughout his career, he made great efforts to charm her with skilful blarney, plus the well-chosen present of a Georgian Irish silver teapot. In December 1980 they held a meeting which the communiqué described as extremely constructive, promising to devote their next meeting to discussing the 'totality of relationships between these islands'. Haughey portrayed this as a triumph from the Irish point of view, and Irish ministers started talking about 'new institutional structures', annoying Mrs Thatcher and infuriating the unionists.

Meanwhile, she was having to cope with a serious crisis triggered by the IRA prisoners in the Maze prison in Belfast. A 'special category' status for convicted terrorist prisoners in Northern Ireland had been conceded in 1972. This was, in her view, a bad mistake and it had been ended in 1976. But earlier prisoners continued to have a special category status. Within the Maze prison in Belfast, protest had been constant, including fouling cells and breaking up furniture. In October 1980, they announced plans for a hunger strike, demanding the right to wear their own clothes, avoid any prison work and to consort with other 'political prisoners'. Her response was that there was no such thing as a political murder. Her hatred of terrorism and conviction that terrorists were murderers who should never be rewarded for their terrorism lay behind her resistance to making any concessions to the hunger strikers and in particular her refusal to grant them political prisoner status.

Haughey urged her to make some face-saving concessions. The Catholic Church was persuaded to come out against the hunger strike. When one of the prisoners began to lose consciousness, the strike was abruptly called off. It was then started again in March 1981 by the IRA leader in the Maze, Bobby Sands. Michael Foot, Leader of the Opposition, urged the Prime Minister to make concessions to the strikers. Bobby Sands died on 5 May. In Parliament she said that he was a convicted criminal who had chosen to take his own life. 'It was a choice that his organisation did not allow to many of its victims'. In all, ten prisoners died before the strike was called off in October.

In July 1981, Garret FitzGerald had taken over from Haughey as the Irish Prime Minister. He had first met Margaret Thatcher when she was still Leader of the Opposition. He had been told that she was a convinced unionist and was worried that, under the influence of Airey Neave, she might revert to the idea of a devolved government in Northern Ireland on the basis of majority i.e., Protestant control. He was told flatly by her that there would be no devolution without power-sharing.

In these first contacts with her, FitzGerald came to a very shrewd judgement about her. Most British politicians approached Northern Ireland as gingerly as if it were an explosive device, and were exceptionally fearful of unionist eruptions. He felt that she would be hard to persuade, but that if she were persuaded, 'she had the qualities to do something serious about the North and to stand by what she agreed'. He therefore decided to make an all-out effort with her.

She was impressed by his obvious sincerity and agreed in November 1981 to set up an 'Anglo-Irish Intergovernmental Council' of ministers on both sides to discuss issues of common concern, provoking another furious reaction from the unionists. The return of Haughey to government in Dublin in 1982 brought Anglo-Irish relations back to freezing point. Mrs Thatcher regarded him as fundamentally untrustworthy, a sentiment further reinforced when he sided with Argentina in the Falklands conflict. Chairing a Cabinet committee in July 1982, she heard the sound of a bomb exploding not far away. Bombs had exploded in Hyde Park and Regent's Park, killing eight and injuring fifty-three people.

Midway through the Falklands crisis, David Goodall became Deputy Secretary in the Cabinet Office responsible for foreign and defence matters. He found that the loss of life by British servicemen in the Falklands campaign had caused Margaret Thatcher personal anguish. At the end of 1982, he found himself talking to her about Ireland after a dinner at 10 Downing Street. He observed that it was a scandalous fact that, at the time, the only place in the world where the lives of British soldiers' were being lost in anger was in the United Kingdom itself, in Northern Ireland. He was struck by the seriousness of her interest in Northern Ireland and the extent of her background reading on the subject. The conversation ended with her saying that, 'If we get back next time' (in the 1983 general election), she wanted to 'do something about Ireland'. Robert Armstrong, as Cabinet Secretary, also was told of her determination, once re-elected, to try to do something to change the course of events in Northern Ireland.

The return of Garret FitzGerald as Taoiseach in December 1982 offered hope of an improvement. Following her victory in the 1983 election, talks were engaged between Robert Armstrong and his Irish counterpart, Dermot Nally. In September 1983, David Goodall's counterpart, Michael Lillis, told him that FitzGerald tentatively was thinking of amending Articles 2 and 3 of the Irish Constitution laying claim to Northern Ireland, in return for an Irish political presence in the North, with the involvement of Irish police and security forces there and of Irish judges in terrorist trials. This suggestion was received with scepticism in Whitehall but attracted Mrs Thatcher's interest. The idea of Irish troops or police operating in Northern Ireland was a non-starter, just as a British proposal that the security forces on both sides should have the right to hot pursuit of terrorists within five miles of the border was flatly rejected by the Irish. But she had fully grasped the significance of FitzGerald's readiness to accept publicly, and not just privately, that Irish unification was not a feasible proposition for the foreseeable future.

When they met at Chequers on 7 November 1983, FitzGerald made his case for an 'equation' whereby the Irish government would endorse the Union of Great Britain and Northern Ireland and increase security cooperation in return for an Irish role in the government and administration of justice in the North. He argued for 'joint authority', which she rejected. But he had persuaded her that there was a possibility of progress.

Immediately after the Irish delegation left, she held a meeting with the British participants around the fire at Chequers. She authorised Robert Armstrong and David Goodall, for both of whom FitzGerald had formed a high regard, to engage in secret discussions with their Irish counterparts and to prepare counter-proposals for new forms of cooperation. Robert Armstrong was asked to lead the negotiations because she wanted to keep them firmly under her personal control.

In December, she visited Harrods in the immediate aftermath of an IRA bomb attack there, finding the charred body of a teenage girl lying where she had been killed. The next day, Denis Thatcher was spotted by the press returning to No 10 with a clutch of shopping bags from Harrods. He was not, he declared, going to allow himself to be put off doing his habitual Christmas shopping there by some 'murdering Irishman'.

The Irish put forward proposals for joint policing and mixed courts in Northern Ireland, based on ideas of 'joint sovereignty', which she could not accept. But there followed a series of exploratory meetings between officials. In return for endorsing the Union, the Irish government wanted as much involvement and influence as possible in the North. Mrs Thatcher was not prepared to bargain about an Irish security or judicial presence in Northern Ireland, but recognised the need to address nationalist concerns about the conduct of the security forces and the impartiality of the courts. She had initially been very attracted by the idea of the Irish amending the offending article of their constitution, but the price they wanted from the British for this – 'joint authority' – was unacceptable to her and would have triggered a full-scale unionist revolt. She was prepared to agree a consultative role for the Irish government in Northern

3. Press conference following the signing of the Anglo-Irish Agreement at Hillsborough Castle, 15 November 1985. View of the politicians involved in the signing including Taoiseach Dr Garret FitzGerald and British Prime Minister Margaret Thatcher. *Independent Newspaper Ireland/National Library of Ireland Collection © Independent News and Media*

4. Sir David and Lady Goodall on the occasion of the conferring of an honorary degree on Sir David by the National University of Ireland, Dublin, December 2015.
© NUI Archive

Ireland which, however, would lapse once there was an administration in which nationalists and unionists were genuinely sharing power.

On 12 October 1984 she was working until 2.40 am in her rooms at the Grand Hotel in Brighton on her speech to the Conservative Party conference when the IRA very nearly succeeded in their objective of eliminating her and much of her government. A massive explosion destroyed a whole perpendicular section of the hotel. Her Private Secretary, Robin Butler, was still working with her in her suite when the explosion took place, and helped her out of the rubble of the hotel. She was evacuated to the Brighton police station, then to the Lewes Police College, but refused to return to 10 Downing Street. In the morning she saw television pictures of Norman Tebbit being pulled from the wreckage; his wife was paralysed in the attack. Anthony Berry MP and Roberta Wakeham had been killed; John Wakeham, a member of the Cabinet, was badly injured.

She told Robin Butler: 'We must make sure the conference restarts on time.' He was appalled. How could she go on with the conference when her friends and colleagues were being dug out of the rubble, he asked. 'We can't allow terrorism to defeat democracy,' was her reply.

At 9.30 am precisely, she opened the conference. Having rewritten her speech once more, she knew that what she said was less important than the fact that she was still there to tell her audience that 'all attempts to destroy democracy by terrorism will fail'. Simon Jenkins observed that the foreign journalists present in Brighton were incredulous at her composure and immaculate appearance. She visited her wounded friends and colleagues in the Sussex country hospital. Her daughter, Carol, found her next day at Chequers grimly reflecting that, 'This was the day I was not meant to see.' The IRA declared that she had been lucky, but they 'only had to be lucky once' in their continuing efforts to kill her.

David Goodall felt that Margaret Thatcher would have been only human if she had responded by suspending the negotiations and half-expected her to do so. But he found that he had underestimated her courage and determination.

Her reaction was to respond not with a barrage of emergency measures – she had considered but, in the end, had always rejected internment without trial for terrorist suspects – but with a display of studied normality. 'Outwardly unruffled', she decreed that the negotiations must continue.

By now, Douglas Hurd had become Northern Ireland Secretary. He found that meetings with her on the subject tended to start from square one. She had a great admiration for the people of Northern Ireland, but a poor opinion of unionist politicians. She would begin by saying that the answer might be to redraw the border so as to get rid of the predominantly republican areas. Hurd would reply that the orange and green ethnic map in his office showed that the communities were irretrievably intermingled. She would then denounce Irish ministers and the police for their feebleness in dealing with the IRA. But he too found that the Brighton bombing did not deflect her from her determination to try to reach an agreement with the Irish government. To have any chance of success, the negotiations had to be conducted in secret, though at a very late stage the unionist leader Jim Molyneaux and Enoch Powell were offered briefings as privy councillors, which, at Enoch Powell's insistence, they rejected.

The unionists had been excluded from the discussions because of the implacable opposition of both unionist parties to any Irish government involvement in the North. She liked and trusted Garret FitzGerald, despite complaining about his verbosity, and respected him as someone who was genuinely trying to change the course of events. He spoke both very rapidly and very softly, as a result of which, on one jet-lagged occasion, she fell asleep during a peroration from him, causing Charles Powell to assure him that he had written it all down and would make sure she read it! He complained that she kept calling her Gareth. 'Does she think I am Welsh?' he enquired. But she hijacked him to travel with her on the plane back from Mrs Gandhi's funeral in Delhi in order to continue their very sensitive private discussions.

In a meeting at Chequers on 18 November 1984, she sought to disabuse him of the notion that a 'joint authority' could be established for Northern Ireland. But they had a detailed discussion on ways to involve the Irish in a security commission. She regarded this as the most serious discussion she had ever had with an Irish leader. She discomfited FitzGerald by declaring at her press conference that the options of unification, confederation and joint authority were all 'out', and was genuinely upset that this caused difficulties for him in the Irish Parliament. In the light of hindsight, however, Goodall felt that it probably saved them, by forcing each side to realise the limits of what was potentially feasible for the other.

She then had a further positive meeting with FitzGerald at the Dublin European Council in December. She semi-apologised by saying that when people asked her direct questions, she had a weakness of giving direct answers. Geoffrey Howe felt that an extraordinary personal chemistry had developed between them.

FitzGerald kept trying to persuade her that something radical must be done to overcome the 'alienation' of the Catholic community in Northern Ireland. 'I do wish you would stop using that dreadful word, Garret,' she would reply! But on the substance, she was persuaded.

Secret discussions between the two governments, led by Armstrong and Goodall, continued on the basis of a British draft formalizing consultation with the Irish government about Northern Ireland. The British negotiators pressed the Irish to state publicly that there could be no change in the status of Northern Ireland without the consent of the majority of the people there. FitzGerald was impressed by their obvious sincerity in striving to reach an agreement and by the fact that, despite the reservations of others on the British side, Armstrong and Goodall had her full confidence and backing.

By now both sides had agreed that instead of amending the Irish Constitution, there would be a formal acceptance by the Irish government of Northern Ireland's status as part of the United Kingdom, unless and until its people should freely choose otherwise, in return for which the Irish government could have an institutionalized influence on British decision-making in Northern Ireland without diminishing British sovereignty – a proposition that required skilful drafting by Robert Armstrong and his counterparts.

Garret FitzGerald made the all-important commitment that the Irish government would declare publicly its acceptance of the Union and of the fact that it could not be changed without the consent of the majority of the people of Northern Ireland in a meeting with Mrs Thatcher at the Milan European Council in June 1985, showing in her view the same political courage she was going to have to demonstrate in dealing with the unionist leaders. While this position had been hinted at by earlier Irish governments and the Irish had said at the time of the of the 1973 Sunningdale Agreement that they wanted to see unity 'established by consent', FitzGerald had agreed to express this in a far clearer and more high-profile manner in the form of a treaty. They had a forthright exchange about the composition of the courts in Northern Ireland and ways in which policing could be rendered more acceptable to the minority community.

At the crucial Cabinet meeting on 23 July 1985, she received vital support from Norman Tebbit, whose wife had been crippled in the Brighton bombing. FitzGerald was continuing to press for joint courts and changes to the police and the Ulster Defence Regiment. Nevertheless, dismissing the reservations of the new Northern Ireland Secretary, Tom King, she felt that they were now close to an agreement.

On 15 November 1985 she and FitzGerald signed the Anglo-Irish Agreement at Hillsborough Castle in Northern Ireland. Article 1 affirmed that no change in status could come about without the consent of the majority of the people of Northern Ireland and recognised that the present wish of the majority was for no change. On this basis, it was clear that the Irish government no longer contested the legitimacy of British authority over the North. The agreement allowed the Irish government to put forward its views and proposals in various areas, including security. But decision rested with the British.

Mrs Thatcher was right in regarding this as a huge prize. Any idea that an Irish government might seek to coerce the North into a united Ireland against the wishes of the unionist community was laid to rest. The 'consultative' structures established under the agreement established a degree of joint responsibility between the two governments without which it is doubtful whether the subsequent Good Friday Agreement (following which the Irish Constitution later was amended) could ever have come about.

The Prime Minister had thought that Article 1 and her own well-known attitude to Irish terrorism should have been sufficient to reassure the unionists about her intentions. Instead, to her fury, the unionists launched a general strike and threats of civil disobedience. She was denounced for treachery by Enoch Powell, who compared her to Jezebel. Having previously always taken him extremely seriously, this convinced her that he was more than slightly mad after all. To her disappointment, Ian Gow, who had been a close political friend, insisted on resigning from his position as a junior Treasury minister. At a dinner for her at this time, Charles Moore, editor of *The Spectator*, attacked the agreement. 'What about the

Protestants?' he asked. Leaning across the table, with her usual intensity, she said, 'Yes, Charles, and what about the Catholics?' She told FitzGerald that he had the glory and she had the problems, but she was not going to be deflected by the unionist protests from implementing the agreement. The agreement got a positive reception internationally, especially in the United States, as showing that the two governments were working together. The Irish government's acceptance that unity could only come about with the consent of the Protestant community undercut republican propaganda to the contrary.

But to Margaret Thatcher's bitter disappointment, it did not result in any improvement in the security situation. The French intercepted a ship carrying Libyan arms for the IRA. A bomb attack killed eleven people at a Remembrance Day service at Enniskillen. She insisted on attending the rescheduled service regardless of the risk to her own security. When three Irish terrorists were killed by British security forces in Gibraltar, the funeral in Belfast turned into a mass IRA demonstration. She was appalled when two British soldiers who stumbled into a further IRA funeral were filmed being lynched by a frenzied mob.

Haughey, who had defeated FitzGerald in the 1987 Irish election, infuriated her by making a violently anti-British speech at the UN General Assembly in March 1988, earning a stinging rebuke from her. Nor was she any better pleased when Geoffrey Howe said that 'he did not underestimate the hurt felt by the Irish in recent months.' Security measures were reinforced, but the government rejected bringing back internment and she was persuaded not to seek to proscribe Sinn Féin. A further blow followed when the IRA killed Ian Gow with a car bomb in July 1989.

She had found the results of the Anglo-Irish Agreement disappointing. It had alienated the unionists without resulting in improved security cooperation with the Republic. This was never likely to be feasible with Charles Haughey in control. The unionists were yet to produce, in David Trimble, a leader, in Douglas Hurd's words, with a sense of the future as well as the past.

Margaret Thatcher, for all her formidable qualities, was never going to be the leader best qualified to help bring peace to Northern Ireland. The IRA were right to see her as their most implacable opponent. They would never have agreed to negotiate an end to hostilities with her. Nor would she temperamentally have been able to muster the infinite patience and care which John Major and, later, Tony Blair, devoted to managing Irish sensitivities and helping to overcome the innumerable obstacles to an agreement.

Nevertheless, the Anglo-Irish Agreement was one of the most indispensable building blocks on the road to a more peaceful future for Northern Ireland. Charles Haughey, who had attacked the agreement as Leader of the Opposition, declared his intention to abide by it when he returned to power. The fact that it was concluded solely by the two governments, without the political parties, turned out to be its strength. The earlier Sunningdale Agreement had collapsed when the unionists withdrew their support. But both the British and Irish governments stuck by their commitments under the Anglo-Irish Agreement. It marked a turning point in the relationship between them and provided a foundation on which John Major and then Tony Blair were able to build towards the 1998 Good Friday Agreement and all that followed.

Garret FitzGerald had abandoned the position that a unitary state could somehow be achieved regardless of the wishes of the majority in the North. All future negotiations with the Irish government, resulting eventually in amendment to the Irish Constitution and, later, the discussions with Sinn Féin, started from this point.

She also would claim to have made clear to the IRA that they could never achieve their objectives by the route they had chosen. This was a conclusion that some of the IRA leadership were starting to come to themselves. Opaque messages started to be received to that effect. Two years after Margaret Thatcher's downfall, the Northern Ireland Catholic leader John Hume told me in Washington that there had been a revolution in IRA thinking. They were now interested in discussing a political solution. I hardly dared believe him at the time, but he turned out to be right.

Robin William Renwick, Baron Renwick of Clifton, KCMG, was born in 1937. He is a graduate of Cambridge and the Sorbonne. He served in the army from 1956 to 1959 and joined the diplomatic service in 1963. He had close to a dozen assignments in his career, including ambassadorships in South Africa and the United States. In the Foreign Office, in charge of EU issues during the Thatcher premierships, he played a key role in the negotiation of the correction (reduction) of the British budgetary contribution to the EU. He was made a life peer in 1997 and served in the House of Lords until 2018. He was a director of several companies following retirement from the Foreign Office. He has written *Not Quite a Diplomat: a Memoir* (2019), as well as books on South Africa, before and after apartheid, on Hillary Clinton and on Helen Suzman. His book, *A Journey with Margaret Thatcher; Foreign Policy under the Iron Lady*, was published in 2013.

II

A Commentary

CHARLES POWELL

DAVID GOODALL DID POSTERITY a great service by leaving us his exquisitely polished private account of the negotiations in which he was a key player leading up to the Anglo-Irish Agreement. That in turn became the vital first step on the road to the Good Friday Agreement and peace in Northern Ireland. It is well-travelled ground. Margaret Thatcher provided her own rather churlish account of the same negotiations in her autobiography and Charles Moore a fuller and more rounded version in his magnificent biography of Margaret Thatcher. Various Cabinet ministers of the epoch told their own stories. And that is just on the British side. But none match the eloquence and immediacy of David Goodall's recollections based on private diaries he kept at the time. What marks out his account from others is the emotional commitment to reconciliation in Ireland which sprang both from his Irish connections and his Catholicism. For him negotiation of the Anglo-Irish Agreement was more than statecraft, it was a mission.

I was not personally engaged in the negotiations but witnessed them at close quarters from under Margaret Thatcher's wing as her private secretary in the two years running up to the AIA and thereafter until she stepped down as Prime Minister in late 1990. That was to be constantly exposed to the raw side of her views on Ireland, on terrorism and the absolute importance of preserving British sovereignty in Northern Ireland. It also meant attending all her meetings on the subject including her bilateral or tête-à-tête meetings with Dr FitzGerald, including in one case substituting for her when she fell asleep in the course of the meeting (it had been a hard day in the European Council). Other officials notably David Goodall and Robert Armstrong, the Cabinet Secretary, were on the sharp end of her views too, as well as ministers. But it was a characteristic tactic of hers to make outrageous statements and stake out maximalist positions as a warning to negotiators not to chance their arm and go too far in offering concessions. The art with her was to be able to distinguish theatre from reality.

A book celebrating the successful negotiation of the AIA is not the place to drag too many skeletons out of the wardrobe. Suffice it to say Margaret Thatcher's instincts were not the most promising starting point for negotiations with the Republic. She nurtured resentments against the Republic dating back to closing its ports to the Royal Navy in World War 2. Irish attempts to block sanctions against Argentina after its invasion of the Falklands were cited as a further example of perfidy. She was a self-proclaimed unionist at a time when many Conservatives seemed embarrassed at describing themselves as that. She had a visceral hatred of the PIRA, and indeed all terrorists, not diminished by their near miss in trying to assassinate her in Brighton. She believed the Republic could and should do more to eliminate PIRA facilities and weapons stores across the border and that better cross-border security cooperation was the answer to most of the North's problems. She had a blind eye to continuing discrimination there. She had not a drop of sympathy for the nationalists' visions of a united Ireland, any more than she had any understanding of visions of a united Europe.

But as in so many other cases there was another side to Margaret Thatcher. She said in 1983 that she 'wanted to do something about Northern Ireland' after the UK elections. Intellectually she recognised that Northern Ireland deserved a better future than the bleak cycle of violence and deprivation. She wanted to reduce the level of violence and to stabilise a situation which was a constant distraction and threatened her other priorities for Britain. She knew this could only be achieved by political creativity alongside strong security, always provided there was no weakening of British sovereignty and the Union. She was not overly concerned about the impact of the situation in the North on Britain's international reputation. She found President Reagan, Irish roots or not, a solid ally in opposing terrorism and PIRA fund-raising in the United States. If others failed to recognise the need to fight terrorism that was their affair.

Beyond this she recognised in Garret FitzGerald someone she could do business with, the accolade she also conferred on Mikhail Gorbachev. She trusted his good intentions, while complaining of a tendency to over-promise in the case of removing Articles 2 and 3 of the Irish Constitution and joining the European Convention on the suppression of terrorism, and under-deliver on improved border security. I am not sure she ever fully realised how difficult it was for him politically to recognise the North as part of the UK without a more extensive role for the Republic in the governance of the North. In her mind concepts like joint authority were simply never on the agenda.

In David Goodall and Robert Armstrong, she had two outstanding officials who were motivated to move Northern Ireland back to the top of the political agenda and showed endless creativity and ingenuity in doing so, in which they were well-matched by the mercurial Michael Lillis on the Irish side. It is to her credit that she gave her negotiators considerable latitude even though she knew that their views of what could be achieved ran well ahead of hers and she would frequently need to rein them back in. It often seemed that the gap between them and Irish officials was far narrower than the gap between them and her.

As a result, the negotiations were far from a straightforward experience. Time and again she reined them back from being too conciliatory and too willing to consider Irish proposals on joint authority in the North, on joint patrolling of minority areas, joint policing, joint courts, and similar ideas which would give the Republic a direct involvement in the processes of government in the North rather than a consultative role only. As a result, the negotiations moved in a series of fits and starts, and more than once teetered on the brink of break-down. Garret FitzGerald was subjected to the hair-dryer treatment, especially with Margaret Thatcher's 'Out, Out, Out' at a press conference referring to the proposals for Ireland's future by the New Ireland Forum which Garret FitzGerald had himself set up, a dry run for her later 'No, No, No' to Jacques Delors proposals for the future of the European Union. But the result was an agreement she could live with and believed would eventually benefit all the parties even if it would take time for them to see it that way.

In one major area, David Goodall's account is incomplete and that is the lack of any reference to the views of the unionists whom he seems to have seen as someone else's business and they barely get a mention at all. In terms of Whitehall departmental boundaries, they were the responsibility of the Northern Ireland Office rather than the Foreign Office. But it goes without saying that is not how Margaret Thatcher saw the unionists. For her they were loyal, patriotic citizens of the UK and the bulwark against terrorism. She saw them as 'her' people even when they did not return the compliment. Yet she knew that if they were included in the negotiations being conducted with the Irish government, or had the details shared with them, there would never be an agreement at all. It pained her hugely to exclude them. She hoped they would trust her, given her record, to ensure their interests would be well protected. They did not and some of their leaders engaged in a degree of brutishness towards her worse than any other behaviour I have witnessed. It is wholly to her credit that she rose above her instincts, loyalties and friendships to conclude an agreement which she knew in her mind to be right even if her heart told her otherwise.

Even so she was never at ease with what she had achieved and the disillusion got worse as time passed. She was dogged by doubts: that she had conceded too much, that she had 'betrayed' the unionists and that, as she said to Garret FitzGerald 'you got the glory and I got the problems'. PIRA terrorism continued, indeed escalated, and she never felt that the Republic's heart was in effective cross-border security cooperation. Sinn Féin's rise continued both in the North and the Republic. She came to regard the Agreement if not as a failure at least as a disappointment. It is said that Queen Mary who was held responsible in the sixteenth century for losing Calais as a British possession remarked 'when I am dead and opened you shall find Calais lying on my heart'. Margaret Thatcher would have shared the sentiment. The tragedy is she did not need to. The Agreement she struck with the aid of talented officials like David Goodall was the essential first step to peace on the island of Ireland.

Charles David Powell, Baron Powell of Bayswater, KCMG, was born in 1941. He is a graduate of Oxford; he was a British diplomat and is a businessman. He joined the diplomatic service in 1963. Among his assignments was one as Special Counsellor for the Rhodesia negotiations from 1979 to 1980. While serving as Counsellor at the UK mission to the EU in Brussels in 1983, he was seconded to Downing Street to serve as Private Secretary to Prime Minister, Margaret Thatcher, until she left office in 1990, and then to Prime Minister, John Major until 1991. During his time working for Prime Minister Thatcher, he became one of her most trusted aides. His brother, Jonathan, was chief of staff to Prime Minister Tony Blair. From 1992 Lord Powell has served on the boards of several prominent companies. He was created a life peer in the 2000 New Year Honours.

An Irish View

Northern Ireland and Dublin

STEPHEN COLLINS

IRISH POLITICS IN THE 1980s was largely defined by the rivalry between Fine Gael leader Garret FitzGerald and his Fianna Fáil counterpart Charles Haughey. At the heart of their conflict was a profoundly different approach to the status of Northern Ireland and the appalling violence that beset the region during the period.

Haughey became leader of Fianna Fáil in December 1979 despite the fact that he had been sacked from the cabinet in 1970 for his involvement in a plot to import arms to aid the Provisional IRA. In truth for many in his party it was precisely his involvement in the conspiracy that made him an attractive leader who would stand up to the British and pursue the traditional nationalist agenda of a united Ireland.

By contrast the fundamental motivation in FitzGerald's political career was to build bridges between the two parts of Ireland, between the two communities in the North and between Ireland and the United Kingdom. His book *Towards a New Ireland* published in 1972 outlined this vision of a shared future. When he became leader of Fine Gael in 1977, he embarked on an ambitious project to modernise his party and turn it into a professional political organisation that could rival Fianna Fáil. One of his main objectives in this was to make Fine Gael powerful enough to change the political narrative from an emphasis on Irish unity to an approach centred on cooperation between the two parts of the island and the two communities in the North.

Haughey never made a secret of the fact that he regarded the national issue as the one which was the key to his place in the history books. He reportedly told British Prime Minister Margaret Thatcher during their first meeting in 1980 that no political leader would be remembered for reducing the balance of payments or for adjusting the scale of government borrowing but, the one who came up with a solution to the national question would go down in the history books. His image of himself as a man of destiny was evident at the choreography which surrounded his first Ard Fheis (party conference) as leader in February 1980. He was piped into the RDS by the Transport union brass band to the strains of the old nationalist anthem, 'A Nation Once Again' prompting an ecstatic welcome from more than 5,000 delegates. In his speech, which reflected traditional Fianna Fáil attitudes, his description of Northern Ireland as 'a failed political entity' was greeted with wild applause by the audience.[1]

Haughey's emphasis on the traditional goal of a united Ireland contrasted sharply with FitzGerald's support for a devolved power sharing arrangement in Northern Ireland as the first step towards any solution. Haughey maintained that decisions could only be taken by the two governments over the heads of the squabbling parties in the North. After six months in office, he met Thatcher, herself in her first year in government, for an Anglo-Irish summit meeting in London. He brought her an antique Irish silver teapot as a present and despite the jokes and the ridicule that followed about 'teapot diplomacy' the two leaders got off to a good start. The really significant follow-up summit took place in December 1980 in Dublin Castle. To emphasise the importance she attached to it, Mrs Thatcher brought with her the Foreign Secretary, Lord Carrington, who had just negotiated the Rhodesian (Zimbabwe) settlement. The Chancellor of the Exchequer, Geoffrey Howe, and the Northern Secretary, Humphrey Atkins, made up the high-powered British team. Minister for Foreign Affairs Brian Lenihan and Minister for Finance Michael O'Kennedy were involved on the Irish side though the two prime ministers had a private meeting which lasted more than an hour.

The joint communiqué issued after the meeting described the talks as 'extremely constructive and significant' and went on to say that the 'totality

1. *Irish Press*, 18 February 1980.

of relationships' between the two islands would be considered in a number of joint studies. These covered a range of topics such as new institutional structures for the island, security matters, citizenship rights and economic cooperation. Haughey made it clear that he was even prepared to consider a defence pact with Britain in the context of agreement on the North. 'We would, of course, have to review what would be the most appropriate defence arrangements for these islands as a whole. It would be unrealistic and improvident not to', he told the Dáil.[2] The meeting with Mrs Thatcher heralded a genuinely important breakthrough but Haughey showed poor political judgement by insisting that the constitutional position of Northern Ireland as part of the United Kingdom was now in the melting pot. Lenihan went even further and said that the partition question was on the verge of being solved and a united Ireland could become a reality in the next decade. Thatcher was angry at the gross over-hyping of the summit and denied point blank that the British government had any intention of altering the constitutional position of Northern Ireland. Not for the first time Haughey showed his propensity to go for short-term political gain, thereby sacrificing the possibility of long-term progress on a critically important issue.

Haughey called a general election in June, 1981, and not only did he have to face an unexpectedly stiff challenge from a rejuvenated Fine Gael, he had to contend with an attack on Fianna Fáil's other flank from the IRA hunger strikers in the H Block wing of the Maze Prison. The demands of the hunger strikers for the restoration of special status had been resisted by Thatcher. The hunger strike leader Bobby Sands was elected to the House of Commons at by election in Fermanagh-South Tyrone in April of 1981 and he died less than a month later. The general election campaign in the Republic provided the hunger strikers with an opportunity to put their case before the electorate at a time of deep emotion on both sides of the border. Haughey had made vain efforts to convince Thatcher of the need to compromise but she refused to budge. He suffered politically as the relatives of the hunger strikers demanded firmer commitment from him in dealing with Thatcher. When the votes were counted the hunger strikers, who were committed to a policy of abstention, won four seats, effectively depriving Haughey of a majority.

2. *Irish Press*, 9 December 1980.

A minority Fine Gael-Labour government took office with the support of Independents and had to contend with serious problems in the public finances which had been left in a dreadful state. However, FitzGerald's immediate focus was on finding a solution to the hunger strike impasse. He had numerous meetings with Irish and British officials and a series of communications with Thatcher in an effort to press the British into resolving the issue. He also held a series of difficult and distressing meetings with relatives of the hunger strikers.

Some members of FitzGerald's government felt he was devoting far too much time and attention to the North when the Republic he governed was in the midst of a budgetary crisis. His close friend and special advisor Alexis FitzGerald shared that anxiety and warned the Taoiseach that his obsessive focus on Northern Ireland was getting in the way of his duty to the State. In his first six weeks in office there were 25 exchanges between the two governments about the hunger strikes, 15 of them at prime ministerial level but by early August, FitzGerald decided there was nothing to be gained by pressing the British any more.

When things had calmed a little FitzGerald held a conference of his senior ministers and closest advisors to try and plot a course for a new approach to Northern Ireland. There was a hard headed discussion about the constitutional and legal changes that would be required to convince unionists that the Republic was not a sectarian state. The widely shared view at the meeting was that the territorial claim to the North contained in Articles 2 and 3 and the constitutional ban on divorce were serious obstacles to progress. Whether it would be possible to do anything about them was the issue.

'What appeared to us to be desirable might not, it was felt, be politically feasible. For if a constitutional initiative were undertaken on Articles 2 and 3 and failed the existing situation might be considerably worsened,' was FitzGerald's conclusion but he was convinced that the issues needed to be raised in public discussion.[3]

While he was mulling over the issues, he gave an interview to the *Cork Examiner* in which he argued that Articles 2 and 3 and some of the other constitutional provisions which seemed to him sectarian in character were unhelpful. The response from Fianna Fáil was swift. Brian Lenihan

3. FitzGerald, *All in a Life*, p. 376.

was particularly negative saying in a television interview that he would lead a crusade against the abolition or modification of Articles 2 and 3 and adding. 'We will get the support from nationally minded people of this country and we will win.' [4]

FitzGerald discussed these exchanges with political correspondents at an off the record lunch and decided that, as the debate had started, he needed to give a strong lead. He subsequently gave a radio interview to RTE in which he turned Lenihan's language on its head saying: 'What I want to do, if I may, is to take a phrase from somebody the other night on television: I want to lead a crusade, a republican crusade to make this a genuine republic'. He added that he was not going to rush into a referendum but would try and lead the country towards becoming a pluralist society. [5]

Haughey immediately denounced FitzGerald saying his remarks had 'caused deep dismay among all those of us in every part of Ireland who cherish the ideal of unity.' FitzGerald, though, was heartened by what he felt was a surge of enthusiasm from a large section of the Irish people 'who found inspiration in a political credo that responded to their deeply felt frustration at the narrow and exclusive rhetoric' propounded by so many politicians. [6]

FitzGerald elaborated on his vision in a speech to the Seanad [Seanad Éireann, Upper House of Irish Parliament] in which he invoked the memory of Seán Lemass who had complained about the strait jacket of the Constitution in relation to the North in particular. He also quoted Jack Lynch who had said that the Constitution should try and accommodate the views of people who saw aspects of it as an infringement of their civil rights and their liberty of conscience. He then asked Attorney General Peter Sutherland to undertake a review of the Constitution but the process was interrupted when his government fell on the budget vote in January, 1982. [7]

Haughey returned to power with a minority government whose short life has gone down in history as one of the most chaotic and dysfunctional in the history of the State. One fateful decision Haughey took during that year was to stage an unnecessary confrontation with Thatcher at the height of the Falklands war. Ireland held a seat on the UN security council when the war broke out and initially backed the British sponsored Resolution 502 which called for the withdrawal of Argentine forces from

4. *Irish Times*, 26 September 1981.
5. *Irish Times*, 30 September 1981.
6. FitzGerald, *All in a Life*, p. 378.
7. *Irish Times*, 10 October 1981.

the Falklands. However, after the sinking of the General Belgrano, Haughey withdrew support for EU supported sanctions against Argentina and sought an immediate meeting of the UN Security Council to prepare a resolution calling for an end to hostilities. Thatcher was furious at what she regarded as a stab in the back from her nearest neighbour.

Haughey's precarious hold on power slipped in November 1982 when his minority government lost a vote of confidence in the Dáil. It followed an amazing succession of sinister actions, blunders and bad luck, including the phone tapping of prominent journalists and the arrest of double murderer Malcolm McArthur in the flat of the Attorney General, Patrick Connolly. Haughey's description of this event as 'grotesque, unbelievable, bizarre and unprecedented' prompted Conor Cruise O'Brien to coin the acronym GUBU to describe his 1982 government.

In the general election campaign that followed his Dáil defeat, Haughey sought to distract from his government's disastrous performance by accusing FitzGerald of being a lackey of the British. Reverting to full blooded nationalism he made the ludicrous accusation that the Fine Gael leader was acting in collusion with British Intelligence. A suggestion by FitzGerald six months earlier that an all-Ireland court and all Ireland police force would be the best way to tackle IRA violence were presented as evidence that he was working hand in hand with the British against the interests of his own country.

It was against this background of bitter division about how to deal with Northern Ireland and Anglo-Irish relations that Fine Gael and Labour returned to office with a clear majority. It should not be forgotten, though, that Haughey won a whopping 45 per cent of the vote which indicated that there was still a huge constituency for unvarnished nationalism. While there were some fundamental differences between Fine Gael and Labour about the best way to tackle the economic crisis, they were bound together by a belief that another Haughey led government would be dangerous for Irish democracy and would inflame tensions in Northern Ireland.

As a result, the government operated in an unusual way with a threefold system of decision making. On Northern Ireland FitzGerald was in clearly in charge but on most aspects of domestic policy government decisions were arrived at by consensus. As David Goodall's memoir illustrates, the Taoiseach devoted a great deal of energy to persuading the British and particularly Prime Minister Margaret Thatcher that a serious initiative was needed to end the violence that was causing so much suffering and death.

The intensive behind the scenes activity was matched by highly publicised initiatives. First FitzGerald established the New Ireland Forum which aimed to get a consensus in nationalist Ireland about a new approach to the problem. At the core of his approach was an attempt to modify the nationalist aspiration for a united Ireland to try and win unionist consent to a new approach. SDLP leader John Hume was a strong supporter of the initiative and while some of his ministers doubted that the Forum would achieve anything FitzGerald was determined to proceed with it.

There was a tense struggle at the Forum which pitted Fianna Fáil against all of the other nationalist parties. True to form Haughey stuck rigidly to the traditional demand for a unitary state as the only solution. When the final report published on 2 May 1984, it listed three possible options: a unitary state, a federal/confederal arrangement or joint British/Irish authority. The report also expressed support for any proposals which would further peace and stability and crucially acknowledged the right of unionists to have their British identity and inheritance fully acknowledged in any solution.

At a press conference in December, 1984, which followed an Anglo-Irish summit with FitzGerald in London, Thatcher was asked about the Forum suggestions. She listed the three main options saying 'that is out' to each of them. Her response was abbreviated by the media to 'Out, Out, Out' and it caused a political storm in Dublin. FitzGerald was pressed by his own party to deliver an aggressive response but he refused to do anything of the kind. Instead, he proceeded with the intense round of diplomacy in the first half of 1985 designed to persuade Thatcher to modify her position.

His forbearance paid off handsomely and, as outlined in the Goodall memoir, a reluctant Thatcher was persuaded that new thinking was required to break the cycle of violence. The outcome was the Anglo-Irish Agreement of November 1985 which represented the biggest change in relations between the two countries since the Treaty of 1921. Under the terms of the Agreement the Irish government was given a role through the Anglo-Irish Intergovernmental Conference in representing the views of the nationalist community in the North. A permanent Irish secretariat was established at Maryfield in Belfast to give concrete expression to the

Agreement. It was widely hailed a political and diplomatic triumph for FitzGerald but Haughey denounced it as a betrayal of the constitutional claim to Irish unity. Before the talks reached their conclusion, he even dispatched his Foreign Affairs spokesman Brian Lenihan to Washington to lobby leading Irish American politicians to oppose the outcome. This attempt to undermine FitzGerald's negotiating position was rejected by influential American figures like Speaker of the House of Representatives Tip O'Neill and Senator Ted Kennedy.

Haughey's attempt to torpedo the agreement showed the political risk FitzGerald had taken in his determined effort to develop a nationalist consensus behind a new approach to Northern Ireland. FitzGerald received a short-term political boost as the public rallied behind his approach while Haughey's cynical manoeuvring caused a split in his party which ultimately led to the formation of the Progressive Democrats and deprived him of an overall majority in the 1987 general election. When he took office with another minority government after that election, he abandoned his claim that the Agreement was unconstitutional and instead operated the institutions which it had established.

The process that led to the Agreement was FitzGerald's finest hour. While it did not avert electoral defeat in 1987, over time it forced his political opponents into a fundamental reassessment of their position. Less than a decade later Fianna Fáil under Albert Reynolds accepted the principle of consent in the Downing Street Declaration of 1993 as fundamental to the future of Northern Ireland. In 1995 John Bruton as Taoiseach led the campaign to remove the prohibition on divorce from the constitution. He was supported by Fianna Fáil and the referendum was carried by a small majority. Then in the Good Friday Agreement of 1998 Bertie Ahern committed the Republic to a referendum abolishing the territorial claim to the North and an overwhelming majority of the electorate voted for a new form of wording. Ultimately it was FitzGerald's vision of the island's future, and not Haughey's, which prevailed.

Stephen Collins is a political columnist with the *Irish Times* and the author of a number of books on Irish politics. After graduating from University College Dublin with an MA in Politics he began his career in journalism with the Irish Press group and has been writing about Irish politics since the 1980s. He was political editor of the *Irish Times* for a decade and now writes a weekly column on current affairs for that newspaper. He has authored a number of books on political history including *Ireland Under Fianna Fáil* and *Breaking the Mould,* the story of the Progressive Democrats. His most recent book, co-authored with historian Ciara Meehan, is *Saving the State: Fine Gael from Collins to Varadkar* which was published in 2020.

Appendices

I
A Copy of The Anglo-Irish Agreement 1985

Editor's Note The official texts of the UK and Irish versions of the Anglo-Irish Agreement 1985 are identical save that the UK version (on the following pages) describes the two governments as 'the Government of the United Kingdom of Great Britain and Northern Ireland and the Government of the Republic of Ireland', while the Irish version describes them as 'the Government of Ireland and the Government of the United Kingdom'. It seemed appropriate to use the UK version in this instance in honour of the late Sir David Goodall.

The Agreement was previously published as Republic of Ireland No. 1 (1985), Cmnd. 9657

REPUBLIC OF IRELAND

Treaty Series No. 62 (1985)

Agreement

between the Government of the United Kingdom of Great Britain and Northern Ireland and the Government of the Republic of Ireland

Hillsborough, 15 November 1985

[The Agreement entered into force on 29 November 1985]

Presented to Parliament
by the Secretary of State for Foreign and Commonwealth Affairs
by Command of Her Majesty
December 1985

LONDON
HER MAJESTY'S STATIONERY OFFICE
£1·35 net

Cmnd. 9690

AGREEMENT
BETWEEN THE GOVERNMENT OF THE UNITED KINGDOM OF GREAT BRITAIN AND NORTHERN IRELAND AND THE GOVERNMENT OF THE REPUBLIC OF IRELAND

The Government of the United Kingdom of Great Britain and Northern Ireland and the Government of the Republic of Ireland:

Wishing further to develop the unique relationship between their peoples and the close co-operation between their countries as friendly neighbours and as partners in the European Community;

Recognising the major interest of both their countries and, above all, of the people of Northern Ireland in diminishing the divisions there and achieving lasting peace and stability;

Recognising the need for continuing efforts to reconcile and to acknowledge the rights of the two major traditions that exist in Ireland, represented on the one hand by those who wish for no change in the present status of Northern Ireland and on the other hand by those who aspire to a sovereign united Ireland achieved by peaceful means and through agreement;

Reaffirming their total rejection of any attempt to promote political objectives by violence or the threat of violence and their determination to work together to ensure that those who adopt or support such methods do not succeed;

Recognising that a condition of genuine reconciliation and dialogue between unionists and nationalists is mutual recognition and acceptance of each other's rights;

Recognising and respecting the identities of the two communities in Northern Ireland, and the right of each to pursue its aspirations by peaceful and constitutional means;

Reaffirming their commitment to a society in Northern Ireland in which all may live in peace, free from discrimination and intolerance, and with the opportunity for both communities to participate fully in the structures and processes of government;

2

Have accordingly agreed as follows:

A

STATUS OF NORTHERN IRELAND

ARTICLE 1

The two Governments

(a) affirm that any change in the status of Northern Ireland would only come about with the consent of a majority of the people of Northern Ireland;

(b) recognise that the present wish of a majority of the people of Northern Ireland is for no change in the status of Northern Ireland;

(c) declare that, if in the future a majority of the people of Northern Ireland clearly wish for and formally consent to the establishment of a united Ireland, they will introduce and support in the respective Parliaments legislation to give effect to that wish.

B

THE INTERGOVERNMENTAL CONFERENCE

ARTICLE 2

(*a*) There is hereby established, within the framework of the Anglo-Irish Intergovernmental Council set up after the meeting between the two heads of Government on 6 November 1981, an Intergovernmental Conference (hereinafter referred to as "the Conference"), concerned with Northern Ireland and with relations between the two parts of the island of Ireland, to deal, as set out in this Agreement, on a regular basis with

(i) political matters;
(ii) security and related matters;
(iii) legal matters, including the administration of justice;
(iv) the promotion of cross-border co-operation.

(*b*) The United Kingdom Government accept that the Irish Government will put forward views and proposals on matters relating to Northern Ireland within the field of activity of the Conference in so far as those matters are not the responsibility of a devolved administration in Northern Ireland. In the interest of promoting peace and stability, determined efforts shall be made through the Conference to resolve any differences. The Conference will be mainly concerned with Northern Ireland; but some of the matters under consideration will involve co-operative action in both parts of the island of Ireland, and possibly also in Great Britain. Some of the proposals considered in respect of Northern Ireland may also be found to have application by the Irish Government. There is no derogation from the sovereignty of either the United Kingdom Government or the Irish Government, and each retains responsibility for the decisions and administration of government within its own jurisdiction.

3

ARTICLE 3

The Conference shall meet at Ministerial or official level, as required. The business of the Conference will thus receive attention at the highest level. Regular and frequent Ministerial meetings shall be held; and in particular special meetings shall be convened at the request of either side. Officials may meet in subordinate groups. Membership of the Conference and of sub-groups shall be small and flexible. When the Conference meets at Ministerial level the Secretary of State for Northern Ireland and an Irish Minister designated as the Permanent Irish Ministerial Representative shall be joint Chairmen. Within the framework of the Conference other British and Irish Ministers may hold or attend meetings as appropriate: when legal matters are under consideration the Attorneys General may attend. Ministers may be accompanied by their officials and their professional advisers: for example, when questions of security policy or security co-operation are being discussed, they may be accompanied by the Chief Constable of the Royal Ulster Constabulary and the Commissioner of the Garda Siochana; or when questions of economic or social policy or co-operation are being discussed, they may be accompanied by officials of the relevant Departments. A Secretariat shall be established by the two Governments to service the Conference on a continuing basis in the discharge of its functions as set out in this Agreement.

ARTICLE 4

(*a*) In relation to matters coming within its field of activity, the Conference shall be a framework within which the United Kingdom Government and the Irish Government work together

(i) for the accommodation of the rights and identities of the two traditions which exist in Northern Ireland; and

(ii) for peace, stability and prosperity throughout the island of Ireland by promoting reconciliation, respect for human rights, co-operation against terrorism and the development of economic, social and cultural co-operation.

(*b*) It is the declared policy of the United Kingdom Government that responsibility in respect of certain matters within the powers of the Secretary of State for Northern Ireland should be devolved within Northern Ireland on a basis which would secure widespread acceptance throughout the community. The Irish Government support that policy.

(*c*) Both Governments recognise that devolution can be achieved only with the co-operation of constitutional representatives within Northern Ireland of both traditions there. The Conference shall be a framework within which the Irish Government may put forward views and proposals on the modalities of bringing about devolution in Northern Ireland, in so far as they relate to the interests of the minority community.

4

C

POLITICAL MATTERS

ARTICLE 5

(*a*) The Conference shall concern itself with measures to recognise and accommodate the rights and identities of the two traditions in Northern Ireland, to protect human rights and to prevent discrimination. Matters to be considered in this area include measures to foster the cultural heritage of both traditions, changes in electoral arrangements, the use of flags and emblems, the avoidance of economic and social discrimination and the advantages and disadvantages of a Bill of Rights in some form in Northern Ireland.

(*b*) The discussion of these matters shall be mainly concerned with Northern Ireland, but the possible application of any measures pursuant to this Article by the Irish Government in their jurisdiction shall not be excluded.

(*c*) If it should prove impossible to achieve and sustain devolution on a basis which secures widespread acceptance in Northern Ireland, the *Conference shall be a framework within which the Irish Government* may, where the interests of the minority community are significantly or especially affected, put forward views on proposals for major legislation and on major policy issues, which are within the purview of the Northern Ireland Departments and which remain the responsibility of the Secretary of State for Northern Ireland.

ARTICLE 6

The Conference shall be a framework within which the Irish Government may put forward views and proposals on the role and composition of bodies appointed by the Secretary of State for Northern Ireland or by departments subject to his direction and control including

the Standing Advisory Commission on Human Rights;

the Fair Employment Agency;

the Equal Opportunities Commission;

the Police Authority for Northern Ireland;

the Police Complaints Board.

D

SECURITY AND RELATED MATTERS

Article 7

(*a*) The Conference shall consider

(i) security policy;

(ii) relations between the security forces and the community;

(iii) prisons policy.

(*b*) The Conference shall consider the security situation at its regular meetings and thus provide an opportunity to address policy issues, serious incidents and forthcoming events.

(*c*) The two Governments agree that there is a need for a programme of special measures in Northern Ireland to improve relations between the security forces and the community, with the object in particular of making the security forces more readily accepted by the nationalist community. Such a programme shall be developed, for the Conference's consideration, and may include the establishment of local consultative machinery, training in community relations, crime prevention schemes involving the community, improvements in arrangements for handling complaints, and action to increase the proportion of members of the minority in the Royal Ulster Constabulary. Elements of the programme may be considered by the Irish Government suitable for application within their jurisdiction.

(*d*) The Conference may consider policy issues relating to prisons. Individual cases may be raised as appropriate, so that information can be provided or enquiries instituted.

E

LEGAL MATTERS, INCLUDING THE ADMINISTRATION OF JUSTICE

Article 8

The Conference shall deal with issues of concern to both countries relating to the enforcement of the criminal law. In particular it shall consider whether there are areas of the criminal law applying in the North and in the South respectively which might with benefit be harmonised. The two Governments agree on the importance of public confidence in the administration of justice. The Conference shall seek, with the help of advice from experts as appropriate, measures which would give substantial expression to this aim, considering *inter alia* the possibility of mixed courts in both jurisdictions for the trial of certain offences. The Conference shall also be concerned with policy aspects of extradition and extra-territorial jurisdiction as between North and South.

6

F

CROSS-BORDER CO-OPERATION ON SECURITY, ECONOMIC, SOCIAL AND CULTURAL MATTERS

ARTICLE 9

(*a*) With a view to enhancing cross-border co-operation on security matters, the Conference shall set in hand a programme of work to be undertaken by the Chief Constable of the Royal Ulster Constabulary and the Commissioner of the Garda Siochana and, where appropriate, groups of officials in such areas as threat assessments, exchange of information, liaison structures, technical co-operation, training of personnel, and operational resources.

(*b*) The Conference shall have no operational responsibilities; responsibility for police operations shall remain with the heads of the respective police forces, the Chief Constable of the Royal Ulster Constabulary maintaining his links with the Secretary of State for Northern Ireland and the Commissioner of the Garda Siochana his links with the Minister for Justice.

ARTICLE 10

(*a*) The two Governments shall co-operate to promote the economic and social development of those areas of both parts of Ireland which have suffered most severely from the consequences of the instability of recent years, and shall consider the possibility of securing international support for this work.

(*b*) If it should prove impossible to achieve and sustain devolution on a basis which secures widespread acceptance in Northern Ireland, the Conference shall be a framework for the promotion of co-operation between the two parts of Ireland concerning cross-border aspects of economic, social and cultural matters in relation to which the Secretary of State for Northern Ireland continues to exercise authority.

(*c*) If responsibility is devolved in respect of certain matters in the economic, social or cultural areas currently within the responsibility of the Secretary of State for Northern Ireland, machinery will need to be established by the responsible authorities in the North and South for practical co-operation in respect of cross-border aspects of these issues.

G

ARRANGEMENTS FOR REVIEW

ARTICLE 11

At the end of three years from signature of this Agreement, or earlier if requested by either Government, the working of the Conference shall be reviewed by the two Governments to see whether any changes in the scope and nature of its activities are desirable.

7

H

INTERPARLIAMENTARY RELATIONS

Article 12

It will be for Parliamentary decision in Westminster and in Dublin whether to establish an Anglo-Irish Parliamentary body of the kind adumbrated in the Anglo-Irish Studies Report of November 1981(1). The two Governments agree that they would give support as appropriate to such a body, if it were to be established.

I

FINAL CLAUSES

Article 13

This Agreement shall enter into force on the date on which the two Governments exchange notifications of their acceptance of this Agreement(2).

In witness whereof the undersigned, being duly authorised thereto by their respective Governments, have signed this Agreement.

Done in two originals at Hillsborough on the 15th day of November 1985.

For the Government of the United Kingdom of Great Britain and Northern Ireland:	For the Government of the Republic of Ireland:
MARGARET THATCHER	GEARÓID MacGEARAILT

(1) Cmnd. 8414.
(2) The Agreement entered into force on 29 November 1985.

Printed by Her Majesty's Stationery Office
1155 Dd 601690 12/85 C10 3163631

ISBN 0 10 196900 7

II
Biographical Notes

ACLAND, Sir Antony (born 1930). Permanent Under-Secretary of State, Foreign and Commonwealth Office (FCO), and Head of the Diplomatic Service; attended Chequers strategy meeting with PM, Howe, Prior and negotiating team in January 1984 to determine way forward on negotiations. He joined the Foreign Office[1] in 1953 and, over the course of a varied career, with many assignments at home and abroad, rose to become Permanent Under-Secretary of State and Head of the Diplomatic Service 1982–86. His last assignment was as Ambassador in Washington 1986 to 1991 when he retired. On retirement he served as Provost of Eton College 1991–2000 and Chancellor of the Order of St Michael and St George 1994–2005.

ANDREW, Sir Robert John (born 1928). Permanent Under-Secretary, Northern Ireland Office (NIO); member British negotiating team Anglo-Irish Agreement 1985. Following a spell in the British Army Intelligence Corps from 1947 to 1949, he joined the civil service in 1952 and over service in several ministries, rose to become Permanent Under-Secretary of State NIO from 1984 to 1988. He became part of the British negotiating team from January 1984.

APPLEYARD, Sir Leonard (Len) (1938–2020). Principal Private Secretary to Foreign Secretary, Geoffrey Howe (1984–86). He joined the Foreign Office in 1962; served as Principal Private Secretary to Foreign Secretary, Sir Geoffrey Howe from 1984 to 1986. He had many assignments, at home and abroad, including a secondment to the Cabinet Office, and retired after serving as Ambassador to China from 1994 to 1997. After retirement he served as Vice-Chairman, Barclays Capital 1998–2003.

1. Until 1968, when it merged with the Commonwealth Office, Britain's foreign ministry was known as the Foreign Office (FO) and the Foreign and Commonwealth Office (FCO) until 2020 when it became the Foreign, Commonwealth and Development Office (FCDO).

ARMSTRONG, Sir Robert Temple, Baron Armstrong of Ilminster (1927-2020). Cabinet Secretary Head of Civil Service, and lead British negotiator, Anglo-Irish Agreement 1985. Educated Eton and Oxford; in a long career in the British civil service, he worked in several ministries. He served as Private Secretary to a number of prominent politicians, including Reginald Maudling, R.A. Butler and Roy Jenkins. He became Principal Private Secretary to two Prime Ministers, Ted Heath and Harold Wilson. It is reputed that, while working for PM Ted Heath, he cautioned against the introduction of internment in Northern Ireland. He was appointed Cabinet Secretary and Head of the Civil Service in 1979 by PM Margaret Thatcher, having been selected personally by her, the only person she interviewed for the post. From 1983 to1985 he led the negotiations which culminated in the Anglo-Irish Agreement. He retired in 1987. After retirement, he was Chancellor of the University of Hull from 1994 to 2006; a board member of the Royal Opera House Covent Garden and from 2005 to 2013 he was chairman of the Sir Edward Heath Charitable Foundation.

BARRETT, Seán (born 1944). Attended signing of the AI Agreement Hillsborough Castle. TD[2] (Fine Gael party, 1981-2002, 2007-20); Ceann Comhairle (Chairman/ Speaker) of Dáil Éireann,[3] 2011-16.

BARRY, Peter (1928-2016). Irish Foreign Minister during negotiations of the 1985 Anglo-Irish Agreement. Irish politician, TD (Fine Gael party) from 1969 to 1997, representing a constituency in Cork city, and a businessman (head of the family firm, Barry's Tea). He was Lord Mayor of Cork in 1970-71. Over his political career he served as Minister for Transport and Power; Minister for Education; Minister for the Environment and from 1982 to 1987 as Foreign Minister. During this last-mentioned period he was engaged in the negotiations leading to the Anglo-Irish Agreement of 1985.

BELL, Sir Ewart (1924-2001). Head Northern Ireland civil service: Bell briefed Goodall on NI issues during the latter's visit to NI in late 1983. Joined the Northern Ireland civil service in 1948 and following service in several Ministries in NI finished his career as Head of the Northern Ireland Civil Service 1979-84. As a young man he played rugby at Oxford University, Cheltenham and for Collegians and Ulster. In 1953 he made his international debut for Ireland against France; played in all Five Nations matches for Ireland that year.

2. TD = Teachta Dála (in the Republic of Ireland) a member of Dáil Éireann.
3. Dáil Éireann = Irish lower house of Parliament

BRAMALL, Field Marshal Edwin Noel Westby, Baron Bramall (1923-2019). Supported the visit by Goodall to NI in 1985 to see the UDR. Joined the army in 1943 and served in NW Europe 1944-45. Over his career he served in Japan, the Middle East, on the staff of Lord Mountbatten at the Defence Ministry, in Malaysia and Hong Kong. He was Commander-in-Chief of UK Land Forces from 1976 to 1968 and finished his army career as Chief of the Defence Staff 1982-85.

BRENNAN, Anthony John Edward (Tony) (1927-2017). NIO official and member British negotiating team Anglo-Irish Agreement 1985. He served in the British Army 1946-49 and joined the civil service in 1949. Most of his career was spent in the Home Office although his last assignment was as Deputy Secretary in the Northern Ireland Office from 1982 to 1987. He was a member of the British negotiating team from early 1984.

BRITTAN, Leon, Baron Brittan of Spennithorne, QC, DL (1935-2015). Home Secretary: mentioned in passing in the memoir in the context of a Cabinet reshuffle. Conservative politician and Minister. Educated Cambridge and Yale; President Cambridge Union 1960; Barrister; Conservative MP 1974-88. Served as Minister, junior and senior, in number Ministries, including the Home Office, Treasury and Trade and Industry. He was Vice-President of the European Commission 1989-93. He was Chancellor of the University Teesside from 1993 to 2005.

BUDD, Sir Colin Richard (born 1945). Assistant Private Secretary Foreign Secretary Howe 1984-87: while abroad in September 1985, Goodall was warned by Budd of NIO efforts to row back on the draft Agreement. Joined the Foreign Office in 1967. Over his career he had several assignments, including as Assistant Private Secretary to Foreign Secretary Howe from 1984 to 1987. He was Chef de Cabinet to Sir Leon Brittan when he was Vice President of the European Commission 1993 to 1996, was Deputy Secretary in the Cabinet Office in 1996-97 and retired in 2005, having completed a final assignment as Ambassador to the Netherlands from 2001-2005.

COLES, Sir (Arthur) John (born 1937). Private Secretary to PM Thatcher 1981-84. Educated Oxford and served in HM Forces from 1955-57; joined the Diplomatic Service in 1960. His foreign postings included the EEC in Brussels, Jordan and Australia. On secondment he served as Private Secretary to PM Thatcher from 1981 to 1984. He was appointed Permanent Under-Secretary at the FCO and Head of Diplomatic Service in 1994, retiring in 1997.

Donlon, Seán (born 1940). Secretary General Irish Dept. Foreign Affairs 1981-87 and member Irish negotiating team Anglo-Irish Agreement 1985. Irish diplomat:

joined Diplomatic Service 1963 and served as Consul General in Boston 1968–71; he was involved in Northern Ireland affairs at HQ from 1971 to 1978 when he was appointed Irish Ambassador to the US from 1978 to 1981 during which period, he supported the formation of the Friends of Ireland group in the US Congress and engaged with President Ronald Reagan on Northern Ireland issues. He was Secretary General of the Department Foreign Affairs 1981 to 1987 and Special Advisor to Taoiseach, John Bruton 1994-97. He had earlier been a participant in Sunningdale Conference 1973 and in the negotiation of the Anglo-Irish Agreement of 1985. He resigned from the civil service in 1987. In the private sector he was Executive Vice-President of the GPA Group 1987–94. Later he served as Chancellor of the University of Limerick 2002–07; Executive Director, European Bank Reconstruction and Development 2013-2016; Chairman, Press Council of Ireland 2016–to date.

DORR, Noel (born 1937). Irish Ambassador London 1983–87 and member of the Irish negotiating team, Anglo-Irish Agreement 1985. Former Irish diplomat; served as permanent representative to the UN 1980–83 and Irish representative on UN Security Council 1981–82; Irish Ambassador to the UK 1983–87. He was Secretary General of the Department of Foreign Affairs 1987–95; Irish representative on official-level drafting groups for EU Treaties of Amsterdam 1996–97 and Nice 2000–1. He has written two books on Ireland and UN – *A Small State at the Top Table: Memories of Ireland on the UN Security Council 1981-82*, IPA (2011) and *Ireland and the United Nations: Memories of the Early Years*, IPA (2010); his most recent book is *Sunningdale: The Search for Peace in Northern Ireland.* He was a member of the Irish negotiation team for the Anglo-Irish Agreement of 1985 and provided detailed records of all the meetings of the negotiators.

DUDLEY Edwards, Ruth (born 1944). Writer, historian, biographer, freelance journalist and broadcaster; she was chair of the British Association for Irish Studies from 1985 to 1993.

FITZGERALD, Dr Garret Desmond (1926–2011). Taoiseach[4] 1982–87. Irish economist, barrister, lecturer, politician (member and leader of the Fine Gael party), served twice as Taoiseach in the 1980s. He had been Minister Foreign Affairs 1973-77; served as a TD 1969–92 and previously a Senator 1965–69. As Taoiseach, he advocated the liberalisation Irish society to create a non-sectarian nation;

4. Taoiseach = Irish Prime Minister

but his attempt to introduce divorce was defeated in referendum in 1986. He liberalised Irish contraception laws but a controversial Pro-Life Amendment (anti-abortion clause) was added to Irish constitution in 1983. On Northern Ireland, FitzGerald, on advice from John Hume, set up The New Ireland Forum 1983, which brought together representatives of the constitutional nationalist parties in Ireland. Although its recommendations were rejected in dramatic fashion by PM Thatcher, its work did provide impetus for the resumption of negotiations between Irish and British governments, culminating in Anglo-Irish Agreement November of 1985. He was Chancellor of the National University of Ireland 1997–2009.

GANDHI, Mrs Indira (Nehru) (1917–1984). Prime Minister of India, first and only woman to hold the post; assassinated by her bodyguards 31 October, 1984; PM Thatcher and Taoiseach FitzGerald travelled back together to Europe from the Gandhi funeral in Delhi in November 1984.

GOODISON, Sir Alan C., KCMG, (1926–2006). British Ambassador Dublin 1983–86 and member British negotiating team of the Anglo-Irish Agreement 1985. Educated Cambridge and served in the army 1947–49. He entered the diplomatic service in 1949 and had assignments in the Middle East, Lisbon, Bonn, and Rome, as well as in the FCO, before being posted to Dublin as Ambassador in 1983, where he worked with the team negotiating on Anglo-Irish affairs. After retirement in 1986 Goodison, who had life-long interest in theology (an interest, which, while in Ireland, he shared with Taoiseach, Garret FitzGerald and his wife, Joan), became a Licensed Reader in the Church of England and preached regularly at Hampstead Parish Church, north London.

GORDIEVSKY, Oleg (born 1938). KGB agent and double agent; he was Deputy Head of Station in Copenhagen 1974–78; Acting Head of Station in London 1984–85, having become a double agent for the British secret service in 1974.

GOW, Ian Reginald Edward, MP (1937–1990). Confidant of Mrs Thatcher. Conservative British politician, solicitor; elected MP 1974; joined the Tory front bench 1978; shared the duties of opposition spokesman on Northern Ireland with Airey Neave; developed policy on Northern Ireland favouring integration with Great Britain; he was appointed parliamentary private secretary to PM Margaret Thatcher in 1979 and became her confidant. He resigned as Minister of State HM Treasury in 1985 in protest at the signing of Anglo-Irish Agreement. On 30 July 1990 Gow was assassinated by the Provisional IRA.

GRAHAM, Edgar (1954-1983). He and Goodall met in 1983 at the annual conference of the British-Irish Association at Balliol College, Oxford. Ulster Unionist Party (UUP) politician and academic from Northern Ireland; regarded as a rising star of both legal studies and Unionism and a possible future leader of the UUP until assassinated 7 December 1983 at Queens University, Belfast by the Provisional IRA .

HALLETT, Edward (Ted) C. (born 1947). FCO; Counsellor and Deputy Head of Mission, Ireland, 2003-2006; at the time of the Anglo-Irish negotiations, he was a research analyst in the FCO dealing with Irish affairs and later in 1986 wrote an internal account of the negotiations, on which Sir David Goodall drew for his memoir.

HATTERSLEY, Roy Sydney George, Baron Hattersley, PC, FRSL (born 1932). one of the first MPs to support the AI Agreement in the Commons debate in 1985. British Labour politician, author and journalist from Sheffield; MP from 1964-1997; Deputy Leader of the Labour Party 1983-92; had number junior ministerial posts and was opposition spokesman on variety portfolios, including defence, education, consumer protection, environment, home affairs; columnist *Punch*, *The Guardian*, *The Listener* 1970-2009.

HAUGHEY, Charles James (1925-2006). Taoiseach. Irish politician; served as Taoiseach three times between 1979 and 1992. A barrister and chartered accountant, with an accountancy practice, he joined the Fianna Fáil (FF) political party in 1948 and married Maureen Lemass 1951, daughter of the party's leader and later Taoiseach, Seán Lemass. He entered the Dáil in 1957 and had a number of ministerial posts – Justice, Agriculture, Finance, as well as Health and Social Welfare. Along with another minister, in 1970 he was dismissed from office by Taoiseach, Jack Lynch, amid allegations of abuse of official funds to import arms for the IRA . Both were tried but acquitted. In 1979 he succeeded in the race to replace Lynch when he retired. As Taoiseach, Haughey made initial progress in improving relations with British PM Thatcher but this was reversed by the tensions over IRA hunger strikes and by the position taken by Haughey on the Falklands conflict. There were four unsuccessful challenges to his leadership during his tenure. He resigned in 1992 when implicated in scandal involving the wiretapping of two journalists; he denied the allegations and remained out of public life until 1997 when an official tribunal determined that, while Taoiseach, he had received large sums of money from a prominent businessman.

HERMON, Sir John Charles (1928-2008). Chief Constable Royal Ulster Constabulary, Northern Ireland 1980–89. Hermon decided against a career in accountancy to join the RUC in 1950; he had various posts in the police before becoming Assistant Chief Constable in 1974 and Deputy Chief Constable in 1976. In 1980 he became RUC Chief Constable. He changed the interview processes for terrorist suspects at Castlereagh interrogation centre, making clear he wished no mistreatment of prisoners on the grounds that allegations of mistreatment were harming relations with the wider communities. Although his reputation suffered from allegations of knowledge of a 'shoot-to-kill' policy in the RUC, it is accepted that he helped transform the police into a more independent force, shorn of its worst sectarian sympathies, changes which allowed the RUC to better support the peace process in the 1990s. He wrote an autobiography, *Holding the Line*, in 1997.

Hogg, Quintin McGarel, Baron Hailsham of St Marylebone (1907–2001). Lord Chancellor of Great Britain 1970–74 and 1979–87. Barrister and Conservative politician; during World War 2 he served in the Middle East (wounded). In 1963 he was considered to be a contender for the Conservative Party leadership. He renounced his peerage in order to compete but was passed over in favour of Earl of Home. He was later created a life peer in 1970. He served as Lord Chancellor until 1987 (the Lord Chancellor is a member of Cabinet, responsible for the efficient functioning and independence of the courts); his opposition to the proposal for 'mixed courts' in NI made it impossible for PM Thatcher to deliver on Article 8 of Anglo-Irish Agreement 1985.

Holland, Mary (1935–2004) Irish journalist. A journalist, born in Dover but raised in Ireland, she specialised in writing about Ireland generally and, especially, Northern Ireland. She wrote for *The Observer* and *The Irish Times*.

Howe, Sir Geoffrey, Baron Howe of Aberavon (1926–2015). Foreign Secretary during negotiation Anglo-Irish Agreement 1985. Barrister and politician: he was Thatcher 's longest-serving cabinet minister, successively holding the posts of Chancellor, Foreign Secretary, and finally Leader of the House of Commons, Deputy Prime Minister and Lord President of the Council. As outlined by both Sir David Goodall and by Howe himself in his autobiography, *Conflict of Loyalty,* he played a positive and central role in the Anglo-Irish negotiations. His resignation in 1990 is widely considered to have precipitated Margaret Thatcher 's own resignation three weeks later. Howe's tenure as Foreign Secretary lasted six years 1983–89, the longest tenure since Sir Edward Grey before World War 1. His tenure was made difficult by growing tensions with

PM Thatcher on South Africa, Britain's relations with European Community and in the lead-up to the 1985 Anglo-Irish Agreement.

HUME, John (1937-2020). Leader of the Social Democratic and Labour Party, Northern Ireland and Nobel Peace Laureate. Northern Ireland nationalist politician, who is widely regarded as one of the most important figures in recent Irish political history and as the architect of the NI peace process. He was a native of Derry, a founding member of the Social Democratic and Labour Party (SDLP) and served as its second leader from 1979 to 2001. He was a leading participant in the negotiations of the Sunningdale Agreement in 1973 and became Minister for Commerce in the short-lived power-sharing executive. He also served as Member European Parliament, a Member of the UK Parliament, as well as a member of the Northern Ireland Assembly. Hume engaged in secret talks with Sinn Féin leader, Gerry Adams, in the late 1980s; a process thought to have laid the foundation for the inclusive nature of the peace process that followed and the successful negotiation of the Good Friday Agreement 1998. He was co-recipient of the 1998 Nobel Peace Prize with the leader of the Ulster Unionist Party, David Trimble, and also received both the Gandhi Peace Prize and the Martin Luther King Award – the only person to receive these three major peace awards.

HURD, Douglas Richard, Baron Hurd of Westwell (born 1930). Northern Ireland Secretary of State 1984-85 and involved in the period in the negotiations of the 1985 Anglo-Irish Agreement. Educated Eton and Cambridge, Hurd was President of the Cambridge Union 1952. He was a diplomat from 1952 to 1966; with service in China, the UN mission in New York, Rome and at the FCO in London. In 1966 he left the FCO and joined the Conservative Research Department; He served as Private Secretary to the Leader of Opposition 1968-70 and as Political Secretary to the PM 1970-74. He was elected as a Conservative MP in 1974 and remained an MP till 1997. He was Minister of State at the FCO 1979-83; Minister State Home Office 1983-84; Secretary State Northern Ireland 1984-85; Home Secretary 1985-89; Foreign Secretary 1989-95. He was a member of the House Lords from 1997 to 2016; he is a prolific author of fiction and non-fiction; his autobiography, *Memoirs*, was published in 2003.

INGHAM, Sir Bernard (born 1932). Press Secretary for PM Thatcher. British journalist and former civil servant. After a career as a correspondent for a number of newspapers and media work for a number of ministries, he became Chief Press Secretary to PM Thatcher throughout her three premierships 1979-90; he was knighted in her 1990 resignation honours list; He is was a visiting Fellow at Newcastle University from 1989 to 2004 and a visiting professor at Middlesex University Business School in 1998.

KING, Thomas Jeremy (Tom), Baron King of Bridgwater (born 1933). Northern Ireland Secretary of State 1985–89 and involved in the latter period of the negotiations of the 1985 Anglo-Irish Agreement. Educated Rugby and Cambridge (MA); military service 1951–53. After the military, King worked as a business executive before being elected Conservative MP for Bridgwater in 1970, remaining an MP till 2001. During his career in the House of Commons he served as junior and senior ministers in the areas of Posts and Telecommunications; Industrial Development; Local Government; Environment, Transport; Employment; Northern Ireland and, finally, Defence. He was Chairman of the Parliamentary Intelligence and Security Committee 1994 to 2001. On retirement from the Commons, he was made a life peer; his autobiography, *A King Among Ministers: Fifty Years in Parliament Recalled*, was published in 2020.

LAMONT, Norman Stewart Hughson, Baron Lamont of Lerwick (born 1942). told Goodall on 18 May 1984 that the Tory Party favoured a positive response to the Forum Report and a possible Irish dimension in the North. British politician and former Conservative MP; educated Cambridge ; president Cambridge Union 1964; elected Conservative MP in 1972. In his ministerial career her served in Trade and Industry; Defence Procurement; the Treasury (Chancellor 1990–93). He was made a life peer in 1998. He was Chairman of the G7 Group of Finance Ministers in 1991 and the EU Finance Ministers in 1992. After resignation, Lamont in 1994 became the first leading politician to raise the prospect of Britain withdrawing from the European Union.

LILLIS, Michael (born 1946). Assistant Secretary General Anglo-Irish Affairs, Irish Department Foreign Affairs 1982–87; member Irish negotiating team Anglo-Irish Agreement 1985. Joined Irish Diplomatic Service 1966 and saw service in Madrid, New York, Washington and Brussels. In the Embassy in Washington, he helped negotiate the Carter Initiative on Northern Ireland inspired by John Hume and the 'Four Horsemen' US lobby (House Speaker O'Neill, Senators Kennedy and Moynihan and New York Governor Hugh Carey). It was opposed by London and by the US State Department. In the initiative, in August 1977, President Carter called for human rights and a solution acceptable to both NI communities. It was a precedent for the US – the first time, since Irish partition, that the US Government had taken a position on NI independently of London. In 1981 Lillis was appointed Diplomatic Adviser to Taoiseach, Garret FitzGerald and in September 1983, having consulted

FitzGerald and Hume, he opened talks with Sir David Goodall, Deputy Secretary to the British Cabinet, on a role for Irish Government in NI. This led to secret negotiations over two years under the direction of the Irish and British Cabinet Secretaries, Dermot Nally and Sir Robert Armstrong, culminating in the Anglo-Irish Agreement of 1985 which gave Dublin a significant input into government in NI. The British Government committed for the first time, in a treaty, to support Irish unity in the event a majority in Northern Ireland so wished – a key element in the Hume-Adams discussions in 1990s. Lillis was appointed the first Irish Joint Secretary of Anglo-Irish Secretariat in Belfast, the first Irish Government residential presence in Northern Ireland since partition. In 1990 he retired from the public service and is currently Chairman of the Advisory Board on Latin America for the aircraft leasing company, Avolon. He was co-author, with Ronan Fanning, of *The Lives of Eliza Lynch*, published in 2009.

Lowry, Robert Lynd Erskine, Baron Lowry (1919–1999). Lord Chief Justice Northern Ireland. Educated Cambridge; served in the army 1940–46. He was called to the NI Bar in 1947; Hon. Bencher, Kings Inns, Dublin, 1973; QC in NI 1956; Counsel to HM Attorney-General 1948–56; Judge High Court of Justice (NI) 1964–71; Lord Chief Justice Northern Ireland 1971–88. He was knighted in 1971 and made life peer in 1979. Lowry opposed the plan for the establishment of mixed courts in Northern Ireland, as proposed in Article 8 of the Anglo-Irish Agreement. He wrote to PM Thatcher threatening to resign if implemented.

Mallaby, Sir Christopher Leslie George (born 1936). Member 1985 British team negotiating the AI Agreement 1985. Entered the Foreign Office (FO) in 1960; over his career he served at the UN, in Moscow; Berlin, New York, Bonn, the Cabinet Office (in replacement of Sir David Goodall); he had several placements in the FCO and towards the end of his career served as Ambassador to Germany and then France. While at Cabinet Office he was involved in the latter period of the negotiations of Anglo-Irish Agreement . He is the author of *Living the Cold War: Memoirs of a British Diplomat* (2017).

Mallon, Seamus (1936–2020). Deputy Leader Social Democratic and Labour Party (SDLP). Irish politician; Deputy First Minister Northern Ireland 1998–2001 and Deputy Leader SDLP 1979–2001. Mallon was a school teacher and later headmaster at St James's Primary School in his home town of Markethill, Co Armagh. He played Gaelic football for Co Armagh; during the 1960s he was involved in the civil rights movement and elected to the first power-sharing Assembly 1973 and also to the Northern Ireland Constitutional Convention in 1975 representing Armagh; From May–December 1982 he served as a Senator in the Irish Senate (Seanad Éireann) on the appointment of then Taoiseach, Charles Haughey . He was a strong promoter of non-violent nationalism, strongly opposed the PIRA campaign and was an advocate of RUC reform of and the abolition of the UDR. He was also a member of the SDLP team negotiating the Good Friday Agreement, famously describing the Agreement, when it emerged, as 'Sunningdale for slow learners'. He retired in 2001. His biographical memoir, *A Shared Home Place,* was published in 2019.

McCarthy, Brian (born 1943). Principal Officer, Department of the Taoiseach (1983–93).

Molyneaux, James, Baron Molyneaux of Killead, KBE, PC (1920–2015). NI unionist politician; leader Ulster Unionist Party (UUP) 1979–95; he served in the RAF 1941–46; was Vice-President of the Ulster Unionist Council 1974–79; MP in NI from 1970 to 1997; he was a leading member and sometime Vice-President of the Conservative Monday Club; also Sovereign Grand Master of the Royal Black Institution (linked to the Orange Order) from 1971 to 1995. He and the UUP strongly opposed the 1985 Anglo-Irish Agreement.

Murphy, Dervla (born 1931). Award winning Irish travel writer. Winner American Irish Foundation Literary Award 1975; Christopher Ewart-Biggs Memorial Prize 1978; Irish-American Cultural Institute Literary Award 1985. She was the author of *A Place Apart* (1979), which, according to David Goodall, PM Thatcher found fascinating.

Murphy, John A. (born 1927). Member of the British-Irish Association (BIA). Irish historian and former senator; currently Emeritus Professor of history at University College Cork (UCC); author of many history publications, including *Ireland in the Twentieth Century.*

Nally, Dermot (1927–2009). (Cabinet) Secretary Irish Government; leader of the Irish negotiating team of the Anglo-Irish Agreement of 1985. Irish civil servant; began work for the state in 1947. While lecturing for the Institute Public Administration in 1973, he was contacted by Taoiseach, Jack Lynch, and offered a position in the Department of the Taoiseach as Assistant Secretary. He had a prominent role in the negotiation of the Sunningdale Agreement in 1973 ; he became Deputy Secretary (General) in the Department of the Taoiseach in 1978 and served as Government Secretary (civil servant administering Cabinet meetings). He led the Irish team which negotiated the 1985 Anglo-Irish Agreement. Over his career he worked with ten governments, reporting directly to five Taoisigh (Irish PMs) and reported directly to the Taoiseach of day on wide range of matters, notably Northern Ireland, the economy and European affairs.

NEAVE, Airey Middleton Sheffield, DSO, OBE, MC (1916-1979). Adviser to PM Thatcher on NI. British soldier, lawyer and Member Parliament; during World War 2 he was the first British prisoner-of-war to escape from Colditz Castle. He later worked for MI9 (British Directorate Military Intelligence); he was a member of the British War Crimes Executive in Nuremburg 1945-46 and served indictments on Goering and major Nazi war criminals in 1945. He later became a Conservative MP for Abingdon. He was opposition spokesman on Northern Ireland in 1975 and became a was close adviser to PM Thatcher on NI, among other issues. He was killed in 1979 by a bomb planted in his car at the House of Commons by the Irish National Liberation Army.

NOONAN, Michael (born 1943). Irish Justice Minister during the negotiations of the Anglo-Irish Agreement. Irish politician (Fine Gael party) who served as TD for Limerick from 1981 to 2020. In his ministerial career he served as Minister for Justice; for Industry, Commerce and Trade; for Energy; and for Health. He was Chairman of the (parliamentary) Public Accounts Committee; Leader of the Fine Gael Party 2001-12; Finance Minister 2011-17.

O'BRIEN, Martin (born 1955). Irish journalist, broadcaster, media/communications consultant, speech writer; specialises in religious affairs in *The Irish Catholic newspaper*; won an award for his Queens University Master's dissertation on PM Thatcher 's Irish policy.

PAISLEY, Rev Dr Ian, Baron Bannside (1926-2014). NI unionist politician and Protestant religious leader. He was the Leader of the Democratic Unionist Party (DUP) from 1971 to 2008 and First Minister in NI from 2007 to 2008. He became a Protestant evangelical minister in 1946; he co-founded the fundamentalist Free Presbyterian Church 1951 and was its leader to 2008. He was known for his fiery sermons and regularly preached and protested against Roman Catholicism, ecumenism and homosexuality. He instigated loyalist opposition to the Catholic/nationalist civil rights movement in NI; throughout the Troubles he was seen by many as a firebrand and the face of hard-line unionism. In 1970 he became MP for North Antrim and in the following year he founded the Democratic Unionist Party. In 1979 he was elected to the

European Parliament and in 2005 the DUP became the largest unionist party in Northern Ireland, displacing Ulster Unionist Party (UUP) which had dominated unionist politics since 1905 and had been instrumental in Good Friday Agreement 1998. Following the St Andrews Agreement of 2005, the DUP agreed to share power with Sinn Féin; Paisley and Sinn Féin's Martin McGuinness became First Minister and Deputy First Minister respectively in May 2007. He stepped down as First Minister and DUP leader in mid-2008 and left politics 2011. He was made a life peer in 2010.

PASCOE, Gen. Sir Robert (Alan) KCB, MBE (born 1932). the General Officer Commanding British forces in NI 1985; emphatic, in discussion with Goodall in NI in 1985, that there needed to be an Anglo-Irish Agreement. British Army officer; served as Adjutant-General to Forces 1988-90; two tours Northern Ireland 1971-74; 1979 Northern Ireland special duty with Sir Maurice Oldfield (former Head MI6); appointed GoC Northern Ireland 1985; retired 1990.

POINDEXTER, Vice Admiral John Marlan (born 1936). US National Security Advisor; in Washington in 1985, Goodall briefed Poindexter, then Deputy NSA, on the AI negotiations. Retired United States naval officer (US Naval Academy 1958, classmate of, later Senator, John McCain) and Department Defense official; he was the first Deputy National Security Advisor and then National Security Advisor in the Reagan administration; he served a brief stint as director Defense Advanced Research Projects Agency for the George W. Bush administration.

POWELL, Rt. Hon. (John) Enoch MBE (1912-1998).British politician, classical scholar, author, linguist, soldier, philologist and poet; served as Conservative MP 1950-74; then in NI for the Ulster Unionist Party (UUP) 1974-87 and had been Minister for Health 1960-63. He attracted widespread attention and criticism for an address he made in April 1968 which became known as the 'Rivers of Blood' speech in which he criticised rates of immigration into UK, he resigned from Conservatives and was returned to Commons October 1974 as UUP MP, which he held until defeated in the 1987 election; Powell was close to PM Thatcher until he broke with her over the Anglo-Irish Agreement – he accused her of 'treachery' in the Commons debate on the Treaty. He was a prolific author of works of poetry, history and current affairs.

PRESTON, Brigadier Roger St Clair, OBE, CBE, (born 1935). did National Service with David Goodall and met him while serving as commander of the UDR. Educated Eton and Sandhurst; began military service 1955 King's Own Yorkshire

Light Infantry; later Brigadier and Commander Ulster Defence Regiment (UDR) 1984-86; retired from military 1986.

Prior, James (Jim) Michael Leathes, Baron Prior, PC (1927-2016). Northern Ireland Secretary 1981-84 and involved in the period in the negotiations of the 1985 Anglo-Irish Agreement. British Conservative politician; MP 1959-87; In his political career Prior served as Minister for Agriculture Fisheries and Food 1970-72; Leader of the House of Commons and Lord President Council 1972-74, all under PM Heath. Under PM Thatcher he was Secretary of Employment and Northern Ireland Secretary. While NI Secretary, he introduced an initiative called 'Rolling Devolution' which was boycotted by SDLP and received little support from PM Thatcher . He resigned Cabinet 1984 and Commons 1987; he was made a life peer. His autobiography *A Balance of Power*, was published in 1986.

Quigley, Sir George (1930-2013). Met and briefed Goodall in NI in 1983. After joining the Northern Ireland civil service, he rose in 1974 to the position of Permanent Secretary of Manpower Services. He worked in a similar capacity across a range of departments and went into the private sector as deputy chairman, later chairman of Ulster Bank. At the same time, he served as a director, then chairman of Short Brothers in NI. In addition, he was a director of National Westminster Bank, NatWest Trustees and a director of Independent News and Media (UK) from 2001 until 2010.

Reagan, Ronald Wilson (1911-2004). US President. 40th president of the United States 1981-89; influential voice of modern conservatism; prior to being president, he was a Hollywood actor and union leader and then served as governor of California 1967-75; In 1980 he won the Republican presidential nomination and defeated incumbent US President, Jimmy Carter. He was the oldest, at 69 years, first-term US president; re-elected 1984; survived assassination attempt; in foreign affairs he denounced Communism and invaded the island of Grenada after Communist elements took control. Influenced mainly by House Speaker, Tip O'Neill, Reagan developed an interest in Ireland and took the unusual step of visiting the Irish Embassy on St Patrick's Day 1981; he also visited Ireland in June 1984. Against British wishes, he put Northern Ireland on agenda for meeting with PM Thatcher at Camp David in December 1984, and the National Security Agency provided Reagan with a speaking note advising that, unless there was progress on NI, the US would have difficulty maintaining its bipartisan approach on the issue. Later, re the Anglo-Irish Agreement of

1985, PM Thatcher told Alistair McAlpine 'It was pressure from the Americans that made me sign the Agreement'.

RICHARDSON, Sir Robert (Bob) Francis, Lieutenant-General (1929-2014). General Officer Commanding British forces in NI in 1983, during Goodall's visit; Goodall had known him in Germany. British Army officer; 1949 Royal Military Academy Sandhurst; briefly saw service at the end of the Korean War; Defence Services Staff College India 1960-61; among other posts, he commanded a battalion and a brigade during the Troubles before becoming General Officer Commanding in Northern Ireland 1982-85.

RICKETTS, Peter Forbes, Baron Ricketts of Shortlands (born 1952). Private Secretary to Foreign Secretary Howe 1983-86; he predicted to Goodall that the AI Agreement would be one of the historic landmarks of the Thatcher Administration. Joined FCO, 1974 and saw service in Singapore, Brussels (NATO), Washington and Paris. In London he had various assignments, including as Assistant Private Secretary to Foreign Secretary Howe and an assignment in the Cabinet Office before ending his career as Ambassador to France 2012-16.

RYAN, Richard (born 1946). Official, Irish Embassy London. Irish poet and former diplomat; in the 1980s he served in the Irish Embassy London where, according to Garret FitzGerald, he did very useful work in run-up to the Anglo-Irish Agreement in influencing a wide range MPs, particularly Conservatives, in favour of Irish policy.

SHACKLETON, Edward Arthur Alexander, Baron Shackleton (1911-1994). Expert on the Falkland Islands . Son of the Antarctic explorer and a British geographer, he served as Minister for Defence for RAF 1964-67 and later Deputy Leader of the House of Lords. A report by Shackleton in 1976, commissioned by PM Callaghan, described the economic future of the Falkland Islands. At the request of PM Thatcher, Shackleton updated his report in 1982 after the Falklands conflict.

SPRING, Richard (Dick) (born 1950). Tánaiste (Irish Deputy Prime Minister) involved, with the Taoiseach and Irish Foreign Minister in the negotiations of the 1985 Anglo-Irish Agreement. Businessman and former politician; Labour Party TD Kerry North 1981-2002 and leader of the Labour Party 1982-1997. In his ministerial, career he served as Minister for the Environment; Minister for Energy and Minister for Foreign Affairs. He was Tánaiste (Irish Deputy PM) during three governments. During his period as Foreign Minister, Spring along with the Taoiseach, Albert Reynolds, was involved in the negotiations leading to the Provisional IRA and loyalist ceasefires in 1994 and the Good Friday Agreement in 1998.

STEEL, David Martin Scott; Baron Steel of Aikwood, KT, KBE, PC (born 1938). supported the Agreement in the Commons debate. British politician; member of the Liberal Party and served as the party's final leader 1976–88; his tenure spanned the duration of the alliance with the Social Democratic Party 1981–88; he was an MP 1965–97; Member of the Scottish Parliament (MSP) 1999–2003, during which time he was the parliament's Presiding Officer. He was a member of the House of Lords as life peer 1997–2020. His autobiography is entitled *Against Goliath: David Steel's Story* (1989).

STEPHENS, Anthony William (Tony) (1930–2016). Deputy Under Secretary State NIO. Educated Bristol and Cambridge; military service 1948–50; he worked in the Colonial Administrative Service with a posting in Kenya; joined the Home Civil Service in 1964 and served in the Ministry of Defence, including as Chief Officer Sovereign Base Areas Cyprus 1974–76 before becoming Under Secretary in the NIO 1976–79; from there he became Assistant Under Secretary of State General Staff 1979–83; and Deputy Under Secretary of State (NIO) 1985–90 (during which period he first met David Goodall); from 1984 he was part of the British team negotiating the Anglo-Irish Agreement.

SUTHERLAND, Peter Denis (1946-2018). Irish Attorney General during the AI Agreement negotiations. Irish businessman, barrister and politician; Irish Attorney General 1982–84; served as UN Special Representative for International Migration 2006–17; Chairman of Goldman Sachs 1995–2015; Director-General World Trade Organization 1993–95; EU Commissioner for Competition 1985–89; barrister by profession; Senior Counsel Bar Council of Ireland.

THATCHER, Margaret Hilda, Baroness Thatcher (1925–2013) . British politician; Prime Minister 1979–90; Leader Conservative Party 1975–90; longest-serving British Prime Minister 20th century; first woman to hold the office; dubbed 'The Iron Lady' by a Soviet journalist, a nickname from then associated with her uncompromising politics and style. She studied chemistry at Oxford and later became a barrister; she was elected Conservative MP for Finchley 1959, a seat she held until 1992. She was Education Secretary under PM Heath in the 1970–74 government; in 1975 she defeated Heath for leadership of the Conservative Party and become Leader of the Opposition, first woman to lead major political party in the UK and first woman to hold one of Great Offices of State. She became PM on winning 1979 election and introduced a series of economic policies to reverse high unemployment in the wake of the 'Winter of Discontent' and ongoing recession; her popularity waned amid recession and rising unemployment until victory in 1982 Falklands War. The recovering economy brought a resurgence of support, resulting in a landslide re-election in 1983. She survived an assassination attempt by Provisional IRA when they bombed the Grand Hotel in Brighton in 1984 and achieved political victory against National Union of Mineworkers in the 1984–85 miners' strike. She signed an agreement in 1985 with Taoiseach, Garret FitzGerald, providing a role for the Irish government in NI in return for Dublin accepting the province to remain part of UK while a majority wished it. She was re-elected for a third term with another landslide in 1987 but the Community Charge ('poll tax') was widely unpopular and increasingly her Eurosceptic views on the EU were not shared by others in Cabinet. She resigned as head of government and party leader November 1990. After retiring from the Commons she was given a life peerage. She wrote a two-volume autobiography, *The Path to Power and The Downing Street Years.*

VAN HATTEM, Margaret (1948–89). Journalist; political and lobby (House of Commons) correspondent for the *Financial Times*; wrote frequently on NI issues.

WARD, Andrew (Andy) (1925–99). Secretary-General Irish Department of Justice and a Member of the Irish negotiating team for the Anglo-Irish Agreement 1985. Irish civil servant, Secretary (General) of the Department Justice; he was the longest serving Secretary General of the Justice Department (1970–86) in the history of the State; his appointment as Secretary of the Department of Justice coincided with worst violence in Northern Ireland since partition and a serious deterioration in Anglo-Irish relations; much of his work involved dealing with consequences of Troubles; he served seven ministers and was a significant contributor on Irish side, on justice matters, during the negotiation of the Anglo-Irish Agreement of 1985.

WHITMORE, Sir Clive (Anthony) (born 1935). Permanent Under-Secretary Ministry Defence: met Goodall to discuss the UDR. Educated Cambridge ; began his career in the War Office, gaining successive promotions in the Ministry of Defence until becoming Permanent Under-Secretary of State in the Ministry 1983–88. He served in the Home Office 1988 to 1994 when he retired.

WICKS, Sir Nigel Leonard (born 1940). attended meeting in Downing Street, August 1985, with PM, Hurd and the negotiators to discuss the emerging

Agreement. Long career in the civil service, including an assignment as Principal Private Secretary to PM Thatcher 1985-88; Second Permanent Secretary (Finance) in HM Treasury 1989-2000; Chairman Committee on Standards Public Life 2001-04; board member several companies.

WOODFIELD, Sir Philip John, KCB, CBE (1923-2000). Advisor regarded by Goodall as having invaluable practical experience of policing and administrative problems. British civil servant; military service 1942-47. In the civil service he served as Private Secretary to three PMs – Harold Macmillan, Alec Douglas-Home and Harold Wilson. In 1965 he was Secretary of the Commonwealth Immigration Commission headed by Lord Mountbatten ; he participated in the first meeting between IRA and officials of the British Government in 1972; he was promoted Deputy Secretary in charge of the Northern Ireland Department in the Home Office in 1972; he was Permanent Under-Secretary of State 1981; he retired from the Home Office in 1983 and was knighted in the same year.

Select Bibliography

ADAMS, Gerry, *Before the Dawn: an Autobiography* (Heinemann: London, 1996)

AUGHEY, Arthur, *Under Siege: Ulster Unionism and the Anglo-Irish Agreement* (Blackstaff Press: Belfast, 1989)

BARTLETT, Thomas (ed.), *The Cambridge History of Ireland, Volume IV, 1880 to the Present,* (Cambridge University Press, 2018)

BEW, Paul and Gillespie, Gordon, *Northern Ireland: a Chronology of the Troubles, 1968-99* (Gill & Macmillan: Dublin, 1999)

BEW, Paul, Gibbon, Peter, and Patterson, Henry, *Northern Ireland 1921-2001, Political Power and Social Classes* (Serif: London, 2002)

BLOOMFIELD, Kenneth, *A Tragedy of Errors: the Government and Misgovernment of Northern Ireland* (Liverpool University Press, 2007)

BOURKE, Richard, *Peace in Ireland: the War of Ideas* (Pimlico: London, 2012)

CAMPBELL, John, *The Iron Lady: Margaret Thatcher, from Grocer's Daughter to Prime Minister* (Penguin Books: New York, 2011)

CLARKE, Liam and Johnston, Kathryn, *Martin McGuinness: from Guns to Government,* (Mainstream Publishing: Edinburgh, 2001)

CRAIG, Anthony, *Crisis of Confidence: Anglo-Irish Relations in the Early Troubles* (Irish Academic Press: Dublin, 2010)

COAKLEY, John and Todd, Jennifer, *Negotiating a Settlement in Northern Ireland. From Sunningdale to St Andrews* (Oxford University Press, 2019).

DALY, Mary, *Brokering the Good Friday Agreement* (Royal Irish Academy: Dublin, 2019)

DORR, Noel, *The Search for Peace in Northern Ireland, Sunningdale* (Royal Irish Academy: Dublin, 2017).

DORR, Noel, *A Small State at the Top Table: Memories of Ireland on the UN Security Council, 1981-82* (IPA: Dublin, 2011)

DORR, Noel, *Ireland and the United Nations: Memories of the Early Years* (IPA: Dublin, 2010)

FARREN, Sean (ed.), *John Hume in his own Words* (Four Courts Press: Dublin, 2018)

FARREN, Sean and Haughey, Denis (eds), *John Hume: Irish Peacemaker* (Four Courts Press: Dublin, 2015)

FEENEY, Brian, *A Short History of the Troubles* (O'Brien Press: Dublin, 2004)

FITZPATRICK, Maurice, *John Hume in America: from Derry to DC* (Irish Academic Press: Dublin, 2017)

FERRITER, Diarmaid, *The Border: the Legacy of a Century of Anglo-Irish Politics* (Profile Books Ltd.,: London, 2019)

FITZGERALD, Garret, *All in a Life: an Autobiography* (Papermac/Macmillan: London, 1992)

FITZGERALD, Garret, *Just Garret: Tales from the Political Frontline* (Liberties Press: Dublin, 2011)

FITZGERALD, Garret, *Towards a New Ireland* (Gill & Macmillan: Dublin, 1973)

GANIEL, Gladys and Yohanis, Jamie, *Considering Grace: Presbyterians and the Troubles* (Merrion Press: Newbridge, 2019).

HOWE, Geoffrey, *Conflict of Loyalty* (Pan Books: London, 1995)

HURD, Douglas, *Memoirs* (Abacus: London, 2004)

INGHAM, Bernard, *Kill the Messenger* (HarperCollins: London, 1991)

KELLY, Stephen, *'A Failed Political Entity': Charles Haughey and the Northern Ireland Question 1945-1992* (Merrion Press: Newbridge, 2016)

KING, Tom, *A King Among Ministers: Fifty Years in Parliament Recalled* (Unicorn: London, 2020)

LEWIS, Roy, *Enoch Powell: Principle in Politics* (Cassell & Co.,: London, 1979)

MALLABY, Christopher, *Living the Cold War: Memoirs of a British Diplomat* (Amberly Publishing, Stroud: 2017)

MALLON, Seamus (with Andy Pollak), *A Shared Home Place* (The Lilliput Press: Dublin, 2019)

MCKITTRICK, David and McVea, David, *Making Sense of the Troubles: a History of the Northern Ireland Conflict* (Viking: London, 2012)

MCKITTRICK, David, KEITERS, Seamus, FEENEY, Brian, THORNTON, Chris & MCVEA, David, *Lost Lives: the stories of the Men, Women and Children who died as a Result of the Northern Ireland Troubles* (Mainstream: Edinburgh, 1999)

MILLAR, Frank, *Northern Ireland: a Triumph of Politics* (Irish Academic Press: Dublin, 2009)

MITCHELL, George, *Making Peace* (William Heinemann: London, 1999)

MOLONEY, Ed, *A Secret History of the IRA* (Penguin Books: London, 2007)
MOLONEY, Ed, *Paisley: from Demagogue to Democrat?* (Poolbeg Press: Dublin, 2008)
MOORE, Charles, *Margaret Thatcher: The Authorised Biography. Volume One: Not for Turning* (Allen Lane: London, 2013)
MOORE, Charles, *Margaret Thatcher: The Authorised Biography. Volume Two: Everything She Wants* (Allen Lane: London, 2015)
MOORE, Charles, *Margaret Thatcher: the Authorised Biography. Volume Three: Herself Alone* (Allen Lane: London, 2019)
MURPHY, Dervla, *A Place Apart* (Penguin: Harmonsworth, 1979)
O'CLERY, Conor, *The Greening of the White House* (Gill & Macmillan: Dublin, 1996)
PORTER, Norman, *Rethinking Unionism: an Alternative Vision for Northern Ireland* (The Blackstaff Press: Belfast, 1996)
RENWICK, Robin, *A Journey with Margaret Thatcher: Foreign Policy under the Iron Lady,* (Biteback Publishing Ltd.: London, 2013)
SPENCER, Graham (ed.), *The British and Peace in Northern Ireland*, (Cambridge University Press, 2015)
SPENCER, Graham, *Inside Accounts, Volume I: the Irish Government and Peace in Northern Ireland, from Sunningdale to the Good Friday Agreement* (Manchester University Press, 2019)
SPENCER, Graham, *Inside Accounts, Volume II: The Irish Government and Peace in Northern Ireland, from the Good Friday Agreement to the Fall of Power-sharing* (Manchester University Press, 2019)
SPENCER, Graham, *Protestant Identity and Peace in Northern Ireland* (Palgrave MacMillan UK, 2012)
TAYLOR, Peter, *Loyalists: Ulster's Protestant Paramilitaries* (Bloomsbury: London, 2000)
THATCHER, Margaret, *The Downing Street Years* (HarperCollins: London, 1993)
WILSON, Andrew J., *Irish America and the Ulster Conflict, 1968-1995* (Blackstaff: Belfast, 1995)
WOODHAM-SMITH, Cecil, *The Great Hunger* (Old Town Books, 1995)
WRIGHT, Frank. *Northern Ireland: a Comparative Analysis* (Gill and Macmillan: Dublin, 1992)

Index